A Different Dimension:
Reflections on the History of Transpersonal Thought

A Different Dimension

Reflections on the History of Transpersonal Thought

Mark B. Ryan

Westphalia Press

An Imprint of the Policy Studies Organization

Washington, DC

2018

A DIFFERENT DIMENSION:
REFLECTIONS ON THE HISTORY OF TRANSPERSONAL THOUGHT
All Rights Reserved © 2018 by Policy Studies Organization

Westphalia Press
An imprint of Policy Studies Organization
1527 New Hampshire Ave., NW
Washington, D.C. 20036
info@ipsonet.org

ISBN-10: 1-63391-757-6
ISBN-13: 978-1-63391-757-6
Cover and interior design by Jeffrey Barnes
jbarnesbook.design

Daniel Gutierrez-Sandoval, Executive Director
PSO and Westphalia Press

Updated material and comments on this edition
can be found at the Westphalia Press website:
www.westphaliapress.org

For Ginger,
my beloved partner in life,
co-navigator in earthly realms
and fellow sleuth in numinous ones

The further limits of our being plunge, it seems to me, into an altogether other dimension of existence from the sensible and merely "understandable" world. Name it the mystical region, or the supernatural region, whichever you choose…. [W]e belong to it in a more intimate sense than that in which we belong to the visible world.

—William James

CONTENTS

Foreword

Family Reunion

About seven years ago now, our new Dean of the Humanities here at Rice University, Nicolas Shumway, approached me with a query. He had a friend who was, as he put it, "a big fan of yours." This friend wanted to meet me. Nick went on to explain to me that Mark Ryan had just moved back from Mexico to Houston, where he grew up as a boy. Nick had known Mark when they both taught at Yale University, where Mark was dean of one of the residential colleges. Nick also explained that Mark's field was American Studies, which was the likely reason he was so interested in my books, which orbit around strange and fantastic subjects like the history of the human potential movement and its American "religion of no religion," the esoteric currents of the American counterculture, the religious dimensions of psychedelic experience, and the intellectual history of the paranormal, much of it again explicitly American.

I think I attempted some self-deprecating humor with Nick at the moment of his initial query, as I often do in these situations. I have never quite figured out how to just sit with praise (and shut up). Laughter is avoidance, even denial, here. In any case, I wanted to get to know both my new Dean and his friend, so I agreed to meet them in an Italian restaurant in the city. The restaurant was much too loud, and the food was not that good, but the company was excellent. Most importantly, the conversations begun there would last for many years, and indeed are still going on to this day. I consider this little Foreword to be another moment in that long happy conversation.

There are many things I could say about this book at this point: that it tells an important American story that is seldom told in any remotely adequate or fair way; that it constitutes a history of the rise of "the unconscious" through both the French clinical and English psychical research streams of the nineteenth century; that all sorts of historical gems are strewn about in its pages, from the history of the phrase "cosmic consciousness" to the genesis of the "spectrum of consciousness" analogies; that it provides a succinct history of transpersonal psychology as this project arose in the 1960s out of humanistic psychology, psychedelia, and a growing interest in the Asian religions, especially Buddhism and Hinduism; or that this history of the transpersonal is one of the many psychological and intellectual streams that have flowed into the great demographic river that is now the "spiritual but not religious," whether those who swim in the latter river are aware of these earlier currents or not (okay, they are not).

But I just pointed all of that out, and I see no reason to dwell on what any good reading of *A Different Dimension* will tell the reader much more fully. I want to say something else here, something simple, pointed, and blunt. I want to say that my discipline, the professional study of religion, has unjustly ignored these transpersonal currents and thinkers. No, let me speak just for myself. I have unjustly ignored these transpersonal currents and thinkers. At the very least, I have downplayed them, even when I have also done my best to write about them and have even sounded exactly like a transpersonal intellectual myself. Perhaps I am.

I am hardly alone in this neglect or intellectual snobbery. Oh, all of us in the professional study of religion read William James, particularly *The Varieties of Religious Experience*. He was a "pragmatist," after all, and that sounds oh so reasonable and dismissive of any robust philosophical claims. That's a relief. We can also just politely ignore all of James's significant psychical research projects and writings, pretend that none of it happened, or, if it did, that it was all just a collection of eccentricities that are best left behind now, you know, now that we are enlightened and rational and have figured out that the brain is just a biological computer and all of that "mystical" stuff is just fantasy, hallucination, delusion. As for Carl Jung, well, we barely tolerate him. And few of us would think of teaching Abraham Maslow, much less Ken Wilber.

There are reasons for some of these choices, which I do not want to deny or dismiss, but I am not always convinced that they are finally the real reasons. I mean, we read practically everyone in the past, regardless of their ideas or the ways that they expressed themselves. So why not here, in our own present? At the end of the day I smell a kind of avoidance or denial of something too familiar in order to preserve a sense of our own originality. We are not really that original.

I am reminded in this instance of Max Müller's attitude toward Madame Blavatsky and the Theosophical Society. Müller was one of the undisputed founders of the comparative study of religion. Indeed, he is often considered to be its "father." He despised Blavatsky and all she stood for. The problem is this. Müller's deepest convictions about the divinity of humanity and the humanity of divinity, his focus on comparative mystical literature to make this case, and the many ways he was despised as heretical or blasphemous by orthodox Christians more than resemble the beliefs and reception of the Theosophical Society. As do, by the way, many of the basic ideas of the psychical research tradition: both the psychical researchers and the Theosophists, for example, were deeply committed to those "supernormal" powers believed to be lying latent in the species. They also both ventured into reincarnation theory as a possible model of how we "evolve." In any case, this deep triangulation of the comparative study of religion, psychical research, and the Theosophical Society should not surprise us: all three movements arose at the same time and within the same Euro-American cultural complex. In the nineteenth century, psychical research and Theosophy were the denied first cousins, or siblings, of the comparative study of religion. I suspect something similar with transpersonal psychology in the post-countercultural period up to today. The transpersonal is the denied first cousin or unwanted sibling of the contemporary study of religion.

I do not know quite what to make of all of this, other than express my own regret for not realizing and saying this sooner. I will continue to say it. I will follow up. For now it is enough to observe that I read Mark Ryan's history, *A Different Dimension*, as a moment of healing in this repressed and denied conversation, as a recognition of these shared historical currents, as a kind of family reunion, if you will. That Mark is a dear friend helps immensely. Friends can speak truths to one another and be heard in a way that no one else can. Friendship is the method of all methods here.

Jeffrey J. Kripal
J. Newton Rayzor Professor of Philosophy and Religious Thought
Rice University, Houston, Texas

Preface and Acknowledgements

With accounts of key figures and their seminal ideas, this book traces the development of an expanded view of consciousness—a view that sees the human mind as reaching into realms that our dominant Western outlook either dismisses as fictional or considers beyond its ken. That expanded view is central to the contemporary movement in psychology called "transpersonal," but it has roots in modern psychology going back to the very rise of the notion of a subconscious mind, and even before.

On Jung and the Transpersonal

In general terms, such an expanded sense of consciousness is consistent with the well-known work of Carl Jung, Sigmund Freud's dissident protégé. Jung saw the unconscious as fundamentally wiser, and with far greater capacity, than did Freud. With his delineation of a collective element in the psyche, an unconscious dimension formed not by individual experiences but extending, rather, beyond the personal, Jung distinguished his view of the psyche from that of his onetime mentor. He saw the "collective unconscious" as universal, encountered in dream-life and in legends and mythology. With his theory of "archetypes," Jung began to define the elements of that collective unconscious—and to revolutionize the Freudian tradition in a way that validated a spiritual dimension to the psyche. His interest in the collective domain spurred Jung's interest in the deeper insights of ancient endeavors that the modern, materialistic mind dismissed as primitive fantasy, such as alchemy, Gnosticism, and astrology.

Jung's notion of the Self, articulated after his delineation of the collective unconscious, indicates a center of the individual personality, beyond and more profound than the persona or conscious ego; it is the totality of the psyche, embracing the unconscious, both personal and collective, as well as the conscious mind. The concept was influenced by both Jung's own mystical experiences and his studies in Asian thought (Coleman, 2006, pp. 154–155). It is often expressed in religious symbols, and is associated with the "numinous"—Jung's term, adapted from the German theologian Rudolph Otto, for the emotional quality accompanying a sense of contact with higher powers, or the divine. "Individuation," the goal of Jungian psychotherapy, is the incorporation of the unconscious, both personal and collective, in a more realized and conscious Self.

With that process, the unconscious becomes a source of wisdom, creativity, and insight into the deeper elements of reality. It brings us into contact with realms that we think of as spiritual. While Freud viewed religion largely as fantasy, as wish-fulfillment and psychological projection, Jung saw value in a specific "religious function" in the psyche. That function was both natural and necessary. Religious symbols and rituals could be a means of integrating unconscious with conscious life, of harmonizing our deeper instinctive inclinations with our daily world. The psyche itself might even reach beyond space and time, and thus partake in what we think of as "eternity" (see, e.g., Jung, 1945/1970).

But Jung valued personal experience of the transcendent over institutionally sanctioned systems of belief. "Creeds," he once wrote, "are codified and dogmatized forms of original religious experience" (cited in Main, 2006, p. 304). The symbols of modern religions, he lamented, often have lost connections with experience. In that sense, Jung was, in contemporary terms, "spiritual" rather than "religious."

Ultimately, for Jung, psyche is not a product of individual brains, but a cosmic principle. All of these notions resonate with transpersonal thought; they are reasons that today's transpersonal psychologists readily acknowledge Jung as a predecessor, and often see their own ideas as confirming and extending basic Jungian insights and principles (see Grof, 1985, pp. 188–192).

Like the spiritually oriented ideas discussed in the following pages, Jungian psychology seldom has had a firm home in the mainstream academic world, dominated as it is by the assumptions of modern materialism. Jungian psychology, however, is thoroughly mined outside of that world; Jung has spurred generations of devotees and critics, as well as institutions that keep his ideas afloat. Legions of commentators have thoroughly explored all aspects of his writings. For that reason, I have included no chapter in this volume examining Jung himself; his ideas crop up frequently enough in the text, but largely in passing. My focus, rather, is on the less appreciated contributions of other thinkers, and on a largely Anglo-American contribution to this notion of an expanded view of consciousness.

Acknowledgments

My own personal encounter with that view is presented in the Epilogue. Here I must acknowledge, with deep gratitude, the role in that process of Stanislav Grof. Through his seminal writings and teachings and practices,

Stan has vastly expanded my own sense of the capacities of the psyche, and has been instrumental in helping me to grasp those experiences in a way that resonates with my intellectual understanding and academic training. My thanks are due, as well, to others in the Grof-inspired training in Holotropic Breathwork, especially Tav and Cary Sparks, Diana Medina, and Mireya Alejo Marcet. A special bow of gratitude goes to my partners at Holotropic Breathwork Houston, Pamela Stockton and Rob Park.

Beginning beforehand, but especially since returning to my native city of Houston in 2011, I have been inspired along the path of these explorations by the teaching and prolific writings of Jeffrey J. Kripal, J. Newton Rayzor Professor of Religion at Rice University. With courage as well as exceptional insight, and a radiant gift of communication, Jeff is at the forefront of bringing the perspective captured in this book into the academy, exploring the further implications of many related ideas, and integrating those notions into a more capacious, spiritually aware but intellectually grounded perspective, with significance for all the humanities.

Jeff has done me the honor of writing a forward to this volume, and of closely reviewing and critiquing the initial draft. The final product has benefitted from the careful reading, suggestions, and encouragement of Ginger Clarkson, as well as from observations by Deepesh Faucheaux, John Hanagan, James Ponet, and Carolyn Turner—all of whom, with the rich discussions we have had over the years, have helped me to refine my thoughts.

Several of these chapters were generated from lectures that I gave originally at the C.G. Jung Educational Center of Houston, a marvelously rich cultural asset in our city. My hearty thanks for their support go to the two directors of the Center during these past few years, Jerry Ruhl and Sean Fitzpatrick, and to their assistants Dorothy Weathers, former Program Coordinator, and Jennifer Wilkins, current Manager of Curriculum and Exhibits. I have benefitted from the cheerful aid of others on the Jung Center staff, including Connie Gooden, Elissa Davis, and Michael Craig. Leaders of the Houston Community Group of the Institute of Noetic Sciences, particularly Merri Michaels, Steve Scholl, and Brad Martin, have been steadfast backers of these lectures. My thanks go as well to Joe and Miriam Hirsh, Lydia Duggan, and Jerry and Linda Patchen, all loyal members of the Jung Center community and Houston IONS group, for their encouragement of my turning those lectures into a book. Brooke Summers-Perry, recent director of the Bishop John E. Hines Center for Spirituality and Prayer, has been another source of encouragement for my lectures, as has Nicolas Shumway, recently Dean of the School of Humanities and now Frances Newman Moody Professor of Humanities at Rice University.

Additional chapters are revisions of articles previously published in journals, especially *The Journal of Transpersonal Psychology*. I am grateful to Marcie Boucouvalas, editor of that journal, for her keen observations and suggestions, and for permission to republish articles that are the basis of Chapters 4, 5, and 9. My thanks are due to Cathy McKinney, editor of the *Journal of the Association of Music and Imagery*, for permission to republish the article that forms the basis of Chapter 8. I am indebted, as well, to Lorelette Knowles, Director of Library Services at Saybrook University, Seattle Campus, for locating Anthony Sutich's doctoral dissertation, a key source for material in Chapter 7. Bill Howze has diligently researched copyright issues related to the illustrations, and John Kadlecek, publisher of Velvet Spring Press, has offered counsel on publication and distribution. I am especially grateful to the authorities and editors at Westphalia Press: to Dr. Paul J. Rich, President of the Policy Studies Organization, for suggesting the Press as a vehicle for this book, and to Daniel Gutierrez-Sandoval, Executive Director of the PSO, and Rahima Schwenkbeck, Westphalia's Director of Media and Marketing, for paving the way to publication. Nancy Kern and Kacey Carmichael have been sources of personal support throughout the process of giving birth to this volume.

My most profound bow of gratitude goes to my beloved wife and partner, Ginger Clarkson. She has bravely risked the inevitable conjugal tensions that go with playing the role of annoyingly scrupulous, if ultimately highly valued, editor. On a far deeper plane, our life together has helped to focus my attention, widen my horizons, and mold my perceptions, informing the outlook and ideas embodied in this book in ways that I am sure I only partially understand.

INTRODUCTION
The Transpersonal Vision

William James, at the turn of the twentieth century, stated the core idea: "The further limits of our being plunge, it seems to me, into an altogether other dimension of existence from the sensible and merely 'understandable' world." We might call that other dimension "mystical" or "supernatural"—but whatever the label, it is part of our consciousness; it is one with us, melding with our "further limits." "[W]e belong to it," James went so far as to say, "in a more intimate sense than that in which we belong to the visible world" (1902/1929, p. 506).

Religious thought and philosophical speculations might forever have honored visions from that other dimension of existence, implying that human consciousness has a reach far beyond the visible realm presented to our senses. James, however, was speaking not as a religious philosopher but as a scientifically oriented psychologist, struggling to explain data and experiences encountered in a lifetime of empirical investigation. This was the researcher, after all, who had established the first psychological laboratory in the United States, and whose *Principles of Psychology,* published in 1890, had aimed to set the fledging field of psychology on firm scientific grounds.

In his times, as in ours, James's expansive view of what human consciousness might encompass was a radical vision, challenging the reigning cultural and professional consensus that all knowledge originates, ultimately, with impressions gained through an individual's five senses. In his researches, however, James repeatedly encountered phenomena that by that assumption seemed inexplicable—cases, for example, of telepathy or thought transference, or clairvoyant knowledge about another's family life that could not have been gained through the knower's ordinary experience.

To explain such phenomena, James and a circle of like-minded investigators turned to the newly minted notion of a subconscious mind. The reach of a person's subconscious, they realized, was far greater than that of his or her normal awareness: it could stretch beyond—perhaps far beyond— what was presented to the senses. Under the right circumstances, it could reach into, or be penetrated by, another person's awareness, or some common trove of awareness accessible, perhaps, to all of humanity. Those right circumstances often involved leaving behind everyday consciousness and

1

entering into some form of trance state. "The whole drift of my education," James concluded,

> goes to persuade me that the world of our present consciousness is only one out of many worlds of consciousness that exist, and that those other worlds must contain experiences which have meaning for our life also; and that although in the main their experiences and those of this world keep discrete, yet the two become continuous at certain points, and higher energies filter in. (1902/1929, p. 509)

For James, those higher energies emanated from regions that we think of as supernatural, mystical, or spiritual.

The Field of Transpersonal Psychology

Beginning in the 1960s, the contemporary field of transpersonal psychology has made systematic efforts to delve into such other worlds of consciousness. Utilizing techniques that were unavailable, or scarcely available, in James's time, it has searched out and instigated points in which the two worlds become continuous, bringing into awareness impressions and experiences that may have been available to the subconscious, but that lay far beyond the reach of our senses and this world of our common thoughts. The character of those experiences varies vastly, if not infinitely, suggesting that an individual human mind might have access, potentially, to any element of consciousness that exists. In any case, the experiences themselves reinforce the notion that the further limits of our being do stretch into other dimensions and worlds—and that our consciousness is far more expansive, more encompassing, than we commonly know.

Take, for example, the case of Karl, who participated in workshops led by the transpersonal psychologist Stanislav Grof. With his wife Christina, Grof was the creator of a technique called "Holotropic Breathwork," which utilizes music and deep breathing to induce what he calls a "non-ordinary state of consciousness," promoting dives into deeper layers of a client's subconscious. Karl participated in a series of Holotropic Breathwork sessions, held at the Esalen Institute in Big Sur, California. In his case, the imagery that emerged echoed experiences he had had previously, while attending workshops in "primal therapy," another self-exploration technique, held in Los Angeles.

During those earlier workshops, Karl seemed to relive elements of his own birth process—an experience that is common, as well, in Holotropic Breathwork. At the same time, he began to experience visions of a scene taking place in a distant time and place—set in a fortress, with tunnels, ramparts, and soldiers. For Karl, the images carried a strong emotional charge, and in successive primal therapy workshops, they recurred in greater detail: the fortress seemed to be situated on a cliff overlooking a rocky ocean shore; the soldiers might have been Spanish.

In subsequent Holotropic Breathwork sessions, the imagery continued to unfold, with visions of bloody combat. Karl felt himself in the scene, not as a soldier, but as a priest. At one point, he viewed a seal ring on his finger, with clearly recognizable initials. At another, he experienced himself as impaled by the sword of a British soldier, then cast down from the ramparts to die on the shore. A skilled draftsman, Karl recorded the scenes in a series of finger paintings and drawings, including ones of the fortress atop a rocky cliff from a perspective set in the ocean, and another of the ring with the priest's initials. As these sessions progressed, Karl discerned relationships between the experience of these images of a distant scene and issues in his personal life.

In the course of these sessions, Karl took a vacation. On impulse, with no thought of a relationship to his psychological explorations, he decided to spend his holiday in Ireland. After his return, viewing his photographs of the trip, he noticed with surprise that he had taken 11 shots of the same scenery on the Ireland's rugged west coast—scenery that he did not find especially interesting. But the repetition intrigued him enough so that, with the help of a map, he reconstructed where he had been at the time, and in which direction he was pointing the camera.

Far in the background of those shots, it turned out, stood the ruin of a fortress known as *Dún an Óir*. Today, photographs of the site are readily available on the Internet, showing a massing of cliff and structure strikingly akin to the drawings that Karl had rendered. Researching its history, Karl found that *Dún an Óir* had been the site of a battle in 1580, during the Second Desmond Rebellion, of Irish against British rule. The Irish were aided by Spain, and Spanish soldiers had occupied the fort before being besieged there by a larger British force. Sir Walter Raleigh, attached to the British contingent, negotiated an agreement promising the Spaniards free escape if they surrendered. The Spaniard assented, but once inside, the

British, instead of honoring the agreement, slaughtered the Spaniards and tossed their bodies over the ramparts.

Fascinated, Karl continued his research on the battle, eventually discovering a document that named a priest with the Spanish forces. The priest's initials were the same as those on the ring of Karl's vision. (Grof, 1988, pp. 92–93; 2006, pp. 137–139.)

Karl's experience of *Dún an Óir* was trans-personal: it came into his personal consciousness, emerging from his subconscious mind into his normal, waking awareness; but it seems to have originated outside the bounds of his egoic individuality, his personal experience, his individual five senses, at least in this lifetime. The gamut of perceptions that fit that broad description is, in various senses of the term, boundless. Grof, among others, has attempted a comprehensive classification of them: experiences in which the percipient subsumes a conscious awareness, normally thought of as decidedly *other*, as if it were an element in his or her own awareness and identity. They might include, for example, identification with another person, or a group of people, living or dead; out-of-body experiences; encounters with a universal or cultural archetype; sensations of oneness with all life, or all creation (see esp. Grof, 1988). Most of these experiences come when the percipient has entered some kind of state other than normal, waking consciousness, be it a dream or some form of trance state.

By that system, Karl's vision would be labeled a "past incarnation experience." In such experiences, past events and historical circumstances feel vividly present, as if they were actually in the here and now. Does that indicate that Karl, himself, was a reincarnation of the unfortunate *padre* of *Dún an Óir*—that he was the same spirit, soul, mind, or entity in a later embodied form? Indeed, it *could* imply that, and many a culture would have no difficulty in accepting the premise. But that is by no means the only way to explain Karl's experience. Might it be, instead, a case of *cryptomnesia*, or a hidden, unconscious memory? Perhaps Karl had once read of the Desmond Rebellion and subsequently forgot about it, so that it was buried in his unconscious but unavailable, in ordinary states of awareness, to his everyday, operative mind. Alternatively—to pursue another theory that has been advanced to explain such incidents—might Karl have been tapping into some collective field of memory, some "reservoir" of human consciousness that any of us might draw on in certain circumstances?

Conceivably, Karl's personal issues of the present day, the ones he found resonate with the scene at *Dún an Óir*, could have attuned him to this particular vision, much as an electrical charge might link two widely dispersed but energetically related pockets of force.

Spiritual Experience and the Nature of the Psyche

We are carried here, certainly, into highly speculative realms—and into questions that challenge the common assumptions of our dominant intellectual consensus and mainstream systems of belief. But Karl's vision—and untold numbers of transpersonal experiences—are data not simply to be ignored; they merit exploration and efforts of explanation. They bring us, moreover, into a rich and vital discussion of some of the most fundamental questions of our lives: questions about the nature and capacities of the human psyche, and its relation to ultimate realities. They suggest a certain harmony between our subjective selves and the larger cosmic matrix of which we are a part; they imply that the subconscious mind has a range and capacity that elevates what humanity is and can be; they adumbrate, perhaps, that the reality that we are given is not simply the accidental conglomerate of minute flecks of dust, but the product of a vast, luminous intelligence of which we are intentional components.

From its inception, at any rate, transpersonal psychology has justified concerns that we call "spiritual." It has envisioned the human psyche as embedded in invisible realms, as immersed in a context that extends beyond our ordinary ken, beyond the reality presented by our sense experience. It has seen that wider reality as constituted by consciousness, as governed by and composed of intelligence. And it has validated the notion of transcendence—the notion that we can have some avenue of communication, some form of authentic relationship, with elements of that larger, enveloping consciousness. It has validated, that is to say, spiritual experience (see Lajoie & Schapiro, 1992).

That is not to say that it has stood with traditional religions. Its emphasis has been on the experiential—on direct, personal experiences of those wider levels of intelligence. One of its central preoccupations has been mystical experience, as manifested in all religious traditions, or entirely outside of them. It has viewed such experiences as at the heart, ultimately, of genuine human relationship with the sacred, and as the source of the varying religious traditions that we know. And it has been intrigued by the practices in all those religions that help catalyze religious experiences. But its attitude towards organized religion is less sympathetic: as institutional churches develop creeds, dogmas, and entirely mundane power arrangements, ostensibly on the authority of those religious experiences, the transpersonal perspective grows wary. Mystical experiences, to borrow James's term, are "ineffable": the formulaic creeds and dogmas purportedly based on them are shaped by the limited human cultures of their time and place. Dogmas inevitably fail to capture what is essential about the original experience; their characterizations of its truth are necessarily distorted or partial. The institutions created in its name, with their hierarchies and group interests, are governed not directly by divine will, as they often pretend, but by decidedly human concerns.

With this perspective, the strain of thought that we are naming "transpersonal" is often in sympathy with the growing segment of the population who identify as "spiritual but not religious." It provides, in fact, a philosophical justification and intellectual tradition for that orientation, which now, by the most authoritative accounts, is embraced by some 18–33% of American adults (Gallup, 2003; Pew Research Center, 2012).

Science and Spirit

Follow the mainstream press in our day, and you will encounter discussions that assume a stark opposition between "science" and "religion." "Science," however, is generally taken in these debates to mean a fully materialistic outlook on causality, and "religion" is seen as a system of beliefs drawn from scriptures and creeds. These are disputes that could have been played out a century and a half ago, when Darwinian theories and higher Biblical criticism first began to challenge the literal interpretation of Judeo-Christian scriptures.

Materialism pervades Western intellectual culture, in ways not only explicit but also far-reaching and subtle, shaping not only conscious convictions but also general assumptions and attitudes. It determines what questions are seen as legitimate in academic inquiry and elite intellectual life. In brief, it is a series of philosophical assumptions, naively assumed to be validated by modern science. Science most easily probes the relationship among material *things*, and materialism sees what physical science is best equipped to explore, material things, as the fundamental element of reality.

At bottom, by this outlook, reality is matter, usually conceived of particles and assemblies of particles, occupying three-dimensional space. The complex world that we know—including our conscious awareness—is built, ultimately, from the relationship of those utterly unconscious particles, which, since they are in motion, combine in increasingly complex ways. The combinations, however, are products of random collisions, not a governing intelligence. Consciousness—awareness, intelligence—is a result of chance configurations, an accident of probabilities as the combination of particles reaches a certain level of complexity. The wonders of human consciousness are explicable in terms of the physical assemblage of our brains, as it responds to the physical input from our senses.

Assumptions of this ilk figure in, and limit, much of our public discussion, often in hidden ways. The deeper realms of theoretical science, however, have long since abandoned a picture of the world that would justify adopting these assumptions as an unquestionable philosophical framework. Since the rise of quantum mechanics in the early twentieth century, modern physics may not have demonstrated the ontological reality of a spiritual realm, but it arguably has made room for a view that consciousness is as fundamental to reality as "material" particles. Through that door, it helps to bring spirituality back to the table as the basis of legitimate philosophical constructs. Albert Einstein's demonstration that mass, ultimately, is energy; the concept of particles not as solid objects but as condensations in fields of energy, and simultaneously as waves; the "Copenhagen interpretation," which proposes that observation itself is a factor in condensing waves into particles; the demonstration of quantum entanglement—the interconnection of particles distant from one another; the mathematical pursuit of evidence of multiple and parallel universes, as suggested in string theory: these are only some of the notions that shake the foundations of classical Newtonian mechanics.

As the British physicist James Jeans stated as early as the 1930s, "The stream of knowledge is heading towards a non-mechanical reality; the universe begins to look more like a great thought than a great machine" (1930/1937, p. 137). That characterization is reinforced by trends in system and field theories, where the notion of what is most fundamental shifts from objects to patterns, from substance to process, and aggregates seem to adopt what we think of as mental characteristics. Actions of components are determined not so much by the particular components themselves, but as if they were directed by the aggregate, in an ever-wider web of interconnection.

If the physical world begins to appear not as a random aggregate of particles but as an interconnected web of energies, the mental world, too, must admit of interconnection, of relationship over distance, of direct influence from what is physically afar. Transpersonal psychology studies, among other things, influence from afar, and from the wider reaches of the interconnected web. Or, we might say, from the spiritual realm. In exploring that realm, it draws on the deeper, psychological meaning of religious truths, of what its practitioners refer to as "wisdom traditions."

The resulting conception of spirituality is something apart from, but related to, the eternal realms of religious orthodoxies. Understood in this way, however, that conception can embrace both a scientific and a religious attitude towards life. By and large, science and religion each have their own realms to explore, their own methods of doing it. But at points they cross paths and their terrains overlap. The result need not be conflict, if our conception of each is not reduced to long-outmoded patterns of thought. The transpersonal perspective embraces the validity of an ever-evolving scientific quest, as well as the reality of a spiritual realm that, as Aldous Huxley, who figures in these pages, phrased it, is "substantial to the world of things and lives and minds" (Huxley, 1945, p. vi).

Lives and Minds

It is lives and minds that are the focus of this volume. The questions touched upon here are breathtakingly big, dealing with our most basic outlook towards the real. They may be approached in innumerable ways, through the perspective of a multiplicity of disciplines. They have dimensions that are philosophical, sociological, psychological, physical, biological, neurological, anthropological, cosmological—the adjectival list could stretch on endlessly. My modest purpose here is to glance at a sweep of intellectual history, focusing on the field of psychology, broadly understood. I propose to provide a historical overview of transpersonal thought in the Anglo-American world, from the latter nineteenth century, when psychology first began to emerge as a distinct discipline, to the present. The approach is to present key concepts of this worldview by looking at the ideas of some outstanding figures in the field, against the background of their lives, their intellectual milieu, and cultural trends that contributed to their formation. Each chapter includes, as well, ruminations about how the ideas of these pioneers might fare in the intellectual context of transpersonal thought today. Part I examines the foundations of transpersonal ideas from the latter nineteenth century; Part II takes up the contributions of the field labeled "transpersonal psychology" from its formal founding in the late 1960s.

Keep turning these pages, and you will encounter such figures as Richard Maurice Bucke, the Canadian psychologist who, struck instantaneously with a transformative vision, popularized the notion of "cosmic consciousness"; William James, who produced what still, after more than a century, might be considered the most consequential study of religious experience yet written; and Frederic W.H. Myers, who in attempting to provide evidence for an afterlife, gave us the first comprehensive theory of the unconscious mind. Less extensively, you will glimpse the role of other early explorers of depth psychology, from Jean-Martin Charcot and Pierre Janet to Sigmund Freud, Theodore Flournoy, and Carl Jung. You will glance back, too, at some of the earlier forebears of transpersonal concepts, such as Anton Mesmer, the charismatic and controversial eighteenth-century physician who developed a technique referred to as "magnetism," which later was refined as "hypnotism"; his equally influential follower the Marquis de Puységur; and the early German psychologist Gustav Fechner, who figures in mainstream psychological history as the creator of psychophysics, bringing experimental observation and exact measurement to the study of the psyche, but who harbored notions of panpsychism, seeing all reality as conscious.

Moving forward in the twentieth century, you will consider the influence of Huxley, the remarkable polymath, novelist, philosopher, and social commentator whose blood lineage embodied the conflict between science and religion, and who turned to Asian and mystical thought as a way to resolve that conflict—marking out, in the process, a seminal theory of the relationship between mind and brain. And throughout these chapters, but most amply in Part II, you will meet, and feel the influence, of some of the creators of the contemporary field of transpersonal psychology, as it adopted that label and self-consciously declared itself to the world in the late 1960s: Abraham Maslow, Anthony Sutich, Stanislav Grof, Helen Bonny, Ken Wilber. Their various ideas of mind and reality are not always entirely compatible; they certainly have generated debates among themselves. But together, in the long view, their ideas form a picture of reality cohesive enough to be set in opposition to the dominant materialist paradigm.

The list of participants is by no means comprehensive, and this survey makes no attempt to be. My aim is to introduce the field of transpersonal thought to a general reader; the book is not intended primarily for academic specialists. In one respect, however, I hope that the specialists take note. What this collection brings to the transpersonal field is a broad perspective of intellectual history. History is often not the strength of academic psychologists, and transpersonal psychologists initially presented their findings to the world with limited awareness of the historical precedents for what they thought of as revolutionary ideas and procedures. For that reason, this book casts a strong emphasis on the antecedents, within the field of psychology, of thought that I refer to as "transpersonal." It is innovative, in some measure, in portraying the transpersonal field not as beginning in the "revolutionary" 1960s, but as a vibrant if often marginalized movement stretching from the earliest days of academic psychology. Those earlier manifestations, to my mind, are ripe for fruitful study, to deepen and enrich the field of transpersonal thought as it flowers into the future.

PART I

Foundations of Transpersonal Thought

CHAPTER ONE

Cosmic Consciousness
Illumination Beyond Religion

"Cosmic consciousness": The phenomenon is no doubt ancient, perhaps perennial, but the term is a modern one. It reflects an effort to comprehend a sudden and spontaneous and life-transforming state of mystical awareness, and to do so from a *psychological* perspective: that is, not as a product of divine grace understood within a particular theological framework, but rather as a human experience that might be found in all religious traditions, and among people with little or no religious beliefs, and which perhaps underlies the spiritual strivings of all cultures.

To those who have it, almost universally, that experience seems to reveal that all of reality is somehow a unity, permeated by consciousness and intelligence and purpose—that the reality we know exists in a larger spiritual context. It is an ecstatic experience of oneness, and of our own identity with the larger, sacred whole.

We begin with an instance from our own epoch. Here are the words of astronaut Edgar Mitchell—scientist, military pilot, and the sixth man to walk on the moon—describing his experience gazing out at the earth and the infinite field of stars, as Apollo 14 returned to the earth in 1971:

> And suddenly it settled in, a visceral moment of knowing.... It was not an intellectual realization, but a deep knowing that was accompanied by a feeling of ecstasy and oneness.... In that instant, I knew for certain that what I was seeing was no accident. That it did not occur randomly and without order.... It was as though my awareness reached out to touch the furthest star and I was aware of being an integral part of the entire universe, for one brief instance.... I could reach out and touch the furthest parts and experience the vast reaches of the universe. It was clear that those tiny pinpoints of light in such brilliant profusion were a unity. They were linked together as part of the whole as they framed and formed a backdrop for this view of planet Earth. I knew we are not alone in this universe, that Earth was one of millions, perhaps billions, of planets like our

13

own with intelligent life, all playing a role in the great creative plan for the evolution of life. (Cited in Martin, 2009)

Mitchell may have been looking out at the literal cosmos, but the term "cosmic consciousness," denoting such a life-changing epiphany, permeates our modern discourse of spirituality. My own Internet search for it instantly come up with a million two hundred and eighty thousand results. Its use runs the gamut from sober scholarly studies to popular works of self-help; it is likely to emerge in accounts of near-death experiences or psychedelic drug journeys, in discussions of transpersonal psychology or speculations about the evolution of human consciousness (see, for example, Liester, 2013).

Richard Maurice Bucke

Our use of the term can be traced back now more than a century, to the classic study by that name written by Richard Maurice Bucke and published in 1901. To examine Bucke's ideas, and the context out of which they came, carries us, I believe, into the modern roots of today's transpersonal movement, and of the widespread trend in contemporary culture that we refer to as "Spiritual But Not Religious" (SBNR). That movement, and that trend, are respectful of the findings of modern science, but they challenge the dominant materialism of Western intellectual culture. They perceive a wider spiritual context to our lives, but emphasize the limitations of the dogmas and creeds of religious institutions. They see the individual psyche not only as the product of a particular human brain, but as somehow linked to a broader cosmic intelligence that permeates, or perhaps underlies, the reality that we know. That is implied in the term "transpersonal," which posits a consciousness beyond the person of the individual ego.

At the establishment of *The Journal of Transpersonal Psychology* in 1969, Willis Harman, a kingpin of the movement, pointed to Bucke's *Cosmic Consciousness* as a key forerunner of the field. My purpose in this chapter is to look at the central ideas of Bucke's work, to glance at the influences that helped form them, and to reflect on the way they persist in our own times.

Bucke was a descendent of the eminent Walpoles of England: His father, a clergyman, was a great-grandson of British Prime Minister Sir Robert

Walpole. Richard Maurice was British-born; but in 1838, when he was only an infant, his family emigrated to Canada, and he grew up on a farm in Ontario. He had no formal early education, but he was home-schooled in languages and absorbed much from his family's large library. At age 16, he set out to wander through the United States, working odd jobs like wagon-driving and mining, and losing one foot and half of another to frostbite contracted in the Sierra Nevada mountains. After five years he returned to Canada and eventually studied medicine, first at McGill University in Montreal and then in Paris. (The sketch of Bucke in Figure 1.1 was drawn by a fellow student at McGill.) Maurice (pronounced "Morris"), as he was known, returned from Europe to Canada, married, and began raising a family and building a medical practice; but he was subject to depression— to anxiety and panic attacks—and also to physical ailments. And then, in 1868, he encountered Walt Whitman's *Leaves of Grass*—a book, he later said, that he saw as the "revealer and herald" of a new "religious era" (Bucke, 1883, p. 183).

1.1 Richard M. Bucke, drawn by a fellow student at McGill University, c. 1858. (Western Archives, Western University, AFC 203, Dr. Richard Maurice Bucke and Family fonds, Series 3, File 5, Sketch of Richard Maurice Bucke, c. 1858.)

The Legacy of Walt Whitman

This is where our story connects with the deeper American roots of transpersonalism and Spiritual But Not Religious. Whitman is often taught as a poet of American nationalism and political democracy, and as an innovator in literary form; in current scholarship, he is often construed as a gay poet. But to Bucke and others in that epoch, Walt Whitman was a transcendent *religious* figure, the clarion voice of a radical new religious sensibility suited to the modern age, a prophet on the order of Jesus himself. "I can never think of Whitman as a mere literary man," said one admirer. "He is a mighty spiritual force" (cited in Robinson, 1981, p. 5).

This was a world in which traditional religious teachings had begun to crumble, at least among the intelligentsia. Discoveries in geology and biology had shattered the biblical account of creation; the tale in Genesis was shown to be one creation myth among many; and textual studies of the Bible revealed it as a human document composed in many, often conflicting voices. Whitman had been inspired by the American Transcendentalists, who came into prominence in the early nineteenth century. Ralph Waldo Emerson and other Transcendentalists had recast the spiritual as something to be experienced in the individual human heart, apart from the dogmas and creeds and rituals of religious institutions, which they saw as only perpetuating misunderstandings of original spiritual insights. The Transcendentalists portrayed the natural world as suffused with a divine presence. Whitman sang that new sensibility, embracing the new science, but finding in it evidence of a living universe, and seeing beyond it into mystical realms. In a private letter to Whitman, Emerson himself called the first edition of *Leaves of Grass* "the most extraordinary piece of wit and wisdom that America has yet contributed" (Emerson, 1957, p. 362). To his more fervent admirers later in the century, Whitman carried the new religious sensibility to its highest expression.

Whitman saw divinity in the commonplace and the everyday, in the human body and in sexuality, in the trees and the insects and on the trolley car. He saw oneness with the divine especially in the human Self, and he sensed an embodied intelligence in the universe that worked towards harmony and the greater good of the unified and interconnected whole of which we are a part.

Later, Bucke would say that Whitman was "par excellence, the man who in modern times has written ... from the point of view of Cosmic

Consciousness" (1991, p. 225). It could well have been that Whitman's perspective was shaped by a sudden, spontaneous experience of that sort. Bucke himself thought so, and took as evidence this verse from *Leaves of Grass:*

> Swiftly arose and spread around me the peace and joy and knowledge
> that pass all the art and argument of the earth;
> And I know that the hand of God is the elderhand of my own,
> And I know that the spirit of God is the eldest brother of my own,
> And that all the men ever born are also my brothers
> ....and the women my sisters and lovers,
> And that a kelson of the creation is love.... (Cowley, 1959, p. 29)

("Kelson" here is a nautical metaphor: it refers to the line of timber that supports both the keel and the floor of a boat, holding the structure together.)

Leaves of Grass transformed the life of Maurice Bucke. It was, he believed, responsible for his return to health. Over the next few years, he made a study of it, collecting all that had been published about its author. Then, in 1872, when he was 36 years old, Bucke had the defining experience of his own life.

Bucke's Cosmic Vision

He was in England at the time, in London, and had spent an evening visiting with two literary friends, reading and talking about poetry, especially Whitman's. On his way back to his lodgings, in a carriage, his mind burst into a new level of consciousness. This is how it happened. Allow me to quote a rather long passage, because this experience formed the template for what Bucke called "Cosmic Consciousness," and all the details play a role:

> My mind, deeply under the influence of the ideas, images, and emotions called up by the reading and talk, was calm and peaceful. I was in a state of quiet, almost passive enjoyment, not actually thinking, but letting ideas, images and emotions flow of themselves ... through my mind. All at once, without

17

warning of any kind, I found myself wrapped in a flame-colored cloud. For an instant I thought of fire, an immense conflagration somewhere close by in that great city; the next, I knew the fire was within myself. Directly afterward there came upon me a sense of exultation, of immense joyousness accompanied ... by an intellectual illumination impossible to describe. Among other things, I did not merely come to believe, but I saw that the universe is not composed of dead matter, but is, on the contrary, a living Presence; I became conscious in myself of eternal life. It was not a conviction that I would have eternal life, but a consciousness that I possessed eternal life then; I saw that all men are immortal; that the cosmic order is such that ... all things work together for the good of each and all; that the foundation principle of the world, of all the worlds, is what we call love, and that the happiness of each and all is in the long run absolutely certain.

The vision lasted a few seconds and was gone; but the memory of it and the sense of the reality of what it taught has remained during the quarter of a century which has since elapsed. I knew that what the vision showed was true. (As cited in James, 1902/1929, pp. 390–391)

In his medical practice, Bucke veered towards the newly emerging area of psychology, which was still unformed as a field—practitioners were then called *alienists* (from the French *aliéné*, meaning *insane*). In 1877, he was appointed superintendent of the insane asylum in London, Ontario, a post that he retained for the rest of his life, another quarter century. Shortly before, the treatment of the insane had consisted primarily in restraining them, but Bucke soon supported a far more compassionate regimen of work, recreation, creativity, entertainment, and religious worship (Maynard, 2014, pp. 129–140; Rechnitzer, 1994, pp. 185–194). "We know that the person of a patient is sacred...," he said in one talk.

If we suffer from their evil passions, they suffer ten times more from them, and it is chiefly because they are subject to them that these unfortunate people deserve our deepest pity and our best care; for whether we are sane or insane it is from our own evil passions that we really suffer, and not from those of someone else. (Cited in Maynard, 2014, pp. 133–134)

Bucke rose to the top of the profession, eventually becoming president of the Psychological Section of the British Medical Association, and then president of the American Medico-Psychological Association, now called the American Psychiatric Association.

Throughout that career, Bucke's fascination—indeed, obsession—with Walt Whitman only intensified, and he devoted much of his time to championing Whitman and his work. At about the time of his appointment to the London asylum, on a professional trip to Philadelphia, he met the poet for the first time, dropping in at Whitman's home in Camden, New Jersey. To say the least, Bucke was impressed. "I have never seen any man to compare with him…," he wrote to a friend. "He is an average man magnified to the dimensions of a god." As a result of that meeting, Bucke found himself "lifted to … a higher place of existence," where he felt he stayed, basically, for the rest of his life (cited in Robinson, 1981, pp. 112-113). From that lofty perspective, he completed his first book, which had been germinating for some years. He dedicated *Man's Moral Nature* (1879) to Whitman, as "the man who of all men past and present that I have known has the most exalted moral nature."

Bucke on Whitman

In 1880, Whitman visited Bucke in Canada, staying for four months. (The image of Whitman in Figure 1.2 was taken on that visit.) Drawing on that encounter (and with extensive revisions by Whitman himself), Bucke wrote the first biography of his mentor, published in 1883. It is also an analysis of the poems, a riposte to Whitman's critics, and an exercise in hagiography, aiming to show that Whitman did indeed have the most exalted moral nature that humanity had attained, and that the purpose of *Leaves of Grass*, his ever-growing magnum opus, was above all *religious*—to plant, in Bucke's words, "the germs of a greater religion than has hitherto appeared upon the earth" (p. 158). It is a Christ-like Whitman that walks through those pages, with "a perfect mother," a carpenter-father, a capacity to heal the sick and wounded in Civil War hospitals by the power of his presence—and with a new dispensation for all the world. Whitman's religion, however, "was not comprised in dogmas, churches, creeds," for which he cared little; rather, "it is that habitual state of feeling in which a person regards everything in God's universe with wonder, reverence, perfect acceptance and love" (p. 31). *Leaves of Grass* here becomes a Bible for the new religion; its longest poem, "Song of Myself," says Bucke, "is an expression of Faith, the most lofty and absolute that man has so far attained" (p. 163).

Some years after that biography was published, Bucke was visiting the poet in Camden when Whitman had a series of strokes. In the patient's estimation, Bucke's medical skills saved his life. That incident brought the two closer together for Whitman's last four years. Bucke was Whitman's physician as well as friend, and an advisor on his publications. Eventually, he became one of Whitman's three literary executors, the editor of volumes of Whitman's letters and papers, and the editor of, and a contributor to, a collection of reviews and commentary on the poet's life and work.

1.2 Walt Whitman in London, Ontario, 1880. (iStock.com.)

Edward Carpenter

Meanwhile, Bucke had taken up the writing of his own *magnum opus.* The term "Cosmic Consciousness" was not of his coinage; it came from another Whitman devotee, the British writer and social activist Edward

Carpenter, whom Bucke met in England in 1891. Some ten years earlier, Carpenter had had a mystical illumination of his own, precipitated at the death of his mother and perhaps linked, too, with his readings of *Leaves of Grass* and of the *Bhagavad Gita*, the Hindu sacred text. By the time that he met Bucke, Carpenter had gained fame for his epic Whitmanesque poem "Towards Democracy" as well as notoriety as a Socialist philosopher and activist; later, he was to gain still more notoriety for his open defense, even extolling, of homosexuality.

Carpenter was enthralled by Asian religions: when he encountered Bucke, he had just returned from a long journey to India and Ceylon, where he studied with "*gñáni*"—his transliterated Sanskrit term for esoteric teachers. That experience surely formed a substance of their conversation (Maynard, 2014, p. 245). Carpenter invented the term "Cosmic Consciousness" as an English equivalent of the Sanskrit compound *Sat-chit-ananda*, literally, "Being-Awareness-Bliss," designating the ecstatic subjective experience of Brahman or of ultimate reality. In his reflections on his journey, published the following year, he said this:

> ...[W]hat the Gñáni sees and obtains is a new order of consciousness—to which, for want of a better we may give the name *universal* or *cosmic* consciousness, in contradistinction to the individual or special bodily consciousness with which we are all familiar. (Carpenter, 1904, p. 154)

Carpenter formulated the idea that cosmic consciousness represented a coming stage in the evolution of human awareness, a notion that fit well with Bucke's already formulated theories. Bucke took up the term, and worked on his study of the phenomenon over the next ten years.

Cosmic Consciousness: *the Book*

Cosmic Consciousness is Bucke's attempt to give a universal and historical context to experiences of illumination like his own: sudden visions of what he called "THE WHOLE" or "the meaning and drift of the universe" (p. 74), which come like "a dazzling flash of lightening in a dark night, bringing the landscape which had been hidden into clear view" (p. 75). The book was published in the first year of the new century, in Philadelphia, in an edition of only 500 copies. But it has never been out of print and remains honored as a classic, even as its core ideas have suffered challenge.

Bucke himself saw little of its success: he died suddenly, from a fall, a year after its publication. It is a hefty tome, and I can give only a brief sketch of it here: but it is built, I would say, around two core arguments: the universal commonality of mystical experience, and its place in human evolution.

The great bulk of the work is devoted to accounts of enlightened figures, highlighting what we know of their illuminating experience—all with co-pious quotation, accompanied by Bucke's interpretive notes, which often draw parallels with other figures in the book. Bucke divides those figures into two categories: the "great cases," whose experience he considers es-sentially complete, and more minor ones, whose experience, though pro-found, was partial. He counts 14 in the first category, most of them major prophets, philosophers, or poets; in the second, he gives us another 36, including more prophets and literary figures, but also lesser known people of his own acquaintance.

His clear goal is to establish, from a psychological perspective, the es-sential commonality of all these experiences. They differ in what he calls "detail," but he insists that they "agree in all essentials" (p. 72): "they are all more or less unsuccessful attempts to describe the same thing" (p. 382). His account of the Buddha, for example, draws parallels with teachings and writings in the Upanishads, and of Confucius, Jesus, St. Paul, Dante, Shakespeare, Balzac, Whitman—especially Whitman— and Edward Carpenter. The central teaching of Buddhism, says Bucke, is the possibility of nirvana, which is what Jesus meant by the Kingdom of God, which *is* Cosmic Consciousness. That too, he argues, is what Lao-Tsu meant by the "Tao," what Paul meant by being "in Christ," what Mohammed meant by "paradise," what Dante meant by "Beatrice," what John of the Cross meant by "contemplation." In Whitman's terms, it is "the peace and joy and knowledge that pass all the art and argument of the earth."

For all, it is an experience available in this life. Heaven in the afterlife is a metaphor for what we can find within ourselves in the eternal now: an ineffable vision of the cosmic order, the spiritual underpinning of the order of nature. In that experience, an old "self" is annihilated, as the subject be-comes one with the divine and with all of existence. "[Y]ou are your finite self no longer ..." says Plotinus. "You become one with the Infinite" (p. 123). Or here is John of the Cross, the sixteenth century Spanish mystic:

[A]ll things are mine, God himself is mine.... "[H]uman understanding becomes divine, made one with the divine" (pp. 148, 150). For Bucke, this experience of oneness is not earned by good works nor achieved by practice: it is spontaneous and instantaneous. It does not come from outside us: its font is the divine within us. "The Kingdom of God is within you," says Jesus in the Gospel of Luke. And Plotinus: "...this region of the truth is not to be investigated as a thing external to us.... It is within us" (p. 122).

Bucke identifies the phenomena, the experiences, that often accompany the revelation: not all are universal, but they are common enough to form a pattern. They include a sudden sense of light or flame—like the "great light" encountered by Paul on the road to Damascus, or the "burning bush" met by Moses. There is an ecstasy and sense of assurance or salvation—what Carpenter calls "an indescribable calm and joy" (p. 247). This is the "highest happiness," the "Brahmic bliss" of the Hindus. In the ineffable intellectual illumination, in its farther reaches, all life is seen as divine. The cosmos itself is revealed as a "living presence" (p. 73) exuding infinite love. The teaching of "all the great seers," writes Bucke, is "that God in himself is infinite love ... that divine love is the self-subsisting life of the universe" (p. 285). All things are seen to work together for good. Life is known to be eternal and the human soul in some sense immortal.

Since this is an intensely personal experience, rooted in the individual soul, it is not brought about by dogma, rituals, and the hierarchies of priesthoods. For Bucke, in fact, there is an "incompatibility"—that is his word—between Cosmic Consciousness and organized religion, the churches. "No man with the Cosmic Sense," he says, "will take direction (in the affairs of the soul) from any other man or any so-called God. In his own heart he holds the highest accessible standard, and to that he will and must adhere" (p. 135). Bucke cites Whitman:

> ...the soul emerges, and all statements, churches, sermons, melt away like vapors.... Bibles may convey and priests expound, but it is exclusively for the noiseless operation of one's isolated Self to enter the pure ether of veneration, reach the divine levels, and commune with the unutterable. (From *Democratic Vistas*, cited by Bucke, p. 229)

Evolution: Stages of Consciousness

The subtitle Bucke gave his book was *A Study in the Evolution of the Human Mind*. He saw cosmic consciousness as a fully natural phenomenon, not a supernatural one. It came from the order of nature, but it represented the human nature of the future, a coming stage of human evolution. Essentially, human development traverses three stages of mental evolution: Bucke labeled them Simple Consciousness, Self-Consciousness, and Cosmic Consciousness. Simple consciousness is shared with animals: it is our immediate perception of our bodies and our surroundings. Self-consciousness, on the other hand, is uniquely human: in it, we are aware of ourselves as distinct from the rest of the universe. It allows us to reflect on our own mental states: we know that we know. Self-consciousness gives rise to abstract ideas and language, to human thought, culture, industry, and art. It represents intellect, the conceptual mind.

Cosmic consciousness is the next stage in the natural growth of the mind, a leap beyond self-consciousness as great as the leap of self-consciousness beyond simple consciousness. It represents higher human intuition—not the conceptual but the intuitional mind. It reveals unmistakably what to the self-conscious, conceptual mind is absurd: that the cosmos consists "not of dead matter" but that it is, on the contrary, "entirely immaterial, entirely spiritual and entirely alive...; it shows that the universe is God and that God is the universe..." (p. 17). The apparent differences in mystical accounts—and especially of the religions based on them—spring from the necessity of expressing this core intuition in the limited concepts and language of self-consciousness.

Despite his insistence on a common core of cosmic consciousness, Bucke saw different levels of it; and its highest expression was embodied in Walt Whitman—likely, thought Bucke, "the greatest case of cosmic consciousness to date" (p. 69). What distinguished Whitman from most of his predecessors was his fullness of precisely that sense that "the universe is God and that God is the universe." In their visions of the transcendent, many of his predecessors rejected much of the natural world, but Whitman's pantheistic vision embraced it totally: embraced nature, the body, sexuality, all of life. "[T]he *All* and the idea of *All*," wrote Whitman, "...the pulsations in all matter, all spirit, throbbing forever—the eternal beats, eternal systole and diastole of life in things..." (p. 230).

At any rate, by Bucke's count, instances of cosmic consciousness were multiplying in history; eventually they would become the norm. When that happens, spiritual insight will govern all of life, but institutional religions will be, as he put it, "melted down" (p. 5), as by-products of an earlier stage of evolution. Although they grew out of instances of cosmic consciousness, they are largely products of self-consciousness. "Churches, priests, forms, creeds, prayers," says Bucke, "all agents, all intermediaries between the individual man and God will be permanently replaced by direct unmistakable intercourse" (p. 5).

Historical Importance

Such, then, is Bucke's sense of "the meaning and drift of the universe." So what, now, are we to make of these notions promulgated more than a century ago? Let's look now at Bucke from a perspective of our times.

In retrospect, I would say, Bucke's great and lasting accomplishments were historical; his ideas had an impact on the thought of his times and of posterity. *Cosmic Consciousness* fixed attention on sudden mystical insight, across cultures, as a universal *psychological* phenomenon, independent of religious doctrine. That assessment echoes the astute comment of William James, written in a letter to Bucke just after the book's publication: "I believe," wrote James, "that you have brought this kind of consciousness 'home' to the attention of students of human nature in a way so definite and unescapable that it will be impossible henceforward to overlook or ignore it" (cited in May, 1991, p. 19).

At that time, James was at work on his own yet more significant effort to bring that kind of consciousness "home"—his lectures on mysticism in *The Varieties of Religious Experience.* Together, we might say, those two works launched the modern, phenomenological study of mysticism that persists in our own times, exploring those "further reaches of our being," as James would have it, as they "plunge ... into an altogether other dimension of existence from the sensible and merely 'understandable' world." We can trace that form of inquiry, that psychological investigation of mystical experience, to the present day, through such figures in psychology as Carl Jung, Roberto Assagioli, Abraham Maslow, Stanislav Grof, and Charles Tart, and through such students of mysticism as Evelyn Underhill, Aldous Huxley, Sri Aurobindo, W.T. Stace, Ken Wilber, and Jeffrey Kripal.

Secondly, Bucke implanted a term in cultural discourse that has been with us ever since: surely its tenacity implies a cultural utility. However loosely used, "cosmic consciousness" has signified, over decades, the highest attainment of spiritual insight—or nearly that. You can find it in book titles from over the past century: *Cosmic Consciousness: One Man's Search for God* (1974); *Cosmic Consciousness Revisited: The Modern Origins and Development of a Western Spiritual Psychology* (1991); *Chaos, Creativity and Cosmic Consciousness* (1992); *Cosmic Consciousness: The Man-God Whom We Await (1996): Cosmic Consciousness: The Personality of God upon Creation (2012); The Age of Cosmic Consciousness* (2013). The term is sometimes used to refer to Absolute Mind, the consciousness of the divine or of the universe itself, as well as, perhaps with more historical accuracy, to an experience of unity with that Absolute.

Claims: Commonality, Evolution

What, then, of Bucke's more specific claims: the commonality of mystical experience, and its place in human evolution?

Claims about the essential sameness of mystical experience are woefully out of fashion in academic discourse these days: the current known as "constructivism" points almost exclusively to differences. Constructivists will grow apoplectic over statements such as Bucke's assertion that Paul, Mohammed, Dante, Jesus, and the Buddha were all trying to say the same thing. And really, there is no doubt that Bucke vastly exaggerated the commonality of the cases he examined: all those experiences, as he described them, looked very much like his own. He interpreted them, understandably, through the lens of the central experience of his own life, and no doubt, in the process, often played loose in his interpretations of their accounts. Nevertheless, any human phenomena can be compared both for their similarities and their differences, and the search for each can bear noble fruit.

Bucke's trumpeting of sameness was a keynote in the twentieth-century movement known as "perennialism," which looked for a common core in the world's diverse religious traditions; and that movement has produced a remarkably rich literature, encompassing writings of such towering religious thinkers as William James, Aldous Huxley, W.T. Stace, and Huston Smith. Over a century ago, James pointed out that quite different ideas can immediately be attached to mystical experiences that do, in fact, have a similar psychological pattern and feeling, in widely dispersed cases.

We can dive into the ocean from different points on the globe, and find very different forms of aquatic life; but the experience of hitting the water is very much the same—*and* it gives us a powerful conviction that the ocean exists. To call attention to the dive itself is no small matter in a cultural ambience dominated by materialism, which often denies that the spiritual ocean enveloping us is indeed a reality. To look for commonality in widely diverse religious experiences remains a defensible—I would say, essential—endeavor. The contemporary philosopher Ken Wilber sums up the argument this way: "One Taste or 'cosmic consciousness'—the sense of oneness with the Ground of all creation—is the deepest core of the nearly universal consensus of the world's great wisdom traditions.... It is very simple, very obvious, very clear—concrete, palpable, unmistakable" (Wilber, 1999, pp. 56–57). For all his exaggerations, Bucke gave that endeavor a mighty push, and he identified elements that, whether or not they are universal, continually reappear in like experiences: the loss of a sense of a separate self, identity with the universal One, the joy and ecstasy of illumination, a perception of love as the sustaining energy of the divine.

Some of Bucke's ideas of social evolution, likewise, now seem to us painfully naïve; some of his science is clearly faulty and some of his social attitudes now seem crudely prejudicial. He wrote in a flush of scientific optimism that was common in intellectual circles after the publication of Darwin's *On the Origin of Species* but before the industrialized carnage of World War I. Bucke believed that the world was then on the verge of a social revolution, which he deemed "indescribably hopeful," "a new heaven and a new earth" (p. 4), when socialism and scientific advances would abolish both riches and poverty, air travel would dissolve national boundaries, massive urban centers would melt away, people would live in the most desirable climes, and religious conflict would dissipate in the face of direct contact with the divine.

Naïve as those notions might be, Bucke's focus was the broader one of spiritual rather than social evolution, and there he might be on more solid, or at least more lasting, grounds. He gave impetus to the idea that the basic human story is about the evolution of the human mind to higher levels of spiritual insight; and in one form or another, true or not, that idea has flourished since and is alive and well in our times. It is consistent with the "integral" Indian philosophy, so popular in the West, of Sri Aurobindo; we find it in the thought of the visionary French Jesuit paleontologist and philosopher Pierre Teihard de Chardin. Among our contemporaries, it figures in the work, for example, of Michael Murphy, founder of the Esalen Institute and mainstay of the human potential movement; of Ken Wilber, whose *magnum opus* is subtitled "The Spirit of Evolution"; and of Barbara Marx Hubbard, whose vision is influenced directly by Bucke (see Hubbard, 1998, pp. 176–177; Rechnitzer, 1994, p. 228). "I see now," Hubbard says in a statement currently posted online, "that what has been intuited...may indeed be life after this stage of evolution..., a state of being that normalizes direct apprehension of the divine, of the implicate order, and that sees ourselves as expressions of that unfolding pattern of creation...." (2006).

Spiritual But Not Religious

For a final word in this chapter, let us glance at Bucke's notion of illumination beyond religion, of spirituality without churches, priests, and dogmas. At a time when up to one-third of Americans self-identify as "spiritual but not religious," this posture, emphasizing direct experience over prescribed ritual, seems well worth reflection. The heart of it, I would say, is a psychological re-interpretation of experiences traditionally cast in religious language—a re-interpretation of religious archetypes as states of consciousness.

As an instance, let's consider Bucke's account of the Christian gospels. To Bucke, Jesus was a man who had cosmic consciousness: it occurred suddenly at the time of his baptism by John, when, according to Mark, "straightway coming out of the water, he saw the heavens rent asunder, and the Spirit as a dove descending upon him; and a voice came out of the heavens saying, 'Thou art my beloved Son, in Thee I am well pleased.'" Those words are a recognition of the divinity of the Self, in all people—just what Whitman meant when he wrote, "I know that the spirit of God is the brother of my own." Before that transformative moment, Jesus was quite ordinary: hence the astonishment of those who knew him earlier: "Is this not the carpenter's son?" Jesus's words and parables about entering the Kingdom of Heaven are lessons about the moral characteristics of those who achieve "the Cosmic sense": they are "born anew," and they are "poor in spirit," which here means not dominated by the self-conscious ego. Pointedly, Bucke observes that this moral character is outside of traditional religious observances: "I say unto you that the publicans and harlots go into the kingdom of God before you"—and even more pointedly, "except your righteousness shall exceed the righteousness of the Scribes and Pharisees, ye shall in no wise enter into the kingdom of heaven." Traditional religious forms are even antagonistic to cosmic consciousness: "woe unto you scribes and Pharisees, hypocrites! Because ye shut the kingdom of heaven against men: For ye enter not in yourselves" (pp. 97–111).

To a believer, these interpretations might seem to eviscerate the story, and to deny the worth of a like-minded community; but they, and Bucke's psychologically oriented renderings of the accounts other mystics, could allow minds formed in the modern world, who perhaps find little sense in traditional creeds, to relate to the wisdom in the world's sacred literature. Edgar Mitchell, walking on the moon, viewing the earth from afar and gazing at the infinite field of stars, may not have seen a place to call Heaven; but he found a "visceral moment of knowing," "a feeling of ecstasy and oneness," that revealed a "whole," a "unity" infused and governed by an inexpressible intelligence. In an instant, the scientist and military pilot saw reality in a radically different way, and he dedicated his life to that new understanding, not by repairing to a traditional church, but by founding the Institute of Noetic Sciences, which investigates scientifically anomalous and expansive experiences and thus gives credence to ideas of a spiritual reality.

Edgar Mitchell thus represents a spiritual sensibility significant in our times; and for all its limitations, Maurice Bucke's notion of cosmic consciousness helps to give it a place in our contemporary field of ideas.

CHAPTER TWO

The Discovery of the Unconscious: A Transpersonal Perspective

To an acute observer immersed in the world of early modern psychology such as William James, it seemed like a *moment* of discovery—the most momentous and revolutionary to take place during his long career in that budding field. It revealed, he said, "an entirely unsuspected peculiarity in the constitution of human nature" (1902/1929, p. 228)—no other step in psychology could make a claim such as that. He traced it, precisely, to 1886: the clinical revelation that, "in certain subjects at least," there is not only normal consciousness, but "memories, thoughts and feelings which ... are outside of the primary consciousness altogether, but yet must be classed as conscious facts of some sort, able to reveal their presence by unmistakable signs" (1902/1929, p. 228).

"Consciousness Beyond the Margin"

"Memories, thoughts and feelings which ... are outside of primary consciousness altogether": the very purpose of the emerging discipline of psychology was to subject the phenomena of human consciousness to empirical, scientific investigation. James's own *Principles of Psychology*, published in 1890, was a defining landmark in the field, which was still struggling for academic recognition. That work is remembered especially for the idea of the "stream of consciousness": James examined the way that our attention shifts, from moment to moment. Initially, psychologists thought of the object of attention as an idea: we have a constant succession of thoughts or ideas that dominate our awareness. But James came to think of that focus not so much as a clear and specific idea, but rather as a "field of consciousness." What we have in our minds at any given moment is not so much one idea as a total mental state, a field of objects, with varying levels of clarity or distinctness. You may be looking at me, but at the same time, you are wondering if your daughter has called back on your cellphone, you know that you are hungry, your elbow itches, the fellow in front of you reminds you of your old boyfriend, and you are worried about a client that you're scheduled to deal with tomorrow—and there are fragmentary notions of much more in your mind.

James used a circular metaphor, speaking of a "center of interest," on which attention is primarily focused, surrounded by other objects of awareness that are less and less distinct, until you get to a margin in the circle where things barely reach awareness at all. Until the 1880s, psychology had largely assumed that consciousness ended with those margins, that beyond the margins there was nothing that we could properly call "consciousness." But with the clinical demonstration of the subconscious, professional attention began to focus on what, in James's terms, is "consciousness beyond the margin"—that consciousness of some kind that is in us, but of which our normal consciousness is unaware. Out of that monumental refocusing of attention came the field of depth psychology—the work of Freud and Jung and all their followers and successors—which assumes that those memories, thoughts, and feelings that are outside of primary consciousness altogether is a major, even the driving, component of the human mind.

A Historical Perspective

What happened in 1886? In that year, to set a context, Queen Victoria still reigned over the global British Empire; the French Third Republic entered its sixteenth year; the Austro-Hungarian Empire was in full flower; and President Grover Cleveland inaugurated the Statue of Liberty in New York Harbor. James's comment about the discoveries of that year came a decade and a half later, in *The Varieties of Religious Experience*. What he had in mind, no doubt, were two streams of investigation, one centered in France, the other in England.

Before we go further with those specifics, however, let me note that not only our individual consciousness, but also our collective one, includes ever-changing fields and frontiers of awareness. In any historical epoch, similar ideas seem to occur almost simultaneously to different individuals, as if emerging from a collective, unconscious field, as it were, beyond the margin. The history of ideas is often told, perhaps naively, as a tale of influences, as if one person's idea gives rise to another's, in virtually a causal fashion. Eventually a way of thinking, retrospectively, gets associated with a particular individual in that chain: many a layman, for example, might think that the idea of the unconscious was originally an ingenious insight of Sigmund Freud. But in fact, particular times seem ripe for certain discoveries. One theory may influence another; one discovery may reference another, but the reality is that similar notions often seem to surface in different contexts and locales, brought to light not only by ingenious individual insights, but by an emerging collective awareness that we can only attribute to a *zeitgeist*, a spirit of the times—some ripeness for attention after a long history of perhaps quieter antecedents. In the terms of Carl Jung, particular archetypes emerge in the collective unconscious. That surely was the case with what we'll call the "discovery" of the unconscious in the latter years of the nineteenth century.

This is a complex story, which can be told in many ways—and has been, in various lengthy volumes. But I aim here to give that story a particular twist and interpretation, with a bow especially to the perspective of William James as he observed those events first-hand, and with a retrospective viewpoint formed by today's transpersonal psychology. James is a pivotal witness, both for his intimate acquaintance with the different strands of investigation, and for his judicious weighing of their contributions. He also prefigures the outlook of contemporary transpersonal thought. I intend to suggest that our own *zeitgeist*, in our times, might well be ripe for the rediscovery of certain ideas put forward in those early days of modern psychology, ideas that were subsequently cast aside in the professional development of the discipline. In brief, I will argue in favor of a larger and more encompassing and more positive view of the psyche than the one that prevailed in mainstream professional psychology.

Pierre Janet and the Coinage of "Subconscious"

One who played a vital role was Pierre Janet, whose work James brought to the attention of an English-speaking public in an essay called "The Hidden Self," published in 1890 in *Scribner's Magazine* (James, 1890a). In that pivotal year of 1886, Janet was a young researcher, still in his doctoral studies, volunteering at the psychiatric hospital in Le Havre; he was working with a patient whom in his writings he called "Lucie." Lucie suffered from what then was known as "hysteria"—today we might see it as a form of post-traumatic stress disorder. She was 19 years old, and subject to inexplicable fits of terror, seemingly without cause—but she had some remarkable traits. To probe her condition, Janet used hypnosis and automatic writing, that is, the patient's writing without apparent conscious attention.

Lucie could be engrossed in a conversation with a third person, all her attention seemingly focused on the discussion, while Janet simultaneously questioned her, asking that she write her responses with her right hand. She did so, signing her responses "Adrienne." Lucie had multiple personalities, and her primary self had no conscious awareness of what Adrienne wrote. She was also anesthetic over her entire body: Lucie would not feel or react to, say, being pinched; but Adrienne, reacting in writing, showed that she felt those pinches acutely.

Eventually, as Lucie underwent hypnosis, a third personality appeared: Janet called the three of them Lucie 1, 2, and 3. Lucie 1 had no consciousness of events that transpired when Lucie 2 or 3 were dominant; Lucie 2 held memories of events that transpired for herself and Lucie 1, but not for Lucie 3. Only Lucie 3—the one who called herself Adrienne—seemed to have an integrated memory fully intact, without anesthesia. It was Adrienne who revealed, in automatic writing, the source of Lucie's terror: a practical joke played to scare her when she was seven years old. Out of such cases, Janet constructed a theory of dissociation, the splitting off of thoughts and memories from the primary personality. In the process, he coined the term *subconscient*, or "subconscious," which appears in his doctoral dissertation (Ellenberger, 1970, p. 406; see Janet, 1903).

Cases of divided personality had been observed in medical settings for years, and the use of hypnosis to study hysterical subjects did not begin with Janet. It was a focus of the famous psychological schools at Nancy and at the Salpetriere Hospital in Paris, particularly as promoted by the eminent Jean-Martin Charcot, who pointed to the role of "ideas" split off from the normal mind in the development of neuroses. But a salient achievement of Janet's studies was to demonstrate that these different trains of memories and modes of behavior existed in the same person simultaneously—they were always there, but in a submerged state. Lucie 1 could carry on a conversation while Adrienne wrote; while Lucie 1 or 2 was dominant, Adrienne still observed. This indicated that the subject was not being invaded by an outside consciousness, as was the traditional explanation of, say, demonic possession or of mediumistic trances that apparently relayed messages from the dead. Rather, the split-off trains were in fact part of the same personal consciousness—a sub-consciousness, not an intrusion from afar.

Elsewhere in France, other young researchers were making similar observations. In that year of 1886, Sigmund Freud completed a four-month visit to the Salpetriere; and both Alfred Binet, another psychologist at the Salpetriere, and Henri Bergson, who was then teaching philosophy in the Auvergne region, published writings that pointed to hypnotism's revelation of unconscious mental life. Like Janet, all three of those figures were then in their late 20s.

As James well recognized, there had long been vague talk about "unconscious" mental activity, but the observations in Janet's dissertation, which was published in 1889 as *De l'Automatisme Psychologique*, or *Psychological Automatism*, seemed to him especially effective in casting on the subconscious an experimental and clinical light that made it a worthy subject of investigation for a field striving for scientific legitimacy. It suggested, James thought, that the time might be ripe for the reconsideration of a whole panoply of experiences that had been labeled "mystical" and simply dismissed by scientific minds, including "divinations, inspirations, demonical possession, apparitions, trances, ecstasies, miraculous healings and productions of disease, and occult powers..." (James, 1890a, p. 362). "It often happens," he wrote,

> that scattered facts of a certain kind float around for a long time, but that nothing scientific or solid comes of them until some man writes just enough of a book to give them a possible body and meaning. Then they shoot together, as it were, from all directions, and that book becomes the center of crystallization of a rapid accumulation of new knowledge. Such a book I am sure that M. Janet's ought to be..." (1890a, p. 373).

By the time of his remarks in *The Varieties*, just over a decade later, James could refer to a robust and international set of investigators who had explored very fruitfully the subliminal consciousness of patients with hysteria; they included, besides Janet and Binet, Morton Prince, who was based in Boston, as well as Josef Breuer and Sigmund Freud in Vienna. Collectively, these researchers revealed what James called "whole systems of underground life," memories that do not ordinarily penetrate primary consciousness but show themselves, demonstrably, in a gamut of mental and physical symptoms.

A Universal Trait?

For all his praise of Janet's seminal role, James took issue with him on one crucial question. The issue was fundamental, and the implications boundless. For Janet, these memories, thoughts and feelings hidden from primary consciousness were symptoms of a disease, confined to cases in which the primary consciousness was abnormally weak, unable to integrate the full range of thoughts, memory, and feelings. James, however, suspected that something more universal was at play. While Janet and others had shown that hypnotic suggestion, aimed at the subconscious, could lead to cures of hysterical symptoms in clinical settings, Christian scientists and "mind-curers," he observed, using very different means, often had striking results with more normal populations, perhaps drawing on the same subconscious faculties. "My own decided impression," he said, is that M. Janet's generalizations are based on too limited a number of cases to cover the whole ground" (1890a, p. 373).

James had in mind a very different kind of case, a woman, healthy and decidedly not hysterical, who nevertheless could enter trance states and display knowledge that her ordinary personality simply could not know—facts, for example, about people she had never met. Janet's theories held that primary and secondary consciousness, added together, could never exceed the normally total consciousness of the individual. But James's observation about the woman in trance implied that the subconscious—that "hidden self"—might have a much wider and more mysterious range than had been revealed by clinical observations of very troubled patients. "A comparative study of trances and subconscious states," he concluded in 1890, "is ... of the most urgent importance for the comprehension of our nature" (1890a, p. 373). It was, in his view, not simply our picture of dissociative disorder that was at stake, but of human nature itself.

James's own explorations of the subconscious were focused on a very different group than hysterics—people with traits that could be considered not abnormal but in fact, supernormal, such as the woman who knew facts about people she had never met. They were mediums, who would enter into trance states and then, purportedly, transmit messages from the dead. These observations guided James and others to a very different view of the subconscious than had emerged from the studies of hysteria, a view that perceived the subconscious not only as universal—an element in the psychic constitution of us all—but also as having a collective as well as a personal dimension—a humanity-wide psychic dimension to which we all have access. This hidden side of the mind, moreover, was capable of extraordinary perception and insight. Carl Jung later became associated with these notions—but in 1886, mind you, young Carl would turn 11 years old.

36

The Study of Mediums: The SPR

In that year, which we take as an *annus mirabilis*, Pierre Janet received at his clinic in Le Havre associates of James, from a group based in England that had taken the name the Society for Psychical Research, the SPR; it was founded in Cambridge just four years earlier to coordinate studies in parapsychology, bringing rigorous scientific approaches to claims of paranormal phenomena. They were drawn by their common interest, with Janet, in hypnosis and its potential revelations about the psyche. Among the visitors was Frederic Myers, cofounder of the Society with Edmund Gurney. Together, that very same year, Myers and Gurney concluded a thoroughgoing effort to investigate, experimentally and empirically, the phenomenon of "telepathy"—a term that Myers coined—indicating direct communication from mind to mind, bypassing the physical senses.

By that time, Myers had begun to think in terms of a different order of unconscious mind: a universal "secondary self, or second focus of cerebration and mentation, which ... manifests itself occasionally by certain supernormal physiological or psychical activities" (cited in Hamilton, 2009, p. 127). For that secondary, unconscious self, Myers soon coined the term "subliminal." But whereas Janet and his successors explored these realms through psychopathology, focusing on mental deficiencies, Myers and his associates explored them through parapsychology, focusing on supernormal capacities. Both attempted to be rigorously empirical, following the scientific modalities and cannons of the time; but examining very different kinds of subjects, they soon pointed towards very different views of the unconscious mind.

In contrast to Lucie, for example, was the clairvoyant woman to whom James alluded; her name was Leonora Piper. By all accounts, she seemed a rather ordinary Boston housewife, married to a shopkeeper; when James attended his first séance with her in 1885, she was pregnant with her second child. The skeptical James had come to that session at the behest of his mother-in-law. In it, apparently with no previous knowledge of the James family, Mrs. Piper referred by name to his young son who had recently died (Blum, 2006, p. 100).

James was intrigued, and in the following months he attended a dozen sessions with her, encouraging other observers, including several members of his family, to do the same. In that year of 1886, he submitted a report on

MARK B. RYAN

those séances to the SPR, stating that she "showed a most startling inti-
macy with this family's affairs, talking of many matters known to no one
outside.... I am persuaded," he said, "of the medium's honesty, and of the
genuineness of her trance; ... I now believe her to be in possession of a power as yet unexplained" (James, 1986, pp. 15–16).

Over the subsequent decades, James and his colleagues in the SPR subjected Mrs. Piper to myriad tests, often with strict controls, both in America
and England. They did not take at face value that she was communicating
messages from the dead; but they were convinced that she had a capacity to
absorb, through some unconscious means, information that she had never
encountered in ordinary awareness.

Apparitions, mediumistic trances, clairvoyance, secondary personalities,
possession, and witchcraft—the investigators of the SPR delved into all of
it, attempting to examine objectively phenomena that had been subject to
naïve credulity on the one hand, or unreflective scientistic dismissal on the
other. For James and Frederic Myers, they were all windows into the mysterious extent of the psyche, and the character of what Myers had dubbed
subliminal consciousness. They were, as James put it, "so many ways of putting the Subliminal on tap" (James 1901/1986, p. 196).

By the latter 1880s, then, we have two streams of empirical, scientific research into what was then being referred to as "subconscious" and "subliminal" awareness—clinical studies of hysteria and mental disorders on the
one hand, and studies of the parapsychology and supernormal capacities
on the other.

Antecedents: The Idea of the Unconscious

For all James's emphasis on a moment of discovery, the general idea of an unconscious mind did not begin with these empirical studies. As he recognized,
there had been, for decades before, vaguer talk among psychologists of an
unconscious—and that talk itself rested on prior *philosophical* speculations.

In a broad perspective of the history of ideas, the discovery of the unconscious was a long evolution. Leaving aside its role in other civilizations, we
can trace some notions of an unconscious mind back to the early stages of
Western thought. The Platonic idea that the most profound knowledge
is a recollection or remembrance implies an unconscious knowledge, at

38

least in the collective. And the notion that mental life encompasses more than conscious knowledge was intrinsic to strains of pantheistic thought, Neo-platonism and medieval mysticism. Gottfried Leibniz's philosophy of mind, elaborated at the turn of the eighteenth century, pointed to perceptions that are underneath a threshold of consciousness, but which nevertheless play a strong role in mental life. His idea of a threshold was elaborated early in the nineteenth century by Johann Friedrich Herbart, and subsequent German Romantic philosophers developed a notion of unconscious life as linking the conscious human psyche with the basic energies of nature, a linkage sometimes expressed in symbols and dreams. What Arthur Schopenhauer, early in the century, called "will" was essentially the unconscious, driving forces of human existence. In 1846, four decades before Janet met Myers, Carl Gustav Carus, a painter as well as physician, highlighted the term: his *Psyche: On the Evolution of the Soul* begins with this declaration: "The key to the knowledge of the nature of the soul's conscious life lies in the realm of the unconscious" (cited in Ellenberger, 1970, p. 207). Just over two decades later, Eduard von Hartmann published *Philosophy of the Unconscious*, which posits an unconscious at work in the development of all life, a factor fundamental in the formation of human culture. All of these philosophical speculations, however, pointed more to the existence of a collective unconscious than to the specific operations of an individual psyche.

Magnetism and Hypnosis

Nevertheless, it is a recurring truth in intellectual history that seemingly new ideas are often less radically innovative than their enthusiasts know. Innovators invariably have their predecessors, who sometimes have developed concepts well beyond what the successors assume, and who may have left a legacy in the cultural and disciplinary background on which later figures unconsciously draw. Take, for example, the discoveries of Pierre Janet. Janet knew of the philosophical notion of the unconscious; his coinage of the term "subconscious," in fact, was an attempt to distinguish a more precise and scientifically verifiable notion from vaguer philosophical speculations. In his work with a patient named Leonie, however, Janet found that she had previously been—"magnetized."

"Magnetizing" derived from the work of the eighteenth-century healer Anton Mesmer, who purported to work with a fluid or energy that pervaded the universe. Mesmer used magnets, music, passes, and contraptions meant to concentrate that energy; his follower the Marquis de Puységur, refining the technique, included a collective treatment using ropes tied to a tree and an iron rod. It worked, and Puységur discovered that some of his patients fell into a state that was originally called "magnetic sleep"—a trance-like state in which they could sometimes diagnose their own diseases and prescribe treatments for themselves and others. Once roused from that state, they had no memory of what transpired in it. This might be taken as the first physical demonstration of an alternate level of individual consciousness distinct from our normal, rational awareness (Crabtree, 1993, pp. vii, 87–88). Years later, the English physician James Braid gave this state the name "hypnosis."

Janet began to look into the work of Puységur's generation of magnetizers, which by his day was largely forgotten in professional psychological circles. To his astonishment, he found that they had previously discovered, in the eighteenth and early nineteenth centuries, many of the conditions and effects that Janet and his contemporaries had seen themselves as bringing to light for the first time, including dissociation, post-hypnotic suggestion, dual personalities, psychogenic anesthesia, and clairvoyant self-diagnoses. Janet may not have emphasized it, but some magnetizers also reported cases of thought-transference, clairvoyant awareness of events distant in place or time, and ecstatic spiritual experience.

A Qualitative Leap

Yet for all these prior speculations and experiences, some qualitative leap in the conception of the unconscious took place around 1880. We find the values of it in the well-known painting by André Brouillet, depicting Jean-Martin Charcot with a patient under hypnosis, which was first exhibited in 1887 (Figure 2.1). The leap had to do, first, with the experimental investigation of these insights—the scientific demonstration of specific behaviors and symptoms that suggested dynamics and operations of the unconscious. Theorems alone, James noted, can be barren, but "observations of fact lead to new issues *in infintum.*" With those observations of fact, moreover, came the potential for advances in clinical therapy—for, as James put it, "application to the relief of human misery." "... [T]he subtler knowledge of subconscious states which we are now gaining," he wrote, "will certainly increase our powers in this direction many fold" (1890a, pp. 371–372). An example that impressed him was Janet's treatment of a patient named Marie, whose fits of terror and delirium were alleviated when subconscious memories came to light and were apparently altered under deep hypnosis.

2.1 André Brouillet, "A Clinical Lesson at the Salpêtrière," first exhibited in 1887. ([110 in × 170 in] Pierre Aristide André Brouillet. Paris Descartes University, Paris.)

So when he spoke about a "discovery" of the unconscious, James was referring to a more concrete phenomenon than imagined in speculative theories, something demonstrable in specific behaviors, and repeated in controlled settings. That, in turn, led to new efforts in psychology to depict the contours of this unconscious territory—in effect, to map it out.

Two Streams of Investigation

Let us now take a closer look at these two streams of investigation and the picture of the psyche that each of them produced. The first thing we might say is that the studies of hysteria were more influenced by the rise of positivism in the later nineteenth century, more committed to tying psychological responses to an organic base, which would be accepted as more strictly scientific. The investigation of the paranormal, on the other hand, had more kinship with the philosophical speculations of earlier in the century, and although it adhered to scientific procedures, it was less quick to discard the notion of a spiritual reality behind the material world.

Janet was frankly suspicious of parapsychological research and spiritual-ism, and although he had religious inclinations and interests, he aimed to use a strictly scientific method in his psychology. After the publication of his book, he joined Charcot at the Salpetriere, working to uncover forgot-ten and traumatic and hallucinatory memories, subconsciously retained by hysterical patients. "... [I]n the human mind," he noted, "nothing ever gets lost" (cited in Ellenberger, 1970, p. 366). What was never lost, however, could concretize around "subconscious fixed ideas" or disruptive obses-sions. The subconscious elements that Janet was working with, then, were predominantly pathogenic: they were causes of mental imbalance.

Meanwhile, in Vienna, Josef Breuer and Sigmund Freud were working in a similar framework. Freud had been steeped in scientific subjects: he delved into zoology and other natural sciences as he undertook studies for his medical degree, and he worked for six years in the research laboratory of Ernst Brücke, who aimed to find physiological laws behind psychological processes. He was atheistic and thought that human immortality was mere illusion.

Returning to Vienna after his studies with Charcot at the Salpetrier in 1886, Freud took on the study of other psychological ailments and ad-vanced his analysis of dreams; over the next decade, he worked out his therapeutic methods, first employing hypnosis, but then moving away from it to the technique of free association. His and Breuer's "Preliminary Communication" was published in 1893, and their *Studies on Hysteria*, presenting the prototypical cure of Breuer's patient Anna O. (1895/2004), two years later. They emphasized the pathogenic role of what they called "subconscious ideas," and of the "splitting of the psyche" into conscious and unconscious elements. In their picture, the unconscious remained largely a territory of repressed traumas, of socially unacceptable sexual and aggressive impulses, and of thoughts too distressing to admit to conscious-ness, giving rise to neuroses and disorders and physical maladies. As they speak of it, it is almost entirely personal, not collective; and it looms largest in unhealthy minds.

The subliminal that emerged from the psychic research conducted by Myers and the SPR was far more spacious, and often more benign. 1886 again: in that year, Myers wrote a paper that, while acknowledging the connec-tion between hypnotic states and hysteria, also drew an analogy between such states and genius. Studies with hypnosis, he predicted, could lead to rich discoveries about human nature. The book on telepathy that he and Gurney published that year, *Phantasms of the Living*, included hundreds of closely examined reports of crisis apparitions: that is, immediate perceptions from a distance of loved ones at a moment of crisis, often their death. Demonstrably, the subliminal mind could be shown to have a capacity for super-normal communication and perception. As conceived by Frederic Myers, it was not only a "rubbish heap," as he put it, but a "treasure house," capable of vast intuitive reach and transcendent insight (1903/1954, v. 1, p. 72).

Beginning in 1892, Myers wrote a series of nine articles, in which he outlined what James saw as the first comprehensive theory of the unconscious mind, built on empirical evidence. While others had recognized the existence of the unconscious, Myers, said James, was the first to try to delineate its extent, to "map it out" (James, 1901/1986, p. 196). "Each of us," Myers declared, "is in reality an abiding psychical entity far more extensive than he knows" (Myers, 1892). Our supraliminal selves, our ordinary consciousness, merely makes selections from a far more encompassing and profound consciousness. Those selections are our way of adapting to normal life, but hypnosis, trance experiences, clairvoyance, and other phenomena often classified as occult are windows into a far wider world of potential awareness.

Myers's model, as James put it, "quite overturns the classical notion of what the human mind consists in" (1901/1986, pp. 195–196); it makes the unconscious not only universal, but far more than something just on the periphery of our normal awareness. It is, in fact, the far greater part of who we are. Myers compared consciousness to what science had recently learned about the electromagnetic spectrum: just as only a small band of that spectrum is visible to the human eye, so does normal, supraliminal consciousness encompass only a small range of the mind's potential perceptions and processes. The spectrum of consciousness may be viewed as reaching from organic processes in one direction—the consciousness, for example, that guides our physical movements—to higher mental faculties in the other. It could encompass the repressed memories uncovered in hysterical patients, but also remarkable insights and transcendent visions. Beneath its "realm of dream and confusion," he wrote, lies a "wisdom profounder than we know," one "wiser than sanity itself" (1903/1954, v. 2, p. 100). Strokes of genius and inspired creations represented an "uprush" from the subliminal mind; telepathy and clairvoyance demonstrate that elements of our consciousness, normally hidden, are unbound by the constraints of space and time.

In Myers's imagery, the subliminal, in its profounder reaches, extended beyond individual consciousness into a collective domain; ultimately we extend into what he called "a plenum of infinite knowledge of which all souls form part" (1903/1954, v. 2, p. 273). Our deepest plunges carry us into experiences of the spiritual, mystical experiences in which we have direct knowledge of the transcendent.

By the turn of the twentieth century, then, these two major modes of investigation into the unconscious had produced two very different images of its realms and capacities.

A Bridge: The Role of Carl Jung

In retrospect, the bridge between them came in the person of Carl Jung. Like Janet, Breuer and Freud, Jung was a clinical investigator working with hysterical patients.

He gained fame with his exacting and quantitative word association experiments at the Burghölzli Psychiatric Hospital in Zurich. But Jung also had more ethereal inclinations: he chose to write his medical dissertation about a medium, his cousin Helene Preiswerk, and a source of inspiration for him was Theodore Flournoy, whom he called "my revered and fatherly friend" (1961, p. 162). Flournoy (pictured with William James in Figure 2.2) studied mediums in great depth; his best known book, *From India to the Planet Mars,* published in 1900, delves into the psychological world of a medium who often expressed herself in automatic writing. Jung reported that the work "made a great impression" on him (1988, p. 378), and in fact, Jung kept investigating mediums throughout the 1920s and '30s.

With his eventual delineation of a collective unconscious, with his interest in alchemy, Gnosticism and astrology, in religious myths and Asian scriptures, in synchronicity and what he called the "numinous," with his affirmation of a "religious function" in the psyche and his insistence on the need to account for the infinite in the process of individuation, and in still other ways of being open to what we might term spiritual dimensions, Jung's thought proved to be at least as akin to the romantic and philosophical notions of the unconscious as to the Freudian psychoanalysis with which he was associated early in his career.

Jung met Flournoy's friend William James on only one occasion, at the conference held at Clark University in Worcester, Massachusetts in 1909. The rapport between them was instant. James wrote to Flournoy of the "very pleasant impression" he had gotten of Jung (cited in Perry, v. II, p. 122); Jung, for his part, reported that James "made a profound and lasting impression on me...." They spent what Jung referred to as "two delightful evenings" alone, leaving him "tremendously impressed by the clearness of [James's] mind and the complete absence of intellectual prejudices" (Jung, 1949). From Jung's notes and letters we know something of the substance of their conversation. They "got along excellently," Jung reported, "with regard to the assessment of the religious factor in the psyche" (cited in Bair, 2003, p. 167). The talk centered on the importance of parapsychology—including topics such as spiritualism and faith healing—for understanding the unconscious.

W.J. and Theodore Flournoy, May 18, 1905

2.2 William James and Theodore Flournoy, Geneva, 1905. (MS Am 1092 [1185 no. 111], Houghton Library, Harvard University.)

Such topics, however, were pointedly not on the conference program at Clark. Freud gave five lectures at the Clark conference and Jung—who was soon to be named first president of Freud's International Psychoanalytic Association—gave another three. In retrospect, the conference is viewed as a triumph for Freudian analysis.

A Transpersonal Perspective: Loss and Resurgence

In a professional milieu eager to affirm its scientific credentials, Freudian psychoanalysis came to dominate depth psychology for most of the new century. The other main strain in academic psychology, behaviorism, was thoroughly materialistic in its assumptions; and even the thought of Carl Jung, despite its originality after his break with Freud and its lasting popular appeal, was relegated to the academic sidelines. Meanwhile the research of the SPR was largely forgotten—much as the discoveries of magnetizers had been forgotten a generation earlier.

My assertion, however, is that the later rise of transpersonal psychology—which has always taken Jung as a forebear—compels us to take another look at the psychical research tradition of William James and Frederic Myers. Transpersonal psychology marks its beginnings in the later 1960s, with the work of Abraham Maslow on peak experiences and Stanislav Grof and others on research with psychedelic drugs. It took as its subject matter the higher potentials of the mind, including direct spiritual experiences, transcending the normal boundaries of the personal, that is, of the personal ego, with its strict limitations in time and space.

One of its central concepts was actually described by William James nearly seven decades earlier. It is the notion of "non-ordinary states of consciousness." This is what James wrote in 1902:

> ... [O]ur normal waking consciousness, rational consciousness as we call it, is but one special type of consciousness, whilst all about it, parted from it by the filmiest of screens, there lie potential forms of consciousness entirely different. We may go through life without suspecting their existence; but apply the requisite stimulus and at a touch they are there in all their completeness, definite types of mentality which probably somewhere have their field of application and adaptation. No account of the universe in its totality can be final which leave these other forms of consciousness quite disregarded. (1902/1929, pp. 378–379).

The unconscious mind, in other words, has vast potential, with different orders of perception than we normally experience in everyday reality; but the realization of that trans-personal potential often requires different states of consciousness than our common, rational awareness. James's conviction of the validity of these non-ordinary states was prompted by the use of a drug, nitrous oxide. Plants and substances, however, are only one way of many that different cultures, throughout human history, have used to enter them, from music to dancing to breath control to managed pain. The hypnosis undergone by Lucie and Anna O., and the trance states of Leonora Piper and Helene Preiswerk, were also non-ordinary states: they prompted deep dives into the subliminal, deeper, perhaps, than one could go through any purely "talking cure." From this perspective, Freud's abandonment of hypnosis for free association was a wrong turn in psychotherapy; it kept the patients' experience, and our own understanding of the subconscious, on a relatively shallow plane, limited to the personal unconscious.

For a more curative form of therapy, and for a far vaster understanding of the unconscious mind, non-ordinary states must be subject to methodical and controlled probing—that is the stance of transpersonal psychology. When that probing is condoned and done, the map of the subliminal created by Frederic Myers might achieve a new level of relevance; it might form a theoretical base that allows and encourages insights into the paranormal, the collective mind, and transpersonal and transcendent experiences. In the end, it might provide a basis, at least provisionally, for a still greater understanding of the unconscious—for a deeper awareness of the "hidden self" that around the year 1886 came, with a sense of monumental discovery, so vividly to the fore in the world of modern psychology.

CHAPTER THREE

The Psychical Research Tradition
Looking for Afterlife

To paraphrase Hamlet: Is there an undiscovered country from whose bourn no traveler returns? Are there dreams that come when we have shuffled off this mortal coil? Do we then be or not be?

In Search of the Afterlife

Is there an afterlife? More precisely, can consciousness, or some element of it, survive bodily death? With its foundations in materialism, mainstream Western thought often ignores or dismisses the question, as have the dominant strains of Western psychology. To Freud, for instance, the idea of an afterlife was founded in wish fulfillment; it was mere illusion. But a distinctive characteristic of the psychical research tradition of William James and Frederic Myers, with its sense of a continuity between material and spiritual realms, was that it not only took the question seriously but strove to investigate it empirically. Myers's major legacy, his massive two-volume *Human Personality and Its Survival of Bodily Death*, opens by calling human immortality "the question for man most momentous of all" (1903, v. I, p. 1). To answer that question was the ultimate aim of his scholarly labors.

Historically, the vast majority of human cultures have assumed that consciousness does survive, in some form. But in our modern, materialistic worldview, the enlightened culture of our academies, even raising the question can be seen as delusory, since allegedly, it has been firmly answered in the negative. We do not survive, and the reason seems straightforward: science has shown that consciousness is a product of physical processes in the human brain. Perceptions are channeled to our brains through our five senses. Thinking and awareness come from the actions of chemicals, brain cells, neurons, and synapses. When the brain disintegrates, then, clearly its consciousness can no longer exist. Ultimately, in the materialistic outlook, matter produces consciousness. In the world of psychical research, however, that assumption was not so fixed, even among the most scientifically literate.

The Clark University Conference

There is an iconic photograph of the participants in that conference at Clark University, called in 1909 to celebrate the twentieth anniversary of the founding of the ambitious, psychologically oriented graduate school in Worcester, Massachusetts (Figure 3.1). The occasion of Sigmund Freud's only visit to the United States, the conference was hosted by G. Stanley Hall, president of Clark, founder of the *American Journal of Psychology*, and creator of one of the first research laboratories of experimental psychology in the country. In this portrait, next to Hall stands Freud, and at Freud's other side stands Carl Jung, then 34 years old, at a moment in which he and Freud were in close contact. Down the line from them is William James, then 67, a year before his death. It was a crucial moment in the history of modern psychology, as the field was taking its turn towards what was to be its dominant strains in the twentieth century, behaviorism and psychoanalysis.

PSYCHOLOGY CONFERENCE GROUP, CLARK UNIVERSITY, SEPTEMBER, 1909

Beginning with first row, left to right: Franz Boas, E. B. Titchener, William James, William Stern, Leo Burgerstein, G. Stanley Hall, Sigmund Freud, Carl G. Jung, Adolf Meyer, H. S. Jennings. *Second row:* C. E. Seashore, Joseph Jastrow, J. McK. Cattell, E. F. Büchner, E. Katzenellenbogen, Ernest Jones, A. A. Brill, Wm. H. Burnham, A. F. Chamberlain. *Third row:* Albert Schinz, J. A. Magni, B. T. Baldwin, F. Lyman Wells, G. M. Forbes, E. A. Kirkpatrick, Sandor Ferenczi, E. C. Sanford, J. P. Porter, Sakyo Kanda, Hikoso Kakise. *Fourth row:* G. E. Dawson, S. P. Hayes, E. B. Holt, C. S. Berry, G. M. Whipple, Frank Drew, J. W. A. Young, L. N. Wilson, K. J. Karlson, H. H. Goddard, H. I. Klopp, S. C. Fuller

3.1 Participants at the Clark University Psychology Conference, Worcester, Massachusetts, 1909. In the front row are William James, Sigmund Freud, and Carl Jung. (Clark University Archives.)

The participants were acutely aware that their field was still a new science. The first experimental laboratories in psychology had been formed only in the 1870s and '80s'; the first American doctorate in the field was granted in 1886. Before then, studies of the psyche had been seen as an aspect of philosophy. The field was struggling for its identity, and for recognition as a legitimate scientific enterprise. For that purpose, the more empirical it could be—and the more materialistic its foundations—the better.

However, there were divisions on this issue among its practitioners, highlighted by the harmonious meeting of minds at this conference between James and Jung. In one crucial way, they resisted a consensus of the group.

James was the author of what was then seen as the most significant book of the field, *Principles of Psychology*, published 19 years previously, and of what perhaps is still, over a century later, the most important study of spiritual life yet written, *The Varieties of Religious Experience*, at that point seven years in print. Yet Jung noticed that James was "not taken quite seriously" by some of his colleagues at the conference, including James's former student Hall, because of his openness to religious experience, and especially because of his research on extra-sensory perception and on the medium Leonora Piper, who seemed to make contact with spirits of the dead (Jung, 1949). Already the field was reflecting the conflict between those who saw science as inevitably implying a materialistic worldview and those who did not.

James had come over to Worcester, Massachusetts from Cambridge, he said, "to see what Freud was like," but the person he chose to spend his two evenings there with was the younger man who had accompanied Freud on the trip, Carl Jung. What they talked about in those two meetings were themes that were outside the bounds of the conference program: parapsychology, spiritualism, faith healing, and the psychology of religious life. In that meeting of minds, we find seeds of the impending split between Freud and Jung. James hoped that Freud and his followers would, in his words, "push their ideas to their utmost limits," but in a letter to his friend Theodore Flournoy, he complained that Freud had dismissed American faith healing as "dangerous" because it was "unscientific" (cited in Perry, 1935, v. II, pp. 122–123). For James, the frequent effectiveness of faith healers was what needed scientific explanation.

To probe into this division more deeply, we look now at why James, Jung and some of their colleagues were so fascinated by the likes of Leonora Piper and some of her fellow mediums.

The Rise of Scientism

The decades after Charles Darwin published *On the Origin of Species,* in 1859, witnessed a tremendous enthusiasm for natural science among the intelligentsia, and a bitter conflict between spokesmen of the new scientific outlook and defenders of traditional religion—a conflict launched by the celebrated exchange between T.H. Huxley and Bishop Samuel Wilberforce at Oxford in 1860. We get a sense of the heated ambience in the titles of two major books published in the 1870s: John Draper's *History of the Conflict between Religion and Science* (1875) and Andrew White's *The Warfare of Science with Theology in Christendom* (1876). Young people of talent were flocking into scientific fields, which were newly established in the universities. Scientific rationalism, along with higher biblical criticism, seemed to give the lie to age-old religious myths. Henry Adams, the historian and man of letters, wrote of his generation in the Adams family that "the religious instinct had vanished, and could not be revived" (1918, p. 34).

That scientific enthusiasm often went hand-in-hand not only with the disparaging of religious myths, but with a thoroughgoing materialism: the idea, as James put it, "that the deeper order of Nature is mechanical exclusively, and that non-mechanical categories are irrational ways of conceiving and explaining even such a thing as human life" (1896/1986, p. 134). The corollary was that religion is only an anachronism, "an atavistic relapse"—James again—"into a mode of thought which humanity in its more enlightened examples has outgrown" (1902/1929, p. 480). He called that the "survival theory" of religion.

But not all the scientifically oriented minds in that generation abandoned religion gleefully; many also felt a nostalgia for the comforts of a lost faith. That may have been especially true for some who were drawn into the newly emerging science of psychology: Like Carl Jung, Frederic Myers was the child of a parson; William James was the son of a religious thinker, and Theodore Flournoy attended a school of theology for a term before he decided to study medicine. These were scholars who had absorbed the scientific ethos and who had devoted themselves to scientific procedures in their research—but who were not so quick to accept the all the tenets of scientific materialism. They took notice of phenomena that could not be readily explained by those tenets, especially paranormal psychological phenomena, such as telepathy and telekinesis, the apparent power of mind over matter.

Spiritualism

One cultural movement, in particular, captured their attention: the then still widespread popular vogue of *spiritualism,* the experience of mediums in apparently making contact with the dead. There had always been spirit-seekers and reports of apparitions and related phenomena; but the vogue of modern spiritualism began in 1848 in western New York, a region of the state known for its religious enthusiasm. Two young sisters, Kate and Maggie Fox, began to hear raps in their house in Hydesville, a small hamlet within the township of Arcadia. They took those sounds to be communications from a man whose remains were buried in their cellar. In the following decades, thousands would flock to séances with mediums, and the movement spread internationally. (At the invitation of Mary Todd Lincoln, there were even séances in the White House.) These séances often were a paying proposition, and without question, spiritualism was rife with charlatanry and fraud. But some of the people involved seemed credible, and some of the peculiar phenomena around them were difficult to dismiss as mere trickery, even to scientifically oriented skeptics.

At the least, those phenomena—or the apparent perception of them—deserved some form of investigation and explanation. They purportedly included apparitions, a strong sense of the presence of someone when that person was distant, or even dead; apports, or sudden materialization of objects; and inexplicable movement of objects, such as tables. With the medium usually in a trance state, they included psychological phenomena such as telepathy and "telesthesia" or clairvoyance—direct knowledge accessible without use of rational or sense faculties. Such clairvoyance might involve medical diagnoses and prescriptions; precognition, or knowledge of an event before it occurs; location of lost objects; remote viewing, or perception of events from a distance—the investigators called it "traveling clairvoyance"; retrocognition, or revelations about the past; and psychometry, gaining historical information from a material object. The phenomena also included incarnations, or apparent embodiments of deceased persons by mediums, either through voice or automatic, unconscious, writing—we might call it "channeling." None of that was conceivable according to the reigning tenets of scientific materialism.

The group of friends who founded the Society for Psychical Research in 1882 aimed to put those supposed phenomena to scientific test. James joined the organization the following year, and then helped to found an American Branch. The protagonists in this account had some association, at least indirect, with the SPR: Besides James, they included Myers, who was one of the original founders; Flournoy, who was greatly influenced by Myers and James, and whose best-known book was a study of a medium who talked of previous lives as Marie Antoinette, as well as in India and on the planet Mars; and more peripherally, perhaps, Jung, who was influenced by Flournoy and who began attending séances in 1895. Jung's doctoral dissertation, focusing on the medium Hélene Preiswerk, bore the title *On the Psychology and Pathology of So-Called Occult Phenomena* (1902/1970). Throughout his life, Carl Jung gave credence to, and experienced, paranormal events.

In the culture wars between science and traditional religion, all of these figures had cast their lot with science. Myers referred to "modern science" as "the most effective [method] of acquiring knowledge" [I, 1]; James's *Principles of Psychology* had sought to subject the study of the psyche *to* that method—to establish psychology as a science; and Flournoy's and Jung's studies of mediums rejected supernatural explanations of psychic powers—they didn't accept the idea of visitations from the dead. But at the same time, these researchers looked for a science that would encompass all discoverable fact, and that would not simply ignore data that conventional scientific views could not explain.

In their own minds, they were marking a middle ground between, on the one hand, the superstition and credulity of spiritualists, who too readily attributed all strange phenomena to interventions of spirits and ghosts, and on the other, the rigidity of scientific materialists, who just as readily denied that any such phenomena could possibly exist.

A Pioneering Model of the Psyche

Here is the heart of our story: Their quest drove them towards a view of the human psyche that was far larger in scope than the reductive model of the materialists, and even than the psychoanalytic model of Freud—a view that made room for the validity of spiritual experience.

Myers and his co-investigators in the SPR insisted on rigorous empirical procedures of investigation, corroborating all personal testimonies, tossing out testimonies that could not be corroborated, and examining as many cases of similar phenomena as possible before suggesting hypotheses. They always rejected supernatural explanations when natural ones would suffice. Some of them were skeptics who saw their primary mission as exposing the fraud in spiritualism, which they frequently did.

Yet for some, including Myers, spiritualism offered an intriguing hope: it held intimations of the reality of a spiritual realm. But unlike religious faith or subjective religious experience, the phenomena of spiritualism could be subject to empirical investigation—they implied that manifestations of a spiritual world could be put to scientific test. To Myers personally, the study of spiritualism and related phenomena might even offer, in the end, scientific proof of life after death. Some of his colleagues pursued that end with high optimism. The English translator of Flournoy's most celebrated book said it this way: "The scientific demonstration of a future life may be one of the great triumphs of the twentieth century to win, and...Professor Flournoy may ultimately appear to have contributed largely to its accomplishment" (1900, p. 7). In any case, these investigators associated with the SPR were demonstrating empirically that the human psyche was a much broader and more encompassing entity, with a far greater reach, than the scientistic worldview implied.

The SPR: Methods and Approach

In their research, Myers and his colleagues were inclined to acknowledge the existence of strange phenomena, but to attribute most of them to natural causes that are as yet poorly understood. They assumed a continuity between the material and spiritual realms, and a unity in the governing laws of the universe. They largely rejected the notion of miracle, the idea that there are exceptions to those laws. Their effort was to expand our sense of what, in fact, is natural. Myers, who was a genius at coining terms, began to use the term "supernormal" in place of "supernatural," implying that these strange occurrences, although not ordinary, were governed by natural laws—if we expand our view of what the psyche is and can do.

An example of the kind of phenomena the SPR was interested in, and their way of investigating it, was the subject of their first book, a massive, two-volume study called *Phantasms of the Living*, published in 1886 and authored primarily by Myers's friend and colleague Edmund Gurney. Much of it is a study of "crisis apparitions": instances in which someone has a dream or a vision of a beloved person, at the moment when that person is undergoing a major crisis, often death. That, it turns out, proved to be a quite common experience. Gurney and his colleagues, including Myers, studied hundreds of such cases, drawing only on ones that could be in some way verified by others besides the percipients—for example, cases in which the percipient had reported the experience to other witnesses, before news came by telegram of the death. Myers began to see such experiences as a key to understanding the nature and capacities of human consciousness. The simple spiritualist explanation was that these apparitions were a direct visitation of the spirit of the departed, but Myers and Gurney suggested that they could be explained as a form of "telepathy."

That was another term that Myers coined, from the Greek roots *pathos*, or "feelings" and, *tele*, or "afar." He defined it as "the transference of ideas and sensations from one mind to another without the agency of the recognized organs of sense." For Myers, telepathy was, as he put it, a "Rubicon between the mechanical and spiritual conceptions of the Universe," because it implies that the materialist view that all information comes to the brain through the senses is incomplete; it suggests that consciousness has a dimension that can exist independently of senses, and perhaps of the brain (1903/1954, v. 1, p. 24). Researchers associated with the SPR conducted experiments that showed, to their satisfaction, that telepathy occurs, and that it seems to be enhanced under hypnosis and in trance states, when a part of the mind was operative that was not available to ordinary consciousness. Myers called that aspect of mind "subliminal," or below the threshold of consciousness.

Whether or not they were in direct communication with spirits, mediums, who usually entered trance states, could sometimes demonstrate extraordinary powers. The SPR uncovered thousands of instances of fraud, but in some cases, mediums were subject to such control, and were of such a character, that fraud simply was not a viable explanation. Flournoy certainly found that to be true with the medium he studied, Catherine-Elise Muller, as did James with Leonora Piper.

James and the SPR conducted scores of controlled séances with Leonora Piper, and James eventually wrote a report detailing 69 of them, in which a deceased former colleague in the SPR, Richard Hodgson, seemed to be speaking through her. Years before, he had acknowledged that he could not "resist the conviction" that in her trances, Mrs. Piper had access to knowledge "which she has never gained by the ordinary use of her eyes and ears and wits" (1896, p. 131). Often she knew of incidents in the personal lives of those present, or could describe places in their past—information to which, James was certain, she had never had previous access. Either a spirit—they called it a "control"—*was* speaking through her, or her subliminal mind was somehow able, telepathically, to tap memories of sitters, or of distant people, or possibly what James called "some cosmic reservoir in which the memories of the earth are stored..." (1909b, p. 355).

That is an idea worth examining. Well before Jung began to speak so effectively of it, James and his colleagues had come to a notion of a collective unconscious. Here is how James expressed it in the year of the conference at Clark University:

> [O]ur lives are like islands in the sea, or like trees in the forest.... [T]he trees ... commingle their roots in the darkness underground, and the islands also hang together through the ocean's bottom. Just so there is a continuum of cosmic consciousness, against which our individuality builds but accidental fences, and into which our several minds plunge as into a mother-sea or reservoir. (1909a, p. 374)

Frederic Myers had a similar notion, a "plenum of infinite knowledge of which all souls form part." And Flournoy wrote of "that deep and mysterious sphere into which the deepest roots of our individual existence are plunged, which bind us to the species itself, and perhaps to the Absolute...." (1900, p. 65). Through whatever mechanism, mediums apparently had a way of tapping into that mother-sea. Whether or not spirits of the dead were part of it, this implied conscious life beyond the individual brain.

If Myers's spectrum model, with its notions of a collective mind reaching into spiritual realms, is potentially valid, what of our extensive researches showing the effect of brain over consciousness? How do we reconcile this wider view of the psyche, as extending beyond the brain, with research indicating that functions of the brain produce our mental states? Our protagonists had their answer to that question, and it was James who best formulated it, most fully in an invited lecture at Harvard in 1898. He called it the "transmission theory"; we shall examine it in the following chapter.

The Question of Afterlife

So—what did these studies of mediums demonstrate about the possible existence of a future life? Or better said, what conclusions about that question did these investigators draw from their research? In their trance states, mediums such as Leonora Piper would have visions of, and seem to embody, returning spirits, from whom they apparently would gain uncannily accurate information about the lives of others, information that they could not know through ordinary sense experience. Myers provided a theory that showed that information as coming through the subliminal mind, often through a secondary personality that the subliminal somehow encompassed—the "control." But what was the source of those visions?

For many spiritualists, who often were provoked by the skepticism of these investigators, the visions were what they pretended to be: *ghosts*, surviving personalities visiting from another realm, bringing information that they were privy to, but that the mediums, in their ordinary state, could not know. Psychological investigators such as Flournoy and Jung, however, looked for a source within the medium herself. Flournoy coined the term "cryptomnesia": perceptions absorbed through, and then forgotten in, a highly creative unconscious mind. Such memories never surfaced in the medium's ordinary consciousness, but they could be reasserted through secondary personalities that were part of the medium's own unconscious life. Catherine-Elise Muller, Flournoy's subject, could create fantastic scenes of life in fourteenth-century India, or even a language supposedly spoken on Mars, out of material that she had forgotten that she knew. The same could be true of knowledge she exhibited about sitters in her sessions.

Influenced by Flournoy, Jung gave a similar explanation in his study of Helene Preiswerk, who exhibited little in the way of extraordinary knowledge. The unconscious, he said, could take in far more than the conscious mind, and Helene's incarnations were "nothing but dramatized split-offs from her dream ego" (p. 78). They therefore gave no evidence of spirits. Flournoy, however, acknowledged that there were cases in which he had no idea how the information might have been acquired in the medium's life.

In principle, he accepted the existence of telepathy, clairvoyance and tele-kinesis, although he seemed to conceive of them almost materially: in an age that was discovering such physical phenomena as x-rays, he could envision brain waves of some kind traveling through what was then thought of as ether, and what we might now refer to as energy fields.

As for the spiritualists' notion of returning spirits, Flournoy did not dismiss it as impossible, but he saw it as improbable. For him, that was an immature conception of afterlife, too bound by notions of space and time, too much like our own existence. On the other hand, he viewed himself as Christian, and accepted the possibility of some form of indefinable eternal life beyond space and time—but not one that was proven.

The spiritualists, of course, were quite impatient with such skepticism; and there were investigators, very sophisticated thinkers, who while initially skeptical, ended up believing that the spiritualists were right, at least in some instances. SPR member Richard Hodgson, for example, began his work with a fervent attempt to expose fraud, and revealed a great deal of it; he looked assiduously for natural explanations, and disputed spiritually oriented findings of some of his fellow investigators. Eventually, however, Hodgson decided that some of these appearances were what the spiritualists took them to be: communications, through the medium's subliminal mind, from still extant departed spirits. At least two other initially skeptical, scientific investigators, William Crookes and William Barrett—both physicists—came to the same conclusion.

More enthusiastically, Myers agreed. While much of the phenomena, he thought, could be explained as telepathy from a living person to the medium, some of it could not. The best evidence of survival, he thought, was when a medium assumed the identity of someone deceased relatively recently, who was known to some of the sitters. At one point in her career, Ms. Piper's control became a presence announcing himself as "G.P.," or one George Pelham, never encountered by Mrs. Piper during his lifetime, but known by some of the investigators. According to them, Mrs. Piper's "G.P." exhibited striking private memories and personal characteristics of the original George Pelham.

Myers ultimately argued for what he called "the ancient hypothesis of an indwelling soul," which had an existence beyond this plane even during earthly life, and which persisted afterwards. In fact, he argued that such a hypothesis had been proven by "direct observation" (1903/1954, v. 1, p. 35).

For his part, James was not ready to acknowledge that. He was willing to see actual spirits as a possible explanation for mediumistic clairvoyance and visions, but he did not see it as proven. To explain the supernormal knowledge of Mrs. Piper, where the information was sometimes uncannily detailed, James was more inclined to turn towards telepathy from living people, from their unconscious, or the possibility of the medium's unconscious delving into the reservoir of common consciousness. One counter-argument to survival, in James's mind, was the triviality of the spirits' information: if you were coming back after death to meet your long-lost wife, would you really be focused on the fact that she had changed the place of your photograph in the living room? Controls such as Ms. Piper's Phinuit had "every appearance of being a fictitious being," or a "dream-creation" of the medium: he was a French doctor with an astonishingly detailed memory, but with very limited French (1909c, p. 254). Almost never, James observed, did mediums have anything to say about the character of the afterlife.

His own temperamental inclinations, I suspect, were revealed in James's enthusiasm for ideas of the early nineteenth-century German physicist and philosopher Gustav Fechner. In 1904, James wrote a sympathetic introduction to an American edition of a book that Fechner had published nearly 70 years before, called *The Little Book of Life after Death*; and he included a warm and extensive appreciation of Fechner in *A Pluralistic Universe,* one of his later philosophical books. Fechner was a "panpsychic," that is, he believed that consciousness permeates the whole universe, and that consciousness and matter are different sides of one reality. In this view, our individual lives are momentary expressions of a larger consciousness of the earth. When they pass, they are absorbed back into that larger consciousness; the immortality they achieve is in *its* memory, the way it is affected by their lives—but not in their persistence as individual personalities.

Nevertheless, near the end of his life, James experienced one series of séances that gave him pause. In that case, the spirit of the now-deceased Richard Hodgson, his former colleague and fellow investigator, seemed to be speaking through Mrs. Piper, coming back to prove the point. In some of those 69 séances, he acknowledged, the presence of Hodgson felt real, and the notion that an actual visiting spirit was indeed there might be as plausible an explanation as any other he could propose. The phenomena were so complex, however, that he admitted he was baffled and not ready to draw a conclusion.

Reflecting back very late in his life, Carl Jung considered it an unresolved question whether mediums spoke only out of some element in their own unconscious, or whether, in some cases, they might actually be in contact with the dead. Although he had argued for the former explanation in the case of Helene Preiswerk, he later had at least one experience of his own in which the actual presence of a deceased friend seemed conceivable (see 1961, pp. 312–313). In individual instances, he remained skeptical, but "in the long run," he reported privately, "I have to admit that the spirit hypothesis yields better results in practice than any other" (1973, p. 431).

Jung affirmed the psychological value of worldwide myths of an afterlife, even if the reality behind them was unknowable. Yet the possibility that consciousness survives death remained open, he thought—and likely enough for him to venture some speculations about its forms. Modern critical rationalism denies survival, but the reach of rationalism, Jung argued, is strictly limited. We are far more than what we know about ourselves; in actual fact, through the unconscious, "we live far beyond the bounds" of our rational awareness, penetrating into realms unrestricted by the normal functions of space and time (1961, p. 302). Mediumistic phenomena, foreknowledge of events in dreams, premonitions and synchronicities demonstrate rationalism's limitations, and point towards a dimension beyond the one that we readily observe. "We must face the fact," Jung asserted, "that our world with its time, space, and causality, relates to another order of things lying behind or beneath it" (1961, p. 305). Into that order, we gain occasional gleanings.

About the question of afterlife, then, these investigators had varying ideas. But all of them recognized that they had come upon a conception of the psyche that pushed it far beyond the bounds of the materialistic assumptions of figures such as G. Stanley Hall and later behaviorists of the twentieth century. Consciousness was something more than the product of individual human brains, at least as we ordinarily conceive of their operations. The vast reaches of the subliminal mind, opening now to further investigation, made the idea of some form of afterlife a reasonable hypothesis and a valid inquiry, even for scientifically oriented minds of the post-Darwinian era.

CHAPTER FOUR

The Transpersonal William James[1]

"100 Years of Transpersonal Psychology": that was the title of an Association for Transpersonal Psychology conference in September, 2006, and it represented a milestone in the recognition of William James's place in the origins of modern transpersonal thought. As the conference's official announcement declared, James made the first recorded use of the term "transpersonal" in 1905. The conference's title took its measure of a century from that coinage, suggesting a major role for James in the founding of the field.

The occasion of James's use of the term was modest: an unpublished document, merely a printed course syllabus at Harvard University for an introductory course in philosophy. In truth, the meaning he attached to the term was far more restricted than our usage of it today. James was attempting to clarify a technical, philosophical point: exactly what might be meant by the term "objective." The object to which an idea refers, he wrote, might be "Trans-personal" (James hyphenated the term) if two people both perceive it—or, as he put it, "when my object is also *your* object" (Perry, 1935, v. II, p. 445; Vich, 1998, p. 109).[2]

James's invention of the word serves as a convenient symbol, but his significance for transpersonal psychology far transcends that coinage. The intent of this chapter is to explore and clarify that significance.

Historical Accounts of Transpersonal Psychology

Contemporary transpersonal psychology is usually traced to Abraham Maslow's investigations of peak experiences and of self-actualized individuals in the 1960s; to investigations of non-ordinary states of consciousness by Stanislav Grof and others in the same period; to meetings of humanistic psychologists hosted by Anthony Sutich to discuss what they first called "transhumanistic" ideas, and their adoption of the term "transpersonal psychology" in 1967; or to the formation the following year of the Transpersonal Institute, later the Association for Transpersonal Psychology. In the first issue of *The Journal of Transpersonal Psychology*, published in 1969, Sutich, as editor, spoke of "a new frontier of psychological inquiry" that was applying an "empirical approach" to "extraordinary subjective experience," thus providing an early definition of the field (Sutich, 1969a, p. iv).

The pioneers who set out towards this new frontier knew that they had predecessors. Willis Harman, writing in the *Journal*'s second issue, spoke of this empirical study of subjective, especially "transcendental," experience as "a new Copernican revolution"; but the revolution, he acknowledged, had its precursors, earlier figures who had investigated what he called "supraconscious processes." Harman explicitly acknowledged three ground-breaking works from early in the century: Bucke's *Cosmic Consciousness*, Myers's *Human Personality and its Survival of Bodily Death*, and James's *The Varieties of Religious Experience* (Harman, 1969, pp. 22–23).

Among precursors, the one who is most commonly acknowledged is Carl Jung. In his monumental *Beyond the Brain*, Grof refers to Jung as "the first representative of the transpersonal orientation in psychology" (Grof, 1985, p. 188), and the chapter on Jung in the now standard *Textbook of Transpersonal Psychiatry and Psychology* calls him "the first clinical transpersonal psychiatrist and depth psychologist" (Scotton, 1996, p. 39). That image persists: an article in a more recent edition of the *Journal* opens with the observation that Jung "is widely considered to be the first prominent transpersonal psychologist" (Miller, 2005, p. 164), and in Kevin Page's historical film on the movement, Monte Page makes a similar observation (Page, 2006).

James, however, is not ignored for such honors. In that same *Textbook*, Eugene Taylor, in a brief chapter on James, calls him "arguably the father of modern transpersonal psychology" (Taylor, 1996a, p. 21), and the earliest excerpt included in Roger Walsh and Frances Vaughan's defining anthology, *Paths Beyond Ego*, is a passage from James's *Varieties*. In that same volume, Robert McDermott refers in passing to James's philosophy as "transpersonal" and to James himself, along with Jung, as a "forebear" in the field (1993, p. 209). More recently, Michael Daniels traces the birth of transpersonal psychology to James's delivery of the Gifford Lectures, subsequently published as *The Varieties*, at the University of Edinburgh in 1901–1902 (Daniels, 2005, p. 16).

All of these statements may be defensible, but claims of primo-generation, of firstness and fatherhood, have real meaning only when the sense of exactly how that is so is more fully defined.

In the days of the formal launching of the field of transpersonal psychology in the late 1960s, the psychological milieu was still dominated by behaviorism and Freudianism, and, despite the advances of humanistic psychology, by materialistic assumptions and a largely anti-spiritual temper. But those trends, as we have seen, had won the day only after a struggle. Some of the initial luminaries in the field of psychology were intensely interested in questions that might seem quite contemporary to today's transpersonal psychologists. They stood vehemently in defiance of biological reductionism and were fascinated by phenomena that we would call "spiritual." That being the case, the question of who was first tends to lose its meaning and to dissolve into a fascinating intellectual ambience, shared by a number of prominent investigators who certainly recognized the spiritual dimension of the psyche and who held a more extended notion of the nature of consciousness.

James's role in that spiritually oriented conversation was pivotal. Well before the turn of the twentieth century, this magnetic thinker who was both psychologist and philosopher developed a transpersonally inclined psychology and laid philosophical foundations for a transpersonal worldview. Out of a tension between scientific and religious outlooks embodied in his own life and thought, James had embraced and articulated the principal elements of a transpersonal orientation by the early twentieth century, and had given them a metaphysical and empirical justification on which they still can stand today.

James in Historical Context: Science and Religion

James was born in 1842 and came to intellectual maturity in materialistic and newly industrializing times, when the post-Darwinian enthusiasm for natural science had driven spiritual concerns from the minds of many intellectuals of the Western world. In higher education, new scientific studies were challenging the old classical curriculum, and scientific schools were being established at America's venerable universities. German-derived idealism, with its impersonal if divinely tinged "Absolute," continued to reign in British and American philosophy departments; but in the general intellectual atmosphere, traditional theism was in retreat.

William James profoundly engaged the ascendant scientific intellectual milieu. He entered Harvard's Lawrence Scientific School, initially studying chemistry, then anatomy, before training in medicine and physiology at

Harvard and in Germany. His first appointments to the faculty of Harvard were to teach anatomy and physiology. As a pioneer of modern psychology, he was instrumental in setting its studies on empirical foundations, and in divorcing its findings from a traditional concept of mind or soul as a distinct metaphysical entity. The psychological laboratory he established at Harvard, modeled on experimental laboratories in Germany, was arguably the first in the United States. James's first great work, the masterful and literate *The Principles of Psychology*, published in 1890, was physiological in emphasis, thick with neurological detail and focusing on the bodily correlates of psychological experience (1890b/1952). Although it relied heavily on introspection and ventured away from strictly positivistic psychophysics, it treated consciousness as dependent on brain function, always examining the connection between mind and body. It was intended, as James said in a subsequent article, to help psychology become a natural science by treating it as one: the comment appeared in a short article titled "A Plea for Psychology as a Natural Science" (cited in Richardson, 2006, p. 331).

4.1 William James as a graduate student, on a geological research trip to Brazil, 1865. (MS Am 1092 [1185 no. 8], Houghton Library, Harvard University.)

Later in his career, James was known for his defense of "radical empiricism" in philosophy, and as a founder of the philosophical school of pragmatism, which he himself saw as bringing the influence of Darwin to philosophy. With the weight and validity that it gave to sense experience, to the experiential and concrete, radical empiricism reflected his scientific bent, and pragmatism took scientific procedures as the model for the measure of truth. Subsequent scholarship on James has often emphasized those more scientifically oriented elements of his career.

But William James had spiritual inclinations that were not to be denied. His father, Henry James Senior, was a religious philosopher, prominent in the era of American Transcendentalism, who was greatly influenced by the Swedish mystical visionary Emanuel Swedenborg. Ralph Waldo Emerson and other Transcendentalist luminaries were part of the James family's social circles, and William James had been steeped in his father's intellectual milieu. On an emotional level, James struggled with bouts of depression, some of which were alleviated only when he took refuge in religious thoughts and intellectually made room for spiritual life.

His most serious psychological crisis occurred in the first months of 1870, just as he was entering his twenty-ninth year. One focus of his thoughts at the time was the burden of determinism—what he found to be a personally crushing sense that all that we do might be only a product of material processes, with no place for free choice. "I feel ... that we are wholly conditioned," he had written in a letter, "that not a wiggle of our will happens save as a result of physical laws" (cited in Richardson, 2006, p. 101). His cousin Minnie Temple, a great love of his life with whom he had had probing conversations about religion, had recently died of tuberculosis when James hit the depths of his crisis. He suddenly was overwhelmed, he later wrote, by "a horrible fear of my own existence," leaving him with "a sense of the insecurity of life that I never knew before." But the struggle had, he said, a "religious bearing." "...[I]f I had not clung to the scripture-like texts," he said, "like 'The eternal God is my refuge' ... 'I am the resurrection and the life' etc., I think I should have grown really insane" (James, 1902/1929, pp. 156–158).[4]

James did not see himself as prone to direct spiritual experience, but, at the same time, he was a seeker: He sought out and studied non-ordinary states; he experimented with what we would call "alternative medicine," from homeopathy to hypnotism and "mind cure"; and his curiosity about the potential of the psyche prompted him to experiment occasionally with mind-altering substances. In 1898, in the Adirondack woods, he had what could be described as a mystical experience—he described it as "a state of spiritual alertness of the most vital description" and "one of the happiest lonesome nights of my existence" (cited in Allen, 1967, pp. 390–391)—and his letters refer to a previous if lesser one in the Swiss Alps (Richardson, 2006, p. 210). The tension between materialistic and spiritual viewpoints, as he felt it in the culture and, even more, in himself, was a key factor that drove both his psychological investigations and his philosophical speculations.

Some of James's most powerful and penetrating writings attempt to make spiritual experience acceptable to a scientific frame of mind. In that effort, James laid the foundation for a transpersonal worldview. We can see that foundation first in what he chose to study, especially in his interest in psychic and religious experience; second, in his definition of true science and his refutation of materialism; third, in his concept of consciousness, with its broad, collective dimensions; and fourth, in his acceptance of the validity of spiritual experience. Our task is now to examine those elements more closely.

The Study of Psychical and Religious Experience

Throughout his professional life, James was fascinated by psychic phenomena that could not be explained in the context of the prevailing materialistic worldview. For much of his career, he was absorbed, as investigator or knowledgeable scholar, in empirical research on "extraordinary subjective experience," "supraconscious processes," and subjective experience of the transcendental. As early as 1869, he had published a review of a book on spiritualism, calling the subject of "transcendent interest" and noting that such phenomena, "if once admitted, ... must make a great revolution in our conception of the physical universe" (James, 1869, p. 4). Traveling in England in 1883, he became involved with the Society for Psychical Research—with its investigation, as he once put it, of "all sorts of 'supernatural' matters" (cited in Allen, 1967, p. 281)—helping to found an American version of the society the following year. Several years later, the American organization merged with the British; James eventually became president of the combined society, and was a long-term vice president. He took an active research role with its Committee on Hypnosis (using Harvard students as subjects), and especially with its investigations of spiritualism. For a span of two decades, he contributed reports and reviews to the Society's journals.

Soon after he became involved with the SPR, James met Leonora Piper, beginning his investigation of mediumistic experiences. Besides trance states, hypnosis, mediumship, and clairvoyance, his psychological research interests, especially in the 1880s and '90s, included automatic writing, supposed apparitions, thought-transference, and multiple personalities, and he studied and commented on demonic possession, witchcraft, and genius. In all of this investigation, his attitude was both open and skeptical, emphasizing the need to accumulate data but to reserve interpretation. Repeatedly, he urged his colleagues to ferret out more facts before formulating theories. In the 1890s, James argued against proposed bills before the Massachusetts state legislature that would restrict the activities of mental healers and effectively limit the practice of psychotherapy to doctors of medicine. Faith healers, he argued, were accumulating a body of facts that, however they might be explained, deserved study (James, 1894). Wherever the facts might lead, James was convinced that the study of what he called "exceptional mental states" would vastly deepen our notion of the psyche.

The great culmination of James's psychological research into spiritual life was *The Varieties of Religious Experience*. In the sense indicated by figures such as Sutich and Harman as they announced the founding of a new field, the book is certainly transpersonal in subject and approach. James's definition of his topic followed an innovative new trend: he would examine religion not as ideational beliefs, or theological dogmas, or moral dictates, or ecclesiastical institutions, but as psychological experience—as propensities, feelings, and impulses. Moreover, he was interested in the most intense varieties of such experiences, those that were felt as "an acute fever," rather than in the mere acceptance of the "ordinary religious believer" (1902/1929, pp. 7–8). With its massive abundance of personal testimonies, *The Varieties* is a great anthology of peak and non-ordinary experiences, providing an empirical approach to extraordinary subjective experiences, especially of the transcendental.

As psychology moved in an implacably more positivistic direction, some of James's later contributions to the field were relatively ignored. In fact, though, the articulation of transpersonal principles that we can now see in James is a product of his abiding interest in spiritual experience and psychical phenomena. Much of his writing on these matters initially was published for a restricted audience associated with the SPR and not republished for more than half a century after his death. Some key lectures were never published at all.[3] For helping to revive interest in this aspect of his work, and for the resurrection of some of the unpublished material, we are much indebted to the scholarly labors of Eugene Taylor of the Harvard Medical School (1982, 1996b).[5]

In James's writings on psychical and religious experience, we find a full articulation of the modern transpersonal worldview. That worldview entails particular beliefs or attitudes about the nature of science, of consciousness, and of spiritual experience; its orientation on those questions form the core of a transpersonal philosophical framework. In each of those spheres, James anticipated the movement's modern-day outlook. In brief, that outlook scientifically argues the limitations of materialism; it acknowledges what Stanislav Grof calls an "enlarged model" of human consciousness, and it accepts the value and validity of spiritual life. James not only supported those positions but gave each of them a philosophical foundation on which they can still rest. The nature of this essay allows me to give only an compressed account of his positions on these matters, but even a glance at them reveals how, in defending these broad notions, James was a precursor of some more specific ideas that are very much alive in our own contemporary discussions.

Science and Materialism

While James was certainly a believer in science, he made a sharp distinction between the method of scientific inquiry and the philosophy of positivism or materialism. True scientific procedures, he argued, require that we take account of whatever we might observe, even if we have no framework with which to explain it—that was a basic stance of his radical empiricism. Orthodox science largely ignored phenomena for which it had no explanation, even if such phenomena occurred repetitively. But if in their trance states Mrs. Piper and other mediums sometimes revealed knowledge that they could not have known in their ordinary states of consciousness, if faith healers sometimes seemed to help bring about seemingly miraculous cures, if thoughts sometimes seemed to be directly transferred from one person to another, the most *un*scientific response would be to deny or discount what had been observed (see especially James, 1896, 1909a).

For all its accomplishments, science itself was still in its nonage, a recent development in human history, and no match for the infinite complexities of existence. It can give us still only a minute glimpse of unending intricacies of the universe, which may well extend far beyond the reach of human intelligence. "Our science is a drop," James wrote, "our ignorance a sea" (1897, p. 54). In supporting his case against a simplistic materialism, he offered an account of the progress of science that foreshadowed the notion of scientific paradigms advanced nearly seven decades later by Thomas Kuhn (1962). Perhaps his clearest statement of that critique was in a version of "What Psychical Research has Accomplished," included in *The Will to Believe and Other Essays in Popular Philosophy*, published in 1897. Once a scientific theory is widely accepted, said James, it is viewed as a "closed and completed system of truth," leaving any other scheme "unimaginable." But in any science, investigation produces a set of "exceptional observations" that cannot be accounted for with the dominant theories, no matter how entrenched they might be. Such observations usually crop up only occasionally and irregularly—and are more easily ignored than incorporated. In this phase of what Kuhn was to call "ordinary science," such observations that are "unclassifiable within the system...," wrote James, "must be held untrue." So long as they seem oddities or "wild facts," researchers neglect or deny them. But, initiating the phase that Kuhn was to call "extraordinary science," some geniuses become fascinated by this "unclassified residuum" of phenomena, and, delving more fully into it, propose new formulas that "break up the accepted system" and renovate the field. "No part of the unclassified residuum," wrote James, "has usually been treated with a more contemptuous scientific disregard than the mass of phenomena generally called mystical" (1897, pp. 299–303).

For too many scientists, a fact was only a phenomenon that could be explained with a materialistic paradigm. But James wanted to pursue observed facts wherever they lay, even if conventional scientific opinion found them unthinkable. To do so was the very purpose of the Society for Psychical Research, which applied scientific methods to phenomena that, having been left to haphazard observation, were largely disregarded in scientific circles. Claims and manifestations of spiritualistic and psychic phenomena might be rife with fraud and trivia, and subject to naïve and sentimental interpretations. But from those phenomena emerged a core of facts that James found it scientifically irresponsible to dismiss (see 1909a). A truly scientific outlook lay somewhere "between vague tradition and credulity on the one hand and dogmatic denial at long range on the other" (1896, p. 306). "I believe there is no source of deception in the investigation of nature," he wrote, "which can compare with a fixed belief that certain kinds of phenomenon are impossible" (cited in Allen, 1967, pp. 281–282, also in James, 1920, v. I, p. 248). In interpreting such phenomena, naturalistic explanations should be preferred whenever plausible, but at times the suggested ones simply proved inadequate.

James laid out the case against materialism most fully in his Presidential Address to the SPR in 1896: science meant a "dispassionate method" of inquiry, not a philosophical result. Unfortunately, it had, he said, "come to be identified with a certain fixed general belief, the belief that the deeper order of Nature is mechanical exclusively," and that "mechanical" categories are the only valid terms of explanation for both nature and humanity. But such a belief was both limited and limiting, as well as undemonstrated; it converted science into a "sect" and broke violently with ways of thinking that had been accepted throughout the whole of human history. The full truth requires that such "mechanical rationalism" be balanced with a more "romantic and personal view of Nature," which is also fed by fact and experience (James, 1896, pp. 132–136).

In that same address, James presented his metaphor of the white crow. To refute a general belief that all crows are black, you need not show that no crows are: you need only find one white crow. On the question of our ability to know things that we could not have learned in our ordinary experience—that is, through our senses—"my own white crow," he said, "is Mrs. Piper," with the knowledge she displayed in trances that could not have been acquired by "the ordinary use of her eyes and ears and wits" (James, 1896, p. 131). More than any other factor, his observation of Mrs. Piper's supernormal abilities in trance states convinced James of the inadequacy of the reigning scientific explanations of nature. The "most urgent intellectual need" of the times was for a science that could accommodate such anomalous facts (James, 1892, pp. 100–101). They might be baffling and inexplicable in reigning paradigms, but they could push science towards new conquests.

When we step out of a certain paradigm, James argued elsewhere, new facts come into view, or older observed facts reappear that had subsequently been dismissed. On those grounds, while suspending judgment on any single explanation, James was unwilling to deny observations associated even with such occult phenomena as stigmata, diabolical possession, prophecy, and levitation (1902/1929, p. 491). Reality was far more extensive than the materialist dogma was suited to explain. "There are resources within us," he once remarked, "that naturalism ... never recks of..." (1909b, p. 305). What shape the new science beyond naturalism might take, he was not yet prepared to say, but he had no doubt that a paradigm shift, as we might call it, was in the making. "Science, like life," he wrote, "feeds on its own decay. New facts burst old rules; then newly divined conceptions bind old and new together into a reconciling law" (James, 1892, p. 101).

Subliminal and Collective Consciousness

This outlook made the study of what we would call "non-ordinary states of consciousness" especially important, for in such states people encountered different facts of experience. James, as we have noted, was an early advocate of the emerging notion of a subliminal or subconscious mind, calling it "the most important step forward that has occurred in psychology" in his professional lifetime (1902/1929, p. 228). He was intrigued especially by Frederic Myers's conception of the subliminal as a spectrum ultimately connected to a "spiritual world" (James, 1903, p. 207). James found that notion to be reinforced by evidence from such phenomena as post-hypnotic suggestion, automatic writing, crystal-gazing clairvoyance, and thought-transference, as well as by trance states. These non-ordinary states of consciousness—parting, as he said, the "filmiest of screens" that separates them from ordinary consciousness—revealed concretely that the mind encompassed far more than was accessible in our common states of awareness. Over a hundred years ago, James cast his weight behind that expanded model of the psyche that is at the heart of transpersonalism, pointing towards the "mother-sea or reservoir" of consciousness, a "subliminal life belonging to human nature in general" (James, 1903, p. 206), and towards the radically different nature of the "many worlds of consciousness" revealed in exceptional states. As a philosophical pragmatist, James believed that the test of truth for any idea was in its applications in the world of experience, and he had no doubt that these other forms of consciousness "somewhere have their field of application and adaptation" (1902/1929, p. 379).

In 1896, James gave a series of lectures at the Lowell Institute in Boston on such exceptional states: hypnotism, trances, multiple personalities, demon possession, and the rest. The lectures were never published, but they have been reconstructed by Dr. Taylor from James's notes and related writings. They demonstrate James's belief that subliminal consciousness, the subconscious, was the source not only of pathology, as Freud and Breuer portrayed it, but also of higher human awareness—of supernormal consciousness and, on occasion, of transcendent wisdom (Taylor, 1982, see esp. 91–92).

James regarded any effort to discern structure in those wider reaches of the psyche—to create, that is, a map of transpersonal consciousness—as highly tentative. He thought that Myers's conception of a spectrum, and his map of the subliminal, for all their value, still constituted only a vague hypothesis (James, 1903, pp. 204, 207). Late in his career he saw a "probability" in favor of Gustav Fechner's panpsychic notions, which conceived of consciousness as something extending far beyond the human mind (1909b, pp. 309–310). By that outlook, the divine is "indwelling" rather than external to human life; human substance partakes of divine substance. So, too, do other compounds of life and reality, in an ascending order of comprehensiveness. As James sympathetically observed, Fechner regarded the entire universe as "everywhere alive and conscious." Plants had a form of consciousness; so, too, did heavenly bodies and systems. Articulating a notion later to be called "Gaia," Fechner believed in an "earth-soul" and "earth-consciousness" subsuming the consciousness of individual forms of life that are part of its "self-sufficing" system. The awareness and memories of individual persons, even after their passing, become part of that earth-life. Ultimately, at the highest level, there is an all-comprehensive consciousness that we call God (James, 1909b, pp. 131–177).

In the light of later psychedelic research, it bears mention that James's own experience of parting the filmy screen came through the use of a substance, nitrous oxide. On occasion, William James, the iconic Harvard philosopher, experimented with such routes into other worlds; only the "artificial mystic state of mind," he said, gave him a level of insight that seemed closer to ultimate reality (1902/1929, p. 379). For many years he maintained an extensive correspondence with Benjamin Paul Blood, an amateur mystic philosopher and poet, whose plunge into other worlds was first prompted by anesthesia in a dental chair. Blood had written of his experience in a pamphlet called *The Anesthetic Revelation and the Gist of Philosophy*, published in 1874, which James promptly reviewed for the *Atlantic Monthly* (James, 1874). The pamphlet spurred James to experiment with nitrous oxide; he gave an account of his experience in a philosophical journal (James, 1882) and later in *The Varieties of Religious Experience*. That adventure had left him with a persistent sense of "a profound meaning" and was instrumental in revealing the existence of those other worlds of consciousness (1902/1929, pp. 378–379). In *The Varieties*, James also provided detailed accounts of other subjects whose mystical experiences had been sparked by chloroform or ether. The last essay that James published in his lifetime was a spirited appreciation of Blood, who by that time had written numerous tracts on nitrous oxide experimentation and the insights that came from them. Blood's mystical vision involved many worlds, not just one unified reality, and James acknowledged its influence on his own pluralistic philosophy (James, 1910).

James was also, we might note, among the first to characterize alcohol consumption as a misdirected striving for spiritual experience (1902/1929, pp. 377–378). "The sway of alcohol over mankind," he wrote, "is unquestionably due to its power to stimulate the mystical faculties of human nature, usually crushed to earth by the cold facts and dry criticisms of the sober hour" (1902/1929, p. 377). That insight was later sanctioned by Jung and eventually became a key element in the methods of Alcoholics Anonymous. Bill Wilson, who established AA, was directly inspired by a reading of *The Varieties*—so much so that he once stated that James could be viewed as the founder (see Lattin, 2009, p. 76). AA's approach subsequently has been applied with great effect in transpersonal psychotherapy.

Transmission Theory

To admit the possibility of supranormal knowledge in trance states, or of direct experience of other worlds of consciousness, challenged the materialistic notion that all perception comes through the senses and that all consciousness is a product of the individual human brain. Certainly the material conditions of the brain have a great effect on consciousness: James closely followed the burgeoning experimentation that by the 1870s had begun to localize brain functions. But he did not conclude, therefore, that consciousness necessarily begins in the individual cerebrum. In a series of lectures given in 1878, first at the Johns Hopkins University and then at the Lowell Institute in Boston, James argued that the emerging physiological data could not explain consciousness, and that it was more accurate to think of the brain and the mind as interacting, or correlating, rather than as one producing the other.

In his Ingersoll Lecture on Human Immortality, delivered at Harvard in 1897, James defended a "transmission" theory of brain function. The argument goes like this: It is true, James said, that science was demonstrating that particular elements of the brain influenced particular forms of thought—and those discoveries likely would become more and more specific. Consciousness, he acknowledged, was a function of the brain. *Function*, however, does not necessarily always mean *production*, like steam coming from a kettle. In that kind of a function, if you get rid of the kettle, there is no more steam; get rid of the brain, and there can be no consciousness—or afterlife.

But *function* can also denote *transmission,* like a prism affects and transmits a pre-existing light, or an organ pipe transmits air. It is at least logically conceivable, James said, that the brain can sometimes function in that way, transmitting and affecting something that pre-exists. Such a theory, James believed, could explain far better than mere production the data encountered by psychical researchers (James, 1898). On another occasion, James turned to a metaphor drawn from the technology of his times to illustrate the transmission theory: a Marconi wireless telegraph, which received and transmitted radio waves (1909c, pp. 358–359). We now have an array of electronic models we might use to illustrate the point. Think of a television: the image of Sarah Jessica Parker may be dependent on the hard wires and tubes, but she is not located or produced by the flat screen in your living room. That image reflects a reality that comes through it from somewhere else, involving a vast network of operations beyond the conception of most of us looking at the screen.

The main currents of twentieth-century neuroscience flowed in a more materialistic direction, but lately a number of prominent neurological theorists have adopted a posture more like that of James, suggesting an interaction between brain and consciousness and challenging strict materialism in neurobiology.[6]

The Value of Spirituality

As the great psychologist of religion, James was among the first to suggest that genuine spiritual experience comes not through doctrine and ritual, but through the newly identified subconscious mind. Religion, in its most basic form, involved an intuition that we all have a "higher" or "better" part of ourselves, and that this higher part is, as he put it, is "continuous with a MORE of the same quality, which is operative in the universe outside" of us and which we can "keep in working touch with" (1902/1929, p. 499). So he argued in *The Varieties of Religious Experience.* "Whatever this MORE may be on its *farther* side," he hypothesized, "it is on its *hither* side the subconscious continuation of our conscious life" (1902/1929, p. 503). Thus the "further limits of our being plunge" into another dimension of reality that we refer to as "supernatural" or "mystical" (1902/1929, p. 506).

That insight is fundamental to modern transpersonal psychology, growing as it did out of the practices of humanistic psychology and related therapies, when subjects exploring their subconscious began to have spiritual experiences and take seriously a spiritual dimension.

4.2 Ellen Emmet Rand, Portrait of William James. (Harvard University Portrait Collection, Commissioned by the Department of Philosophy for the faculty room, 1910, H111. Photo: Imaging Dept. © President and Fellows of Harvard College.)

On thoroughly pragmatic grounds, James defended what he called "the reality of the unseen" and the reasonableness of giving credence to a spiritual realm. *The Varieties* elaborated arguments he had made five years earlier in "The Will to Believe," his most widely read essay, which defended the right to accept religious notions that may not have persuaded our purely rational intellect (James, 1897). Like Maslow and others who followed him, James recognized that genuine spiritual experience contributes to psychological health. In 1895, he gave an address to the Harvard YMCA entitled "Is Life

Worth Living?" which later was published in a volume with "A Will to Believe." There he defined supernaturalist religion as a sense, a faith, that beyond the order of nature is an unseen world that gives significance and meaning to mundane life. In that view, which can be accepted without dogma or specific creeds, the natural order can be seen as "the external staging of a many-storied universe, in which spiritual forces have the last word...." For those of a certain temperament, such an outlook could indeed "make life seem worth living," bringing "light and radiance" to their worlds (1897, pp. 56–57).

As he stated the case in *The Varieties*, the "faith state"—that is, our feelings and intuitions that there is "something else"—has real emotional effects in our lives and the way we conduct them; it brings us "zest" and "enchantment" (1902/1929, p. 475), a sense of meaning that can engage us more fully with the world around us; it makes "a genuine difference" to us. And whatever produces effects in the world we know must be considered, in some way, to originate in a reality. Many religious creeds may be fanciful and absurd, but spiritual life itself is how we fulfill our "deepest destiny" (1902/1929, p. 507). In its broadest sense, religion is an acceptance that there is an unseen order, and a sense that our highest purpose is putting ourselves in harmony with it (1902/1929, p. 53). Conceived in that way, as he wrote in a letter, "the life of religion ... is mankind's most important function" (cited in Allen, 1967, p. 415).

With this perspective, James elaborated other basic positions that closely anticipate the view of spirituality now widely held in the transpersonal movement. This forum allows me to do little more than define them, but behind each is a rich body of thought and empirical investigation. James believed that all major religions are built on a mystical experience, and he drew a strong distinction between those core experiences and the institutions that grew from them. He identified death–rebirth experience as a central element in those core experiences. And he displayed a fascination with Asian religions for their approach to these essential aspects of religious life.

Personal religious experience, James said, "has its root and center in mystical states of consciousness" (1902/1929, p. 370). Based on his empirical studies of what mystics report, James endeavored in *The Varieties* to define such states, stating that they are "ineffable" but "noetic," that is, they give "insight into the depths of truth unplumbed by the discursive intellect"

(1902/1929, p. 371). In such states, we lose our sense of separate individuality; we become aware of our oneness with the Absolute, the divine (1902/1929, p. 410). "The whole point" he once noted, lies in the sense that "through a certain point or part in you, you coalesce and are identical with the eternal" (cited in Allen, 1967, p. 431). That experience is fundamentally the same across religions—mystics from different traditions describe it in similar terms (1902/1929, p. 410). In essence, it is, as Abraham Maslow would assert more than 60 years later, a core mystical experience (Maslow, 1964). This sense of a core mystical experience is at the heart of what Aldous Huxley, decades after James, would call "the Perennial Philosophy" (1944)—a notion that has had momentous sway in transpersonal thought, and that has been pivotal in the ideas of Maslow, Wilber, Grof, and other principal figures of the movement.

From this point of view, institutional religions, with their theologies and rituals, are only secondary, more mundane growths based on the experience of particular mystics (1902/1929, p. 31). Personally, James found them suspect: They form "corporate ambitions" and political interests that can often corrupt the original visionary experiences of their founders; they generate dogmas that fail to embody the original insight. The "genuine, first hand religious experience" always seems heretical or mad to the orthodox associates of the mystic who has them (1902/1929, p. 328). But ultimately, that experience—or the words in which it is reported—may be converted into a church and an orthodoxy, and when that happens, its inspiration, the inward experience, is inevitably lost (1902/1929, p. 330). James articulated that position—a "spiritual but not religious" posture— more than half a century before it began to be reiterated by Maslow, Grof, and others.

He also saw that a central element in spiritual growth is what later would be called the "death-rebirth experience." The centrality of such an experience was a major theme in Joseph Campbell's studies of mythology (see especially Campbell, 1949), which influenced the transpersonal movement; its therapeutic value is critical in Grof's LSD psychotherapy and Holotropic Breathwork (see Grof, 2000). In his Hibbert Lectures, delivered at Oxford University in 1908, James spoke of "religious experiences ... of an unexpected life succeeding upon death"—death not in the sense of a demise of the body, but rather in the sense of a personal experience of failure and despair. In spiritual literature, James traced the emphasis on renewed life coming from such death experiences to Luther and his successors, but he noted that it was familiar in such modern expressions as mind cure and contemporary evangelical religions. They resulted in breakthroughs in which our egoic props and satisfactions "appear as utter childishness," and we are brought further into "the universe's deeper reaches." "The phenomenon," he explained, "is that of new ranges of life succeeding on our most despairing moments," bringing "another kind of happiness and power, based on giving up our own will and letting something higher work for us...." These phenomena reveal "a world in which all is well, in *spite* of certain forms of death, indeed *because* of certain forms of death...." Those who have such experiences inevitably conclude that "we inhabit an invisible spiritual environment from which help comes, our soul being mysteriously one with a larger soul whose instruments we are" (1909b, pp. 305–308).

And finally, James showed a deep interest in Asian religions and in their psychologies and practices—well before they were widely known in the West, and more than half a century before they became more popular in America and Europe in the 1960s. His acquaintance with those traditions extended back to the influence, in his early life, of the Transcendentalists. Notebooks written in his late teens reflect readings in Indic literature and religion; ones from about the time of his major psychological crisis refer to books that he read on Hinduism and Buddhism (Richardson, 2006, pp. 15, 126). Even his early writings make scattered reference to Sanskrit terms (Taylor, 1996b, p. 61). In *The Varieties*, James's primary example of union with the Absolute, the core mystical experience, is the "Tat Vam Asi" of the Upanishads: "That art Thou!" (1902/1929, p. 410). In that treatise and elsewhere, James wrote observantly about the insights of Buddhism and Hinduism, whose texts he apparently encountered at Harvard, particularly through the History of Religions Club (Taylor, 1996b, p. 62). Moreover, James had personal contact with teachers in those traditions and their Western disciples. Swami Vivekananda, who came to Harvard in 1896, and whom James met there, seems to have made a particularly strong impression on him: James called him the "paragon" of Vedantist missionaries (James, 1907a, p. 58). Vivekananda is mentioned in several of James's writings and is quoted in *The Varieties* (1902/1929, pp. 391–392, 503–504) and in *Pragmatism* (1907a, pp. 58–59).

Although he was not a practitioner, James was intrigued by the possibility of cultivating mystical states through meditation and yoga. At Harvard, he had met other invited meditation teachers besides Vivekananda, and he was impressed not only by their accounts of their practices, but by their presence, calmness, and "imperturbability." In his "Talks to Teachers on Psychology" delivered in 1892, he spoke of the value of their practices and even suggested that meditation might be incorporated into American schools, as a counter to the habitual anxiety and intensity that plagued the national temper (1899/1962, pp. 37–38). His own psychological investigation had taught him the value of holding attention, continually bringing it back to a single focus, and of slower breathing, cultivating a habit of "watchfulness," and attaining a sense of "calmness and harmony in your own person" (1890/1952, pp. 274–275; 1899/1962, pp. 57, 104, 107, 128–129). In *The Varieties*, James cited Vivekananda on the effects of yoga (1902/1929, pp. 391–392); in a later essay, he argued the benefits of various forms of the practice, presenting a lengthy account by a disciple of Vivekananda, the Polish philosopher Wincenty Lutoslawski, who had undergone intensive training in hatha yoga, attaining "a peace never known before, an inner rhythm of unison with a deeper rhythm above or beyond" (James, 1907b, p. 327). James did admit to trying some breathing exercises, but he saw walking as his yoga and writing as his discipline (Taylor, 1996b, pp. 64–65). It is reported that after hearing a Theraveda monk lecture at Harvard on Buddhism in 1904, James declared to the audience that "this is the psychology that everybody will be studying twenty-five years from now" (Fields, 1981, p. 135, cited in Taylor, 1996b, p. 147).

Conclusion

As William James developed and refined a transpersonal worldview, his scientific reputation fell into decline. With its strongly positivistic orientation, the post-Darwinian scientific world resisted his efforts to cultivate a spiritual outlook that would be compatible with its established verities and sounder principles, as opposed to its materialistic prejudices and unverifiable assumptions. James's standing as an icon of American intellectual life rested on his addresses to a wider audience, and to his achievements in the more worldly movement of philosophical pragmatism.

But now, more than a century after he first used the term "transpersonal," a vigorous movement in psychology by that name, with profound philosophical implications, has rediscovered his spiritually oriented insights, and finds new validity in notions that he pioneered about the nature of science, about the domains of consciousness, and about the validity of spiritual life. The transpersonal movement will be enriched as it comes to understand more fully the intellectual legacy that he bequeathed to it.

Having passed the centenary of his death, in 2010, that movement might now recognize William James as a great precursor—who in this respect was a full century ahead of his time.

Notes

1 An earlier version of this chapter appeared as "The Transpersonal William James" in *The Journal of Transpersonal Psychology*, v.40, n.1 (2008).

2 In the same account, James used the terms "trans-visible," "trans-palpable," and "trans-mental" to refer to realities outside of our normal perceptions. The first two terms might sometimes refer to "a panpsychic entity," the latter to an entity "said to be altogether 'unknowable.'" Those terms come closer to the current meanings that we now attach to the "transpersonal" than did James's own definition (cf. Perry, 1935, v. II, p. 446).

3 The account appears in *The Varieties of Religious Experience*, disguised as the free translation of an original in French by an anonymous writer. James later revealed to his son Henry and to his French translator that it referred to his own experience (Allen, 1967, p. 165; Richardson, 2006, p. 543).

4 In 1960, 50 years after his death, Viking Press issued a collection of James's writings entitled *William James on Psychic Research*, edited by Gardner Murphy and Robert O. Ballou. That collection, which stirred little interest at the time, has been superseded by the more comprehensive *Essays in Psychical Research* published by Harvard University Press in 1986, the sixteenth volume in its complete *Works of William James*. The Harvard volume includes a valuable introduction by Robert A. McDermott, which relates James's interest in psychic research to his ongoing effort to define a position that honored scientific procedures but respected religious insights. Convincingly arguing the sustained character of James's involvement with psychical research, McDermott places it in the context of his more widely known philosophical stances. Krister Dylan Knapp has recently published (2017) a thoroughgoing account of James's psychical research, portraying it as "a core part" of his "intellectual disposition" (p. 4): *William James: Psychical Research and the Challenge of Modernity*.

5 *William James on Exceptional Mental States* (1982) meticulously attempts to reconstruct James's lost Lowell Lectures of 1896, which were never published; *William James on Consciousness Beyond the Margin* (1996) offers

a more synthetic view of James's psychic research and its place in his developing thought. My own perspective on James is indebted to Taylor's investigations (although his major studies, which are intended largely for James scholars, do not make explicit comparisons with modern transpersonal thought).

6 The most comprehensive and sophisticated defense of the transmission theory is the recently issued, monumental study by Kelly et al. (2007), which grew out of a study group established at the Esalen Institute's Center for Theory and Research (see especially Chapter 9, pp. 577–643, written by Edward F. Kelly). See also the work of Patrick McNamara of the Boston University School of Medicine, Ann Harrington of Harvard, Andrew Newberg of the University of Pennsylvania, Jeffrey Schwartz of UCLA, Donald Price of the University of Florida, Richard Davidson of the University of Wisconsin at Madison, and the results of the "Mind and Life" dialogues between the Dalai Lama and neurobiologists. All are mentioned in Monastersky (2006).

CHAPTER FIVE

The Resurrection of Frederic Myers[1]

If life after death is not a grand illusion, the soul of Frederic William Henry Myers has cause to celebrate. After a century of neglect, the prolific British psychological investigator, dismissed by successors for his preoccupation with mediumistic phenomena and with demonstrating an afterlife, is once again getting his due, his reputation regaining an earthly immortality, whether or not his spirit is enjoying a heavenly one. The transpersonal orientation in psychology has nourished an intellectual milieu in which Myers's investigations seem courageous, some of his innovative theories ingenious, some of his insights prescient.

At the time of his death in 1901, F.W.H. Myers commanded high esteem from across the still fledgling profession of psychology. A classicist by training, he had collaborated with some of the best-known psychological investigators of his day. He was lionized by prominent colleagues for his wide-ranging knowledge, prodigious memory, mastery of scientific and psychological literature, exacting investigation, and intrepid exploration of less accessible realms of the mind. He had named and intensively explored the phenomenon still now known as "telepathy," and examined many other phenomena that he viewed as related to it; and out of that data he had constructed a far-reaching theory of human personality. In crediting him with the discovery of the subliminal mind, William James recognized that Myers had pulled observations of scattered, anomalous phenomena into a coherent, systematic concept of a subliminal self. The question of how that unconscious territory is constituted, thought James, deserved to be called the "problem of Myers" (James, 1901/1986, p. 196). To Theodore Flournoy, Myers was "one of the most remarkable personalities of our time in the field of mental science" (cited in Crabtree, 1993, p. 327). Although his work was controversial and incited some vigorous criticism, particularly for its more mystical and metaphysical leanings, Frederic Myers was a presence to be reckoned with in the emerging field of psychology.

The driving motivation behind Myers's accomplishments in the field, however, was his absorption with an issue that was increasingly inadmissible in professional inquiry: the question of life after death. As scientific life generally, and psychology in particular, took a resoundingly materialistic turn, Myers endeavored to demonstrate the existence of an autonomous soul, one that outlasted physical demise. In that pursuit, he helped to found the Society for Psychical Research, to coordinate rigorously empirical investigations of psychic and paranormal phenomena; he participated indefatigably in its efforts for over 20 years; he elaborated a pioneering and comprehensive theory of unconscious life, published in the pages of its journal and review; and he assembled his evidence and theories in a massive, posthumously published work, *Human Personality and Its Survival of Bodily Death* (1903), which now, over a century later, is attracting renewed attention. To William James, that work was "a scientific construction of a very high order" and "a masterpiece of coordination and unification" (James, 1903/1986, p. 211).

The admiration of James and his contemporaries, however, was not enough to salvage Myers from the floodwaters of twentieth-century scientific materialism. His theories were often expressed in a florid and now seemingly antiquated prose, and his investigations centered on phenomena that were ever more widely dismissed as illusory. He may have been remembered in certain circles of parapsychological research—and in spiritualistic worlds, where interest was sustained by supposed post-mortem appearances of Myers in séance sessions—but he largely disappeared from the more general psychological literature. Alan Gauld's *The Founders of Psychical Research* (1968) outlines Myers's psychological theories, but the bulk of the book is devoted to the SPR's efforts to confirm or disprove the validity of spiritualistic phenomena. Henri Ellenberger's monumental *The Discovery of the Unconscious*, published in 1970, is still the most comprehensive treatment of the early history of depth psychology. Despite identifying Myers as "one of the great systematizers of the notion of the unconscious mind" (1970, p. 314), Ellenberger's 900 pages grant him only passing references, delving deeply, instead, into the contributions of Janet, Freud, Adler, and Jung. Daniel Robinson's *An Intellectual History of Psychology*, revised a decade later, makes no mention of Myers at all (1981). When not ignored entirely, Myers and his circle in the SPR were sometimes recalled with harsh or dismissive criticism.

Even in the more general literature of the transpersonal movement, until quite recently, Myers has cut a slight figure. As *The Journal of Transpersonal Psychology* was launched in the late 1960s, Willis Harman, as we have noted, included *Human Personality and its Survival of Bodily Death* as among the "pioneering books in the exploration of supraconscious processes" of the early twentieth century (Harman, 1969, pp. 22–23). But while the two other such works that he noted, Bucke's *Cosmic Consciousness* and James's *Varieties*, are widely read and have been republished in numerous editions, Myers's *magnum opus*, until very recently, has scarcely been available. There is nary a reference to Myers in the significant works of such major figures of the movement as Abraham Maslow, Stanislav Grof, and Ken Wilber. Overviews of the field such as *Transpersonal Psychologies* (Tart, 1975/1992), *Paths Beyond Ego* (Walsh & Vaughn, 1993), *Textbook of Transpersonal Psychiatry and Psychology* (Scotton, Chinen, & Battista, 1996), and *Shadow, Self, Spirit* (Daniels, 2005) refer to James and Jung as forebears, but collectively make almost no mention of Myers. Major writings of more parapsychologically oriented researchers familiar in the movement, such as Charles Tart, Russell Targ, and Dean Radin, provide occasional fleeting references to Myers's investigations, but no sustained discussion of his psychological ideas.

Transpersonal psychology, however, has discovered realms, and investigated phenomena, that now are calling Myers back to life. Among historians of psychology, Adam Crabtree signaled the need for a renewed interest in Myers in his notable account of magnetic sleep and the early years of psychological healing. *From Mesmer to Freud* provides an account of the founding of the Society for Psychical Research and of its role in the psychological investigation of phenomena associated with spiritualism, mesmerism, and hypnotism. In a cogent and insightful summary chapter on Myers, Crabtree describes how those and associated investigations ultimately led Myers to formulate his comprehensive theory of the subliminal self (Crabtree, 1993). In recounting Myers's accomplishments, Crabtree observes the incongruity between his former stature and his subsequent neglect, lamenting that he "is today almost unknown in the field of psychology" (p. 327). Since the publication of Crabtree's work in 1993, Myers's name has gained currency.

At the heart of this renewed interest is not so much Myers' psychical studies, nor his success or failure in demonstrating an afterlife, as his comprehensive theory of the unconscious mind. He was among the first visionaries of modern psychology to portray the unconscious as a universal human attribute. In 1893, he had introduced the works of Freud to Britain, but his view of the unconscious was of far greater scope than the one that held sway in Vienna. While Freud saw the unconscious as composed of lost memories and repressed impulses, Myers, as we have seen, viewed it as also a source of wisdom, clairvoyance, genius, and transcendent vision. It may have been the repository of trauma and trivia, but it was also the font of greater human potential. The subliminal that Myers presented extended beyond the individual: it was linked to an evolving collective mind and, ultimately, to a spiritual core in human nature.

Searching for Spirit in Times of Lost Faith: The Life of Myers

Frederic Myers was born in 1843, into an evangelical Anglican household in the town of Keswick, in Cumberland, England. His father was a clergyman, his mother the pious daughter of a prosperous landowner and entrepreneur, owner of flax mills in Leeds. In his childhood, he was steeped in Biblical readings and even then showed a preoccupation with death and afterlife. His father's early death, when Myers was only eight years old, surely reinforced that focus. But Myers came to intellectual maturity at a time in which traditional faith was challenged by historical and textual criticism of the Bible and by the post-Darwinian rise of scientific rationalism. W.H. Mallock characterized the mood of his fellow British intellectuals in the 1870s: "It is said that in tropical forests one can almost hear the vegetation growing," he wrote. "One may almost say that with us one can hear faith decaying" (cited in Gauld, 1968, pp. 63–64).

Nostalgia for the comforts of a lost faith was felt by many in that generation, Myers, for sure, among them. At Trinity College, Cambridge, he distinguished himself as a classical scholar and poet, while undertaking studies in the natural sciences as well. Subsequently he accepted a lectureship at the College, during which he received further recognition for his poetry. For a time, his heretofore waning Christianity was revivified by contact with a beautiful and crusading acquaintance, and perhaps by a conversion experience, but the effects did not last. Nearly dying of pneumonia at the age of 25, he found that although he dreaded the potential loss of his life, his faith had deserted him. But soon thereafter, he grew fascinated with the occult and anomalous phenomena associated with the spiritualist movement, then in high vogue both in the United States and Britain. Intimating personal immortality, those strange and curious occurrences invited empirical investigation.

Together with his Cambridge friend and associate Henry Sidgwick, Myers plunged into the study of alleged spiritualistic phenomena—the mysterious rapping and table-turning, automatic writing, the clairvoyant insights of mediums, their supposed communications from another realm, and even the materializations of ghostly human forms (or parts thereof). Always interested in questions of education, Myers left his lectureship at Trinity to work on behalf of the education of women; subsequently, in 1877, he was appointed school inspector in Cambridge, a position that he retained for the remainder of his professional life. But the investigations of spiritualism and associated phenomena—the effort to test those phenomena empirically and to explain them scientifically—remained the focus of his intellectual endeavors.

In the succeeding years, Myers continued his literary activities, producing long poems, a widely disseminated study of Wordsworth (Myers, 1880), and critical essays on both classical and modern literature (Myers, 1883, 1888). Stimulated in part by a passing interest in the Theosophical Society and its charismatic founder Helena Blavatsky, he also read widely in Asian philosophy. Sometime around 1870, he had fallen deeply in love with the former Annie Eliza, the wife of his troubled cousin Walter Marshall. Annie Marshall committed suicide in 1876. Several years later, Myers married Eveleen Tennant, daughter of a wealthy family who was 13 year his junior; she later became a gifted portrait photographer. Eventually the couple had three children. In 1882, Myers joined with Sidgwick, their friend and associate Edmund Gurney, physicist William Barrett, and various spiritualists and academic investigators in the formation of the SPR. The Society's purpose was the exact and systematic investigation of a wide range of seemingly paranormal phenomena, including thought-transference, effects associated with mesmerism and hypnotism, testimonies about apparitions, as well as phenomena associated with mediumistic trances. By 1890, it had over 700 members, including such prominent figures as William Gladstone, former Prime Minister; Arthur Balfour, future Prime Minister; Alfred Lord Tennyson, John Ruskin, William James, and Lewis Carroll.

Among the Society's first major productions was *Phantasms of the Living*, a study focusing on crisis apparitions, in which people report seeing the figure or hearing the voice of a person at the moment of the latter's death, or of some other major crisis. The study's weighty two volumes examined over 700 cases. Myers collaborated in the investigations, developed, with Gurney, the central thesis, and wrote the long, historical introduction (Gurney, Myers, & Podmore, 1886). In 1892, he began to elaborate his theory of the subliminal mind, publishing a series of studies on the topic in the SPR's *Proceedings* and *Journal*, and introducing his preliminary ideas to a wider public in other forums, including a collection of miscellaneous essays titled *Science and a Future Life* (1893). His effort to assemble this material, and the evidence behind it, into a thorough *magnum opus* was nearing completion when he was stricken with a series of illnesses affecting his heart, arteries, and breathing. In January of 1901, at the age of 58, Myers died in Rome. William James, who accompanied him at the time, remarked that he faced the final transition not only with serenity but eagerness (cited in Gauld, 1968, p. 332). *Human Personality and Its Survival of Bodily Death* was prepared for publication by Myers's colleagues Richard Hodgson and Alice Johnson, and published in 1903.

5.1 Frederic W. H. Myers, by Eveleen Myers (née Tennant) circa 1890. (NPG Ax68396. © National Portrait Gallery, London.)

A New Frontier of Psychological Inquiry: Phase One

Embarking on their empirical investigation of "extraordinary subjective experience" in the late 1960s, the newly denominated "transpersonal" psychologists saw themselves as crossing a "new frontier of psychological inquiry" (Sutich, 1969a, p. iv). But in key ways, the investigators associated with the SPR had crossed that same frontier and trekked through similar territory. Like transpersonal psychologists of more recent times, these researchers aimed to understand spiritual experiences, transcendent states of awareness, and the further reaches of human potential.

Over two decades after the launching of *The Journal of Transpersonal Psychology* in 1969, Denise Lajoie and S.I. Schapiro's surveyed definitions of the field; their integration of those definitions remains an enduring summation of its central concerns. Transpersonal psychology, they wrote, is characterized by the investigation of at least five key interests or themes: states of consciousness; humanity's highest potential; the extension of consciousness beyond ego or self; the notion of transcendence; and the validity and importance of spiritual concerns (Lajoie & Schapiro, 1992). Those very interests and themes permeated the work of Frederic Myers and his confreres.

For Myers, the most profound question of human life was whether "any element" of the human personality might survive bodily death (1903/1954, v. 1, p. 1), and he was radically innovative in arguing that it could be addressed by experimental psychology (1893, p. 44). With the systematic investigation of near-death experiences by investigators such as Russell Noyes and David Rosen in the 1970s, and particularly with the popular accounts of Raymond Moody and Kenneth Ring (Moody, 1975; Ring, 1980), which spawned a new generation of intensive studies, the question has become an admissible one in transpersonal circles, even if it still stands outside the pale of mainstream psychology. Although Ring's classical study makes only passing reference to Myers, and Moody's none at all, the burgeoning study of near-death experiences surely helped forge an intellectual ambience that would be receptive to a renewed interest in his work. (While he did not explore it in detail, Myers was aware of the phenomenon that later became known as "near-death experience." In *Human Personality*, he noted the capacity for "traveling clairvoyance," in which consciousness seems to move away from the location of the physical body, which was sometimes associated with comas preceding death, and he observed that such states could prompt visions of a spiritual realm [v. 2, pp. 129, 218, 525].)

David Fontana's comprehensive review of evidence for an afterlife (2005) builds directly on material collected by Myers and his colleagues. Other recent investigations into the possibility of survival have been to some degree inspired by Myers's work, including studies of reincarnation experiences conducted by Ian Stevenson and his team at the University of Virginia Medical School (e.g., Stevenson, 1970, 1997), the further research on near-death experiences by Bruce Greyson, also of the University of Virginia, and his colleagues (see Holden, Greyson, & James, 2009), and the Survival of Bodily Death Seminar Series at the Esalen Institute (see Kelly et al., 2007).

The thrust of Myers's efforts, however, was not simply to gather evidence of the possibility of survival, but to construct a model of the human psyche that would make survival plausible. In the process, he explored phenomena, developed methodologies, and arrived at concepts that would prefigure central interests and themes of the transpersonal movement. We can recognize Myers as a precursor of transpersonal thought especially in his rigorously empirical methodology; in his assertion of the reality of the spiritual and the inadequacies of materialism; in his expansive concept and map of the psyche, as encompassing a spectrum of states of consciousness; in his view of the unconscious as an avenue to transcendent experience and higher potential, reaching beyond the self; and in his belief in the evolution of consciousness.

Scientific Methodology: Science Beyond Materialism

For Myers, the "method of modern Science" was the most effective way to acquire knowledge, so effective that it merited, in whatever way possible, application to some of the deeper preoccupations of human life, and to questions about human nature, that traditionally had been the province of religion and philosophy. The resulting science may be rudimentary, and inevitably limited, for the most profound questions about reality are not susceptible to scientific inquiry (1900, p. 297; 1903/1954, v. 1, p. 79). But Myers's task, as he saw it, was to expand the reach of science, identifying issues involving mind and reality that could be subjected to dispassionate and systematic study, careful and cumulative observations, and critical analysis of findings (1903/1954, v. 1, pp. 1–2). Like other sciences, such inquiry should be built upon observable facts and whenever possible, on repeatable experiments (ibid., p. 7).

This new science would delve into areas not yet subject to empirical study, ferreting out new facts. Indeed, it would examine phenomena whose very reality had been subject to question. Like his friend and ally William James, Myers saw that science had achieved only a "narrow glance" into infinite realms of the unknown (ibid., p. 249). As it forged forward, it assuredly would uncover facts that were incompatible with inevitably limited reigning assumptions or theory. In Myers's view, anomalous facts clashed with reductive materialist assumptions. But already, in his time, the new psychology had revealed substantive occurrences behind phenomena that scientific minds had previously dismissed as superstition and delusion. Investigations into hysteria and hypnosis had disclosed realities behind unusual manifestations associated with witchcraft and Mesmerism (ibid., pp. 4–5); stigmata, to choose another example, were related to other effects of suggestion on the vaso-motor system (ibid., p. 188).

Myers's own research examined such extraordinary subjective experiences as telepathy, clairvoyance, remote viewing, automatic writing, precognition, inspirations of genius, visions, perception of apparitions, hypnotic states, trances, and spiritual ecstasy. By the systematic study of these phenomena, he aimed to show that they were both real and governed by natural laws, thus marking a middle ground between materialistic outlooks that dismissed them as delusional, and religious convictions that saw them as miraculous. His approach was to classify the evidence into types, track the frequency with which like phenomena recur, and consider how well alternative explanations might account for them. By standards of modern research, his evidence might appear anecdotal and statistically unsophisticated, but as Trevor Hamilton has demonstrated, it was, by the standards of its time, subjected to rigorous scientific canons (Hamilton, 2009, pp. 245–272). Always vigilant against the possibility of fraud, Myers insisted that anecdotal evidence be subject to confirmation, that as many cases as possible be examined before reaching conclusions, and that natural and psychological explanations be considered in advance of any that seemed extramundane. The great bulk of *Human Personality* was given over to evidence rather than theory, to a copious array of detailed case studies accumulated by Myers and his colleagues at the SPR. His expository strategy was to present these accounts in what he saw as a continuous sequence, from the more accepted phenomena of hypnotic suggestion, through various forms of thought transference, leading ultimately to the perception of phantasms, first of the living and then of the dead.

The Reality of the Spiritual

Myers believed that these investigations empirically demonstrated the reality of the spiritual. They showed that humans had faculties that could not be explained in terms of material cause and effect, at least as normally understood—faculties that seemed to operate independently of sense impressions and functions of the brain. For Myers, telepathy, in demonstrating the capacity of consciousness to receive information apart from the physical senses, confirmed that consciousness can function apart from the physical world, and thereby suggested the existence of another dimension. Telepathy, "teleaesthesia" (what we might call remote viewing), precognition and other faculties were not limited by the normal constraints of space and time; their natural milieu was on a different plane, one that interpenetrated but was distinct from the world of matter.

Myers tracked these phenomena extensively, in spontaneous cases, in automatic writing, and in non-ordinary states such as hypnosis and mediumistic trances. They led inexorably, he thought, to a conception of reality that included a spiritual realm, a realm that showed order and elements of consistency with the natural, observable world, but that extended beyond it and was free of many of its constraints. For him, there was a steady progression from the direct transference of ideas from one mind to another, to the well-demonstrated perception of apparitions of a distant person as that person was undergoing a crisis or death, to apparitions of still extant deceased persons, or to their communications with the living in automatic speaking and writing.

Myers pursued the study of all of these perceived phenomena, believing that he had accumulated ample empirical evidence of their reality, though his explanations for them often differed from the popular ones and from the uncritical assumptions of the spiritualists. In them, he saw, in varying degrees, the "disengagement of some informing spirit from the restraint of bodily organism" (ibid., p. 25), and therefore the possibility of life apart from the physical plane. Each of us, he wrote, is "essentially a spirit, controlling an organism" (ibid., p. 217). Though well aware of contemporaneous research linking specific brain functions with mental functions, Myers did not conclude that the former necessarily caused the latter. Much of his research was pitched towards the discovery of instances in which elements of consciousness could be seen as acting on the physical plane, including the brain. True, there was correlation between certain brain functions and mentation, but the relationship could be seen as interactive, or as one in which, to use terminology elaborated by William James, the brain is more of a transmitter than a producer of consciousness (James, 1898). In the final analysis, according to Myers, brain is acted upon by spirit (see, for example, 1903/1954, v. 2, pp. 197, 254). In opposition to the materialistic tenor of his era, he accepted "the ancient hypothesis of an indwelling soul," with an existence beyond the physical plane even during earthly life, and persisting after bodily death. In fact, he believed that such a soul was provable, indeed proved, by "direct observation" (1903/1954, v. 1, p. 35).

The spiritual world existed as the largest context of life, beyond not only the material realm but an intermediate energetic one as well, conceived of as "ethereal vibrations"—we might call it a realm of energetic fields. "That the world of spiritual life does not depend on the existence of the material world," he argued, "I hold as now proved by actual evidence" (ibid., p. 215).

The Subliminal Self: Developing the Spectrum

To explain the anomalous phenomena that he was so heedfully investigating, Myers developed his theory of the subliminal self, his great and original contribution to theoretical psychology. That contribution, first conceived as early as 1885 (Hamilton, 2009, p. 127), deserves far greater recognition than it generally commands, and it is of particular relevance in today's transpersonal studies.

Myers's developing account of the unconscious begins with a series of four articles on automatic writing, published in the Society's *Proceedings*, beginning in 1884. Throughout the series, Myers posed alternatives to the spiritualist assumption that the content of automatic writing emanates from discarnate spirits of the dead. In the first piece (a year prior to the publication of Breuer and Freud's *Studies in Hysteria*) he ruminated about "unconscious cerebration," asserting that it should be seen not as a subsidiary but rather as a *"substantive and primary* operation of our intelligence" (Myers, 1884, p. 219). The following year, in a second article, he wrote of a "threshold of consciousness" and a "secondary self" that, "coincidentally with our normal or primary self," is potentially within us all, linked to the right hemisphere of the brain (Myers, 1885, pp. 27–30, 43). From that secondary self emanate the content of much automatic writing; it can be receptive, too, to telepathic communication from the living. In the final two papers in the series, Myers portrayed a broader range of operations for this "second focus of cerebration and mentation." Out of this "deeper zone" of our being come instinctive motor activity and unconscious control of bodily movements, including, for example, facial expression and activities such as playing a musical instrument, as well as forms of "morbid dissociation"—trains of memory unavailable to a person's dominant states of consciousness (Myers, 1887). But through it, as well, sometimes come highly significant and salutary messages, rising "from one stratum of our being to another..., from the sub-conscious to the conscious or waking self" (Myers 1889, p. 535). Those messages might include admonitions from our wiser self, inspirations of genius, and even clairvoyance or "supernormal" knowledge—access to other information that is beyond the purview of our normal awareness (Myers, 1889).

By 1892, when he launched the first of the nine articles that elaborated his developing theory more fully, Myers had adopted the term "subliminal consciousness" to describe that secondary self below the threshold of normal consciousness, that "abiding psychical entity" that is "far more extensive" than we know (Myers, 1892a, p. 305). With that label, he was reacting against the term "unconscious," intending to convey that this subliminal mind did indeed indicate a form of consciousness, albeit of a different sort than normal waking awareness. It was then, too, that Myers introduced his model of a "spectrum of consciousness," extending from physiological at one end to the psychical at the other. The supraliminal—our everyday awareness—forms a privileged element, well adapted to normal life; but in its subliminal reaches, the mind extends far further and deeper into the individual personality, and even beyond. This subliminal consciousness, he wrote,

> ...may embrace a far wider range both of physiological and of psychical activity than is open to our supraliminal consciousness, to our supraliminal memory. The spectrum of consciousness, I may so call it, is in the subliminal self indefinitely extended at both ends. (ibid., p. 306)

In that psychical extension lay the possibility of "telepathic and clairvoyant impressions," including even those that transcend normal limitations of time and space (p. 306). Myers was well aware of contemporaneous studies linking the unconscious mind with disintegrations of personality, including, for example, the work on hysteria of Janet, Breuer, and Freud. Like others of his time, he knew the unconscious could involve the morbid and destructive; in presenting his own theory, he referred to much of that research. But he saw those morbid aspects as limited manifestations of a universal element in humanity, an element that could also serve the highest human needs and faculties. His distinctive role was to call attention to the benign side of the scale, to the subliminal's capacities for supernormal and transcendent insight, to its indication of what he termed the "evolutive" side of human nature.

Presenting his spectrum, Myers wrote of the subliminal intelligence that controls, or can control, physiological processes—as it were, the "red" end of the spectrum. Included here are not only normal organic functions and physical coordination, but also the capacity of mind, in some way, to gain control over bodily processes, as revealed, especially, in hypnotism. Suggestion in a trance state can anesthetize a patient from pain, slow pulse rate, reduce swellings, calm addictive cravings, and even produce stigmata and other symbolic signs on the skin. Although these suggestions might originally come from a hypnotist—that is, from without—Myers argued that the active agent, more immediately, was the patient's own subliminal mind, and that hypnotism is only a preliminary indication of the subliminal mind's capacity to affect the physical domain.

Myer's greater interest by far, however, was in the psychological or "violet" side of the spectrum—especially in the higher capacities revealed as subliminal consciousness rises into supraliminal awareness. Among those communications from one stratum of mind to the other are hyper-acuity of senses revealed in hypnotism, and musical inspiration, which can come as an unpremeditated "uprush of unsummoned audition" (1892b, p. 344). Other acts of genius, too, can appear full-blown in supraliminal awareness, such as the solving of problems almost instantaneously, without conscious calculation, displayed by child mathematical prodigies. Myers saw a similar dynamic at work, often, in artistic creation.

Dreams are a common form of communication from the subliminal: they sometimes indicate a wider range of memory or awareness than that available to the waking mind, as when they reveal the location of lost objects. They can be prophetic, or monitory—urging an action in everyday life; they can provide a writer with the seed of literary inspiration, and resolve mathematical problems or professional quandaries that had been puzzling to waking awareness. On occasion, they seem to indicate supernormal powers: telepathy, clairvoyance, precognition, retrocognition.

As Myers's analysis progressed, he considered more fully indications of the supernormal. By the fifth article in the series, he examined evidence of such powers in hypnotic states, crystal-gazing and light trances—linking them, always, to operations of subconscious intelligence. Each of these states or techniques was a means of eliciting information from the sub-liminal, bringing it into supraliminal consciousness. "Internal percepts," arising without direct sensory stimuli, he maintained, are "as normal as external percepts" and may, on occasion, present "actual knowledge which external perception could never reach.... [T]he eye," he declared, "is not our only means of seeing, nor is the world around us the only thing that we see" (1892c, p. 528). Evidence that we see by other means pointed to an "Interpenetration of Worlds," a confirmation of "the ancient belief in a spiritual universe, co-existing with, and manifesting itself through the material universe that we know." For our deepest views into the universe, we may need to "gaze within" (ibid., pp. 534–535).

From that basis of affirming the surprising capacity of the subliminal, Myers proceeded to examine cases of apparent telepathy, such as in feel-ing an urgent need to act in order to save a loved one from danger, or be present at a death. Other cases involved the reception of messages from a distant friend or acquaintance revealed in automatic writing, messages not intentionally transmitted by the agent, but with specific and accurate information. Myers took these cases as confirming "a continuously active subliminal consciousness in all mankind" (1893–4, p. 60). Unintentional telepathy from someone present at a séance might also explain messages, including those bearing accurate information previously unknown to the medium, that purport to be from a spirit of someone deceased. But with-out drawing firm conclusions, Myers passed from cases possibly explicable on these grounds, to ones that seem less so—cases in which the automatic writing yields information unknown to those involved, but subsequently verified.

Experiences such as these, which apparently involve perceptions at a dis-tance, seem to transcend normal limitations of space. From them, Myers turned to evidence for retrocognition and precognition—perceptions that seem to transcend limitations of time. In typical fashion, he progressed from ones that are nearer to the present moment to ones more removed. Experiences, he suggested, leave traces on body and spirit, and perhaps on objects in the environment, which, in extraordinary circumstances, may be discerned directly by "sensitives." In some cases, veridical dreams, vi-sions, and automatic writing might have originated in unintentional telep-athy, even if it be from an obscure but living source. From incidents that might be explained in that way, Myers moved to others that the percipi-ents believed involved a disembodied intelligence. More often than not,

Myers argued, the supposed spirit is an "externalized" projection, from a source wholly within the percipient's own intelligence. But in some cases, he held, retrocognitive information likely does indeed come from a surviving departed spirit. Alternatively, it might persist independently of any finite mind, enveloped by a superior intelligence, an "Omnipresent Mind" (1895a, p. 407).

Turning from retrocognition to precognition, Myers begins with rather common premonitions, which might be subliminally extrapolated from a knowledge of present realities, or perhaps from a "hyperaesthetic" extension of ordinary senses—such as in the strong presentiment of a potential accident, resulting in its narrow avoidance. He gives accounts of foretelling by hallucination or apparition, as of a coming death, and of perceptions, often through dreams or automatic writing, that might be explained by unintentional telepathy, or by inference from obscure but subliminally absorbed facts and events. Some cases, however, seem to involve "perception of the future more direct than any which our ordinary minds enjoy" (1895b, p. 485), primarily through premonitory dreams. The "divine inspiration" that tradition ascribes to prophecy, in Myers's view, is "hardly to be distinguished" from messages from subliminal consciousness (p. 585). In certain cases, he surmised, "departed human spirits" might plausibly play a role in the premonitions. In any case, a few of these cases of extraordinary perception brought moments of spiritual ecstasy, which Myers characterized as "the highest condition into which a spirit still incarnate can pass" (p. 568).

Wisdom and the Unconscious

With its capacity for solving problems and dilemmas that confound normal intelligence, for telepathy and clairvoyance, for transcending limitations of time and space—with, in short, its opening to an "interpenetration of worlds"—the subliminal mind potentially was the seat of great wisdom. Messages conveyed from the unconscious to the conscious mind, Myers argued, "may sometimes come from far beneath the realm of dream and confusion,—from some self whose monitions convey to us a wisdom profounder than we know" (1889, p. 543). Far from being only a cause of madness, the subliminal may give rise to impulses that are "wiser than our sanity itself" (ibid., p. 544).

Myers explained genius not as the hyper-development of a rational capacity, but rather as an "uprush" from the subliminal mind, bringing into normal consciousness ideas that had matured in the unconscious, sometimes with little or no conscious awareness on the part of the person involved. Geniuses were individuals who had a low threshold between the supraliminal and subliminal (see 1903/1954, v. 1, pp. 20, 71, 78). Thus great artists often thought of themselves not as inventing, but as recording inspirations that seemed to burst fully blown into their ordinary consciousness.

In its profounder reaches, Myers believed, the subliminal was involved with, and expressive of, humankind's unity and, beyond that, its essentially spiritual nature. He saw the universe as ultimately not a collection of individual experiences, but as "a plenum of infinite knowledge of which all souls form part" (1903/1954, v. 2, p. 273). In that plenum, what we experience as past and future is part of an ever-present reality. Contemplating those nether reaches, Myers turned to Platonic notions, where ideas or archetypes have a timeless presence, and where our profounder realizations are "reminiscences" of truths that we have known in our existence on a spiritual plane. The deepest of those realizations come through religious ecstasy, or mystical experience, which Myers conceived of as a "traveling clairvoyance" to the spiritual realm, and as the supreme uprushes from the subliminal self. "True ecstasy," wrote Myers, "I regard as a condition where the centre of consciousness changes from the supraliminal to the subliminal self, and realises the transcendental environment..." (ibid., p. 572). Such mystical experience was common to all religions, and though it might differ "morally and intellectually" from one to another, in "psychological essence" it was the same in all (ibid., p. 260). Those illuminating experiences were inevitably interpreted, and confused, by cultural constructs and personal beliefs; but however imperfect, they represent "a perception of the Cosmos...wider and profounder than our own" (1895b, p. 568); they remained the highest flights of consciousness that incarnate souls can take.

Evolution of Consciousness

The extraordinary capacities of the subliminal mind pointed towards an evolution of consciousness. Myers wrote at a time when enthusiasm for the idea of evolution, associated with Darwin, was at its apex, despite the resistance of churchmen and others who saw it as a threat to traditional theological convictions. Like R.M. Bucke, he saw possibilities not only of human physical evolution, but of growth in human mental faculties, in perceptual subtlety and powers of concentration. Evolution consisted in "a constant expansion of the span of supraliminal consciousness" (1893–4, p.

15), bringing to awareness more and more of the capacities of the subliminal. Telepathy, for example, could become a universal experience. Genius represented the possibilities of evolutionary development, ways in which common capacities might eventually evolve. While Myers had absorbed the Darwinian concept of natural selection, he also envisioned the possibility of humanity's exerting more control over its future evolutionary development, in part by a wider application of hypnosis and self-suggestion. His notion that supernormal capacities represented glimpses into the direction of evolution was later absorbed by Michael Murphy and others in the Human Potential movement (see Murphy, 1992).

His emphasis on evolution, we should note, did not rob Myers of a respect for the accomplishments of primal cultures. At times his rhetoric reflects a condescending attitude towards the "primitive" that was typical of his era, with its apotheosis of the doctrine of progress and its view of Western civilization as the apex of human achievement. But Myers recognized that his studies were reconfirming notions and experiences that had been part of human culture's earliest manifestations, expressed in healing rituals and such ancient practices as crystal-gazing. Indeed, he saw himself as returning, at times, to "the language of a 'paleolithic psychology'" (1903/1954, v. 1, p. 247) and acknowledged that "the 'humble thinkers' of the Stone Age, the believers in Witchcraft, in Shamanism, have been my true precursors in many of the ideas upheld in this book" (1903/1954, v. 2, p. 218). Spiritual insight was subject to evolutionary development, but supernormal powers and profound spiritual experiences were integral to all cultures, not least that of "the shaman, the medicine man" (ibid., p. 260).

For Myers, the evolutionary trajectory was inseparable from humanity's spiritual nature. It released latent capacities in a subliminal mind that drew sustenance from a spiritual universe. Telepathy, ultimately, is based on a "mutual gravitation or kinship of spirits"—that is to say, on love (ibid., p. 282)—and it gives us a glimpse of the interconnectedness, the final unity, of that ultimate web. As evolution progresses, humanity comes to know a progressively wider environment, which eventually must include the spiritual context of human life. Psychic capacities were a way in which humanity strives to know that context, and a way in which the context strives to be seen. In Myers's vision—influenced, no doubt, by Victorian perceptions of Hindu mystical thought—human life was infused with, was part of, divine life, and was in a process of discovering the nature of, and returning to, its source. Spiritual development was humanity's central purpose;

through it, we co-operate in cosmic evolution. "That which lies at the root of each of us," he wrote, "lies at the root of the Cosmos too. Our struggle is the struggle of the Universe itself; and the very Godhead finds fulfilment through our upward-striving souls" (ibid., p. 277). Citing Plotinus, Myers portrayed the whole evolutionary process as "the flight of the One to the One" (ibid., p. 291).

Myers Reviviscent

In the century following his death, interest in Myers, such as it was, persisted primarily in circles of parapsychology. Occasional books on spiritualism or psychic research examined his role and ideas, and some accounts of his work appeared in his own forum, the *Journal of the SPR*, and in other parapsychological journals. But the centenary of Myer's death and, two years later, of the publication of *Human Personality* sparked thoughtful appreciations that, although addressed primarily to the researchers in parapsychology, asserted his significance in the history of psychology and called attention to ideas that have been central in his twenty-first century revival (Alvarado, 2004; Kelly, 2001).

Although so much of Myers's writing centered on paranormal phenomena and the question of an afterlife, William James had anticipated the focus of more recent interest in Myers's work by highlighting his theory of the subliminal mind. By no means, thought James, had Myers empirically demonstrated all of his claims, nor proven survival. But as early as 1892, James extolled the historical importance of Myers's theory, and of his efforts to subsume within it a wide-ranging spectrum of human capacities (James, 1892/1986, p. 98). Particularly in two essays published shortly after Myers's death, first a eulogy and then a review of *Human Personality*, he elaborated on the significance of these innovative, indeed revolutionary, ideas, and the manner in which Myers arrived at them (James, 1901, 1903). Myers had brought the full array of occult phenomena, normally ignored in scientific investigation, under fair-minded scientific scrutiny (see also James, 1896/1986, p. 132), striking a proper balance between the denial of materialists and the credulousness of enthusiasts. He was "the pioneer who staked out a vast tract of mental wilderness and planted the flag of genuine science upon it" (1901/1986, p. 202). Moreover, he brought the phenomena encountered in that vast tract into relation to one another, arranging them into incremental series, and subsuming them under a general theory, the spectrum view of a universal subconscious mind (ibid., pp.

102

195–196). In the upper reaches of that spectrum, we encounter both spiritual awareness and adumbrations of further evolution of consciousness. James viewed these speculations as preliminary, the first attempt to mark out and map a territory for further study; but whether they would stand or fall in the future, they were the kind of bold and original hypotheses by which "the scientific researches of an entire generation are often molded" (ibid., pp. 199–200).

Through Michael Murphy, the memory of Frederic Myers was revived at the Esalen Institute. According to Jeffrey Kripal's sweeping history of Esalen, Murphy was introduced to the thought of Myers by Willis Harman in 1962, just after the institute's founding, and was inspired by *Human Personality*. Myers's philosophy is reflected in early Esalen brochures, particularly in their emphasis on "psychical research" as one of the institute's three pillars, and in their insistence on applying scientific procedures in the investigation of religious or occultist phenomena. Ultimately, Murphy was influenced by Myers's empirical and comparative approach to religious phenomena in the writing of his own *The Future of the Body*, published in 1992 (Kripal, 2007, 317, 406–408). In that work, Murphy, like Myers, gathers an immensely wide array of evidence related to the supernormal; arranges it in categories that are related but progressively more challenging to conventional explanation, emphasizing their continuity; interprets it with a broad concept of evolution, as demonstrating the emergence of more highly evolved human capacities; and even takes up the question of postmortem survival (Murphy, 1992). Lamenting that "few people today appreciate Myers's work" (p. 10), Murphy draws extensively on *Human Personality* and on the *Journal* and *Proceedings* of the British and American Societies for Psychical Research, examining many of the same metanormal phenomena that fascinated Myers and his circle. Explicitly following Myers and William James, Murphy attributes at least some extraordinary human capacities to "incursions" from a transcendent order that ultimately is part of human identity (Murphy, 1992, pp. 549–551).

A central figure in this revival of a broader interest in Myers has been Emily Williams Kelly of the University of Virginia, who first encountered his writings 1970s, and who was intrigued by their effort to link the particulars of psychic research to a more comprehensive understanding of mind and consciousness, and even of the universe at large (Kelly, personal communications, October 14 and 16, 2009). In the 1990s, Kelly completed a dissertation on Myers at the University of Edinburgh (Cook, 1992), where the ambience was more receptive to her interests than at graduate schools in the United States. She subsequently presented lucid accounts of Myers's approach and theories to the parapsychological world, noting their wider implications for psychology in general (see especially Cook, 1994). Myers, she argued, deserved credit for not abandoning the most basic questions of psychology: the nature of consciousness and the relation between mind and body.

In the year of the centennial of Myers's death, Kelly published an assessment of his influence on psychology in the *Journal of the SPR*, reviving a theme that James had planted in the same journal a century earlier (Kelly, 2001). Like James and others, Kelly praised Myers for the abundance of his research, the range of his subject matter, the breadth and cogency of his theory. But for her, Myers's chief significance lay in how he delineated and approached the territory of his investigations, transcending the debate between naturalism and supernaturalism. His effort to encompass paranormal phenomena within a framework of natural order led Myers beyond the old dichotomy of matter and mind, to adumbrations, supported by the new physics, that the two, in some way yet to be imagined, may be part of a greater unity. Exploring situations in which mental phenomena might be seen to have physical effects, rather than vice versa, Myers portrayed a consciousness that was far greater in extent, with far greater capacities, than we normally assume. In so doing, by Kelly's assessment, he articulated a seminal perspective on the place of mind in the natural world.

Other articles at the time of the centennials asserted that Myers's influence has been greater than commonly recognized. Ann Taves discerned Myers's ideas, especially his concept of the subliminal, behind William James's influential psychological model of mysticism as promulgated in *The Varieties of Religious Experience* (Taves, 2003). A perceptive essay by psychical researcher Carlos Alvarado (2003) argued that many of Myers's ideas had permeated psychological thought, particularly parapsychology, even though they were no longer linked to his name. The notion that extra-sensory perception, telepathy, and other supernormal functions were linked to the subconscious, prevalent in parapsychological studies for a century, could ultimately be traced to Myers. Although his ideas run against the grain of dominant psychological models of our own time, they nevertheless have contemporary relevance, calling attention to a psychology of "optimal functioning" (p. 21); reminding us that materialistic assumptions are subject, at least, to question; emphasizing the evolution of consciousness;

and interpreting certain experiences in terms of a lower threshold between unconscious and conscious activity. *Human Personality*, concludes Alvarado, "helps us to keep open the possibility of a psychology in which the mind is seen as more of a causal agent than is generally assumed" (p. 27).

The paramount contribution to the resuscitation of Myers is a massive study by a team of psychological investigators. *Irreducible Mind: Toward a Psychology for the 21ˢᵗ Century* grew out of a seminar sponsored by the Center for Theory and Research of the Esalen Institute, initiated by Michael Murphy in 1998. Shaped in part by Emily Kelly's longstanding immersion in Myer's thought, the study is structured around issues that Myers had seen as central in the investigation of consciousness. Besides Ms. Kelly, contributors to the volume include Adam Crabtree, neuroscientist Edward F. Kelly, psychologist Alan Gauld, philosopher Michael Grosso, and near-death researcher Bruce Greyson. The seminar involved an annual conference on the question of the survival of bodily death; it regularly drew other prominent researchers, such as Dean Radin and Marilyn Schlitz of the Institute of Noetic Sciences, psychical investigator Charles Tart, and quantum physicist Henry Stapp. For these researchers, as for Myers, the question of postmortem survival hinges on the relationship between consciousness and matter, between mind and brain.

It is that relationship that forms the focus of this nearly 800-page volume, which is dedicated to Myers as "a neglected genius of scientific psychology" (Kelly et al., 2007, dedication page), and which characterizes *Human Personality* as "a great but neglected classic" of the field (p. xiii). (To counter the neglect, the publishers even include a compact disc of Myers's original two volumes on their inside back cover.) In the estimation of these authors, Myers provided the first "effective" description of the unconscious mind (p. 302), and his work represents "the most systematic, comprehensive, and determined empirical assault on the mind-body problem" that psychology has produced (p. xxix). *Irreducible Mind* reviews Myers's contributions, critically examines subsequent research on topics he considered crucial, and on that basis, assesses the current state of the mind–body problem, presenting a radical, empirically based challenge to the dominant materialistic consensus. It offers a thoroughgoing examination of phenomena that are unexplained by physicalist assumptions—by the notion that all consciousness is produced by the brain—even as represented in such advanced and sophisticated fields as cognitive neuroscience and computational theory. Many of those phenomena had been identified and explored by figures associated with the SPR, and the results were most fully synthe-sized by Myers himself. Among them, the authors note, were telepathy, clairvoyance, psychophysical influences, psychokinesis, multiple and alter-nate personalities, near-death and out-of-body experiences, apparitions, genius, and mysticism. Although phenomena such as these continue to be dismissed in mainstream circles, their reality is supported by a steady accu-mulation of evidence that has expanded greatly in the past century. By ex-amining them empirically, the contributors to *Irreducible Mind* continue in the tradition of Myers—in subject matter, in philosophical orientation, in their broad definition of the scope of psychology, and in their faith that the ultimate question of mind's relation to matter can be approached with scientific methodology.

Following Myers's method, the authors arrange discussion of such phe-nomena along a continuum from the most to the least susceptible to con-ventional interpretations. A discussion of the effects of consciousness on physical processes, for example, begins with a discussion of well-recognized psychosomatic factors, such as the effects of mental stress on immune and cardiovascular systems, and the positive effects of meditation on health; it extends to less widely accepted but empirically verifiable occurrences such as various forms of faith healing and placebo effects, then moves pro-gressively through more inexplicable phenomena, passing through such factors as stigmata, physiological changes in the emergence of multiple personalities, hypnotic analgesia and cures, skin writing, and apparent ef-fects of one person's mind on the body of another; it culminates, finally, in discussions of distant mental influence, such as inducing trances, distance healing, psychokinesis, and birthmarks linked to cases implying reincarna-tion (pp. 117–239). The authors argue explicitly that the understanding of any particular phenomenon is best achieved by placing it in the context of related ones (p. 415); and in subsequent chapters they apply that meth-od in analyses of phenomena related to near-death experiences, genius, and mysticism, all the while building on the content and presentation of Myers's studies.

This critique of materialism—or to adopt the authors' updated term, of *physicalism*—has been extended in a sequel volume, growing out of further discussions of the expanding Esalen group. More technical than its prede-cessor, and involving a wider range of contributors, *Beyond Physicalism: Toward Reconciliation of Science and Spirituality* is envisioned as a "progress report" on fruitful if still incomplete efforts to construct a philosophical framework that accommodates the "rogue phenomena" documented in the first volume (Kelly, Crabtree, & Marshall, 2015, p. xxii). In that effort, writes Edward Kelly, "the psychological theories of Myers and James" remain at the "empirical center," amplified by quantum theory, process metaphysics, and mystically oriented religious philosophies (p. xxi).

The renewed interest in Myers's contributions promises to grow apace. He has now become the subject, for the first time, of a full-length biography. Trevor Hamilton's *Immortal Longings: FWH Myers and the Victorian Search for Life after Death* pays far more heed to Myers's investigation of spiritualistic phenomena than to his psychological theories, but it ably sets Myers's life and studies in their social and intellectual context, tracks the progress of his research and the development of his ideas, and provides a valuable assessment of his research methodologies (Hamilton, 2009). Signaling an interest in the academic world, Jeffrey Kripal, of the Department of Religion at Rice University, includes a probing discussion of Myers in *Authors of the Impossible: The Paranormal and the Sacred* (2010). Kripal, whose comprehensive account of Esalen is cited above, recognizes the import of Myers's efforts to construct a *tertium quid* between faith and science, as he and his cohorts examined data "that could not be fully explained by either the theological categories of the churches or the reductive methods of the sciences" (p. 41). Contemplating ongoing attestations of paranormal events, Kripal affirms the explanatory value of Myers's concept of the subliminal Self.

Conclusion

For Frederic Myers, the question traditionally phrased as the "immortality of the soul" was the pre-eminent concern of human life. His investigations were in pursuit, ultimately, of an empirically based answer to that question; his analysis of human psychology, and his map of the subliminal mind, were framed by it. His psychological theories were intended to make the question seem real, and to make the reality of an afterlife plausible to scientifically oriented minds. Subsequent psychology rejected the question, and consequently ignored the theories that seemed tainted by an illusory purpose. Outside of parapsychological circles, Myers's work received little attention in the century after his death.

Transpersonal psychology and associated ideas, however, have once again made the question admissible, however it might be re-construed; and they have established an intellectual milieu in which Myers's innovative theories of consciousness have gained new appreciation. As William James noted in his memorial tribute to Myers, those theories are separable from the question that impelled them. To the ever-judicious James, Myers's conclusions about the demonstrability of life after death ran ahead of the evidence, and his theory of the subliminal mind was inevitably preliminary. In retrospect, James's judgment seems solid. Although Myers resisted the spiritualists' ready inclination to see the intervention of actual spirits as an explanation for many phenomena, he was willing to accept such intervention in certain cases. As he himself recognized, that notion was "unwelcome to modern thought," which he found less resistant to the concept of telepathy (1903/1954, v. 2, p. 194). Contemporary transpersonal psychology, by and large, is more generally (though not universally) inclined to look for explanations of supernormal knowledge in clairvoyant capacities rather than in spirit intervention. Nevertheless, as James also argued, Myers's idea of the subliminal mind, and associated arguments, were ground-breaking, and he was the first to delineate a map of a comprehensive unconscious mind (James, 1901).

A full eight decades before the modern transpersonal movement, Myers was applying rigorous empirical methods in the investigation of extraordinary subjective experience, including such non-ordinary states of consciousness as trance states and hypnotism. In the process, he asserted the inadequacies of materialism and the reality of a spiritual context of human life; he affirmed the significance of spiritual or transcendent experience; he created an immensely expanded model of consciousness, seeing it as a spectrum that reached, ultimately, beyond the ego; and he saw the subliminal as an avenue to higher human potentials, heralding an evolution in human consciousness. In all of that, Myers prefigured aspects of contemporary transpersonal thought. As his newfound recognition attests, Myers, like James, assuredly deserves a place as a major precursor of the transpersonal movement.

Note

1   An earlier version of this chapter was published as "The Resurrection of Frederic Myers" in *The Journal of Transpersonal Psychology*, v.42, n.2 (2010).

CHAPTER SIX

Soul of Spirit
The Perennial Philosophy of Aldous Huxley

In these times, we easily think of the story of religions as a story of warfare, one group's gods against another's, thrashing one another in ideological and even violent combat. Our globalizing world, the ever more intimate contact of each society with others, seems to show how human, how culture-bound, are our notions of the divine, no matter how absolutely they might be promulgated or how passionately held. For many in the modern world, those of a more secular bent, warring religious ideas nullify one another, revealing how limited, if not fallacious, are any and all efforts to attain religious truth. What we believe, it seems, depends on where we were nurtured.

But what if we could see beyond the particular forms of religious worship, beyond the culture-bound dogmas and rituals and priesthoods, to some common fount of religious life, some fundamental wisdom that gives rise to and sustains the enduring religious impulse, at its best, throughout the world? Would that not give legitimacy to humanity's enduring spiritual quest?

Philosophia Perennis

The aspiration to define such a common wisdom, a "perennial philosophy," has a venerable history. In its Latin form, the phrase *philosophia perennis* has often been attributed to the German mathematician and philosopher Gottfried Leibniz, who used it in a letter in 1714, and whose philosophy of concord bolstered his effort to promote harmony, even unity, among discordant religions of his day. But Leibniz was drawing on the work of a renaissance Italian monk by the name of Agostino Steuco, who published *De Perenni Philosophia* in 1540 and who himself was drawing on still older Western philosophical traditions. Those traditions posited a *prisca theologia*, an ancient theology, a primal wisdom, given by God to the earliest peoples, subsequently distorted, perhaps, but still the underlying truth that animates all religions. While it took varying forms, this "ancient wisdom narrative" emphasized direct experience of the divine and the unity of ultimate truth. Steuco referred to "one principle of all things, of which there has always been one and the same knowledge among all peoples" (cited in Schmitt, 1966, p. 517).

In the two centuries since Leibniz used the phrase, it has been conscripted to support various schools of thought, from Platonism to positivism to Catholic neo-Thomism and more. The effort to find a common ground among religions has also grown more complicated, especially as the Western world has come to know more of Asian and other religions. But the philosophical encounter between East and West, which advanced through the nineteenth century, also enlivened with new perspectives the effort to find common ground.

Among American thinkers, the search for a spirituality beyond particular religions, honoring the deepest insights of all but discoverable within, in the individual soul, threads through the writings of Ralph Waldo Emerson and Walt Whitman. In the early twentieth century, William James helped give birth to the academic study of mysticism, conceived of as a psychological experience of oneness with the divine that is at the core of all religions. "In Hinduism," he wrote, "in Neoplatonism, in Sufism, in Christian mysticism, in Whitmanism, we find the same recurring note, so that there is about mystical utterances an eternal unanimity...which brings it about that mystical classics have, as has been said, neither birthday nor native land" (1902/1929, p. 410).

By mid-century, that spirit had flowered into what is now called the "new perennialism," employing the rhetoric of Steuco and Leibnitz, but infused with perspectives drawn from Hinduism, Buddhism, and Sufism, as well as from Western mystics. Behind that thrust were some major philosophers and scholars of religion, including the Ceylonese-born Ananda Coomaraswamy, the Frenchman René Guénon, and the Swiss-born Frithjof Schuon.

The New Perennialism

Both Coomaraswamy and Schuon were active in the United States, but the statement of this orientation with the greatest reach in the Anglo-American world was *The Perennial Philosophy* by Aldous Huxley, published at the close of World War II, a work that now must be regarded as one of the century's great classics of religious thought. It is that volume, and its origins and influence, that are the subject of this chapter. At its release, the *New York Times* called it perhaps "the most needed book in the world" and "the masterpiece of all anthologies." Huxley, too, referred to it as an anthology, for its copious quotations of mystics and adepts of religions across the world, but it is certainly more than that: it represents the personal synthesis and extensive reflections—socio-political as well as spiritual—of a unique figure of twentieth century letters, attempting to delineate what he called "the core and spiritual heart of all the higher religions" (1944, p. 236).

We begin with a look at the man behind it, who was born in 1894, in the county of Surrey, south of London. Aldous Huxley was surely one of the most multi-talented intellectuals of his generation in the English-speaking world. He was a poet, a novelist, an artist and art critic, a social and political commentator, a satirist, a philosopher, a seeker, a visionary, and an early and passionate advocate of environmental sustainability. He wrote at least 47 books in his lifetime, including 11 novels, the best known of which remains the dystopian tale *Brave New World*, published in 1932. Huxley was born into the British intellectual elite, and he embodied in his very bloodline and lineage what was perhaps central cultural conflict of his age: the tensions between science and spirituality.

The Huxley Lineage: Science and Spirituality

Aldous's paternal grandfather was T.H. Huxley, the great spokesman of British science, secretary of the Royal Society, known to the world as "Darwin's bulldog" for his vigorous defense of the theory of evolution. In the years after the publication of Darwin's *On the Origin of Species* in 1859, T.H. Huxley did more than anyone to establish the rising scientific worldview in the mainstream of Western intellectual culture. In 1863 he published *Evidence of Man's Place in Nature,* which before Darwin did so himself, explained the implications of Darwin's theories for the origin of the human species. He promoted what he called "the way of the laboratory" with unbounded optimism, envisioning a future of ever-greater social and intellectual progress. In the process, he approvingly coined the term "agnosticism" to describe the stance that ultimate realities, spiritual realities, are unknowable.

The most bitter responses to Huxley, of course, were from traditional Christians and theists, such as Bishop Samuel Wilberforce. "Is it on your grandmother's or your grandfather's side"—such was the bishop's riposte to his adversary—"that you claim descent from the apes?" But bishops were not alone in their reservations about the rising scientific optimism that T.H. Huxley so forcefully voiced. Aldous Huxley's mother was an Arnold; her uncle was none other than Matthew Arnold, the great Victorian poet, cultural critic and spokesman for the social value of high culture.

Matthew Arnold was no friend of religious dogmatists; he was, in fact, a personal friend of T.H. Huxley, and they collaborated on issues of educational policy. But Arnold remained dubious that the effects of science and technology were purely beneficent. He pointed to the maladies of industrialization and rapid social change, and worried about the moral effects of rising materialism, the view of nature as mechanical and devoid of ultimate meaning. In his famous poem "Dover Beach," he wrote that the ebbing of faith had left us a world with

> ...neither joy, nor love, nor light
>
> Nor certitude, nor peace, nor help from pain,
>
> And we are here as on a darkling plain
>
> Swept with confused alarms of struggle and flight
>
> Where ignorant armies clash by night.

Aldous Huxley grew up steeped in a scientific culture; his older brother Julian became a world-renowned evolutionary biologist. He was a rationalist by temperament, always scientifically knowledgeable; but along with so many of his generation, particularly after the industrialized slaughter of World War I, he lost the buoyant scientific optimism of his Huxley grandfather. "We are living now," he wrote in the 1930s, "not in the delicious intoxication induced by the early successes of science, but in a rather grisly morning-after..." (cited in Sawyer, 2002, p. 105).

Huxley's Early Years

Like a true member of the British elite, Aldous was schooled at Eton and Balliol College, Oxford. In his youth, he endured major childhood crises, including the death of his mother, the suicide of a brother, and the onset of a severe problem with his eyesight, which blinded him for 18 months, kept him out of the war, and affected the rest of his life. With his highly cosmopolitan background, he traveled extensively, living for a time in both Italy and France. As he matured, his interests migrated from science to poetry; by his mid-20s, he had published four volumes of poems and had formed close friendships with figures of literary modernism such as T.S. Eliot and D.H. Lawrence. He married, naming his first son Matthew, after his great-uncle. In the 1920s and '30s, he took up painting and wrote several novels and collections of short stories, along with social commentaries, literary criticism and travel essays.

The tenor of his earlier fiction was often cynical and sardonic, challenging traditional values and social hypocrisy, and portraying a meaningless universe; to many young intellectuals of the time, he was a new "intellectual emancipator." But as the 1930s wore on, he began to search for more meaning, looking for it first, as did Matthew Arnold, in art and culture, and lamenting effects of mass media and industrialization. In *Brave New World*, the search for pleasure, security, and technological improvements creates a robotic society of total conformity.

Turning East

A major turn in his life came with his friendship with the British philosopher Gerald Heard. Heard was a student of mysticism: he accepted that sustaining the phenomenal world was a greater spiritual reality. His route to that acceptance was through the Advaita branch of Vedanta philosophy, based on ancient Hindu texts, the Upanishads. Heard awakened Huxley's latent interests in spiritual experience as a route to meaning, and he inspired Huxley to take up yoga, meditation, and related practices. At just this time, in 1937, Huxley and his family, and Heard, moved to the United States, to southern California.

As an ardent pacifist, Huxley now believed that the way to world peace was through individuals' finding peace within themselves. And Hollywood, he found, could pay the bills, as he turned to writing scripts for movies, and as he and Heard intensified their studies at the Vedanta Society of Southern California. Huxley retained a skeptical posture, and he was wary of gurus and religious devotionalism in any form. But the philosophy he had begun to absorb determined his mature intellectual outlook, especially as he came to know Jiddu Krishnamurti.

Krishnamurti was an Indian holy man, then based in Ojai, California, who shared Huxley's aversion to gurus and established religions. They met within a year of Huxley's arrival and maintained a strong friendship for the rest of Huxley's life. A few years later, Huxley was asked about his own interest in mysticism. "I have lived mainly in the world of intellectual life and art," he replied. "But the world of knowing-about-things is unsatisfactory ... one wants to go further" (cited in Sawyer, 2002, p. 123).

His effort to reveal what it meant to go further was *The Perennial Philosophy*, based on vast compilations of spiritual texts and testimonies that he collected just prior to and during World War II. Although it was heavily influenced by Vedanta, it attempted to define a mystical tradition that stretched across cultures and epochs. That search took Huxley from the stance of a modernist cynic, interested mostly in challenging any belief in value and meaning, to a more hopeful, and compassionate, worldview.

The Perennial Philosophy

At this point in his life, Huxley did not claim to have had a mystical experience. He remained a rationalist, and his book is a rational exploration and organization of the spiritual experiences of others. This is how he defined the perennial philosophy: it is "the metaphysic that recognizes a divine Reality substantial to the world of things and lives and minds; the psychology that finds in the soul something similar to, or even identical with, divine Reality; [and] the ethic that places man's final end in the knowledge of the immanent and transcendent Ground of all being" (p. vii).

A spiritual essence, in other words, infuses and sustains the material world; each of us embodies that spiritual essence, or at least is akin to it, and our highest purpose is to realize that, to know—or better, to experience—the divine both within us and beyond us. That understanding, Huxley tells us, is universal: elements of it are in the "traditional lore" of primal peoples, and it has a place in all of what he calls the "higher religions," at least in their mystical branches. It is what he calls the "Highest Common Factor" of spiritual life.

The book is built, too, on a corollary to this factor: our capacity to grasp it, to achieve this knowing, depends not primarily on intellect, but on who we are as moral beings. The divine is ineffable, beyond the capacity of words to portray, beyond the capabilities of discursive thought to grasp. But it can be experienced, it can be realized on a level deeper than discursive thought; in fact, it *must* be, if it is to be a genuine religious experience. Huxley quotes

Shankara, the Indian sage who systematized the Upanishads: "The nature of the one Reality must be known by one's own clear spiritual perception; it cannot be known through a pandit (learned man)" (p. 5). The capacity for that experience is cultivated through spiritual practice, and especially through love. In the Christian formulation, "Blessed are the pure in heart, for they shall see God."

This is an extraordinarily rich work, and in citing passages of spiritual lore from around the world, Huxley sought not the most familiar, but ones that would be fresh for his readership. He disseminated writings of figures who, in part because of his attention to them, have now grown more familiar to us, such as Meister Eckhart, the medieval German theologian, and Jalal-uddin Rumi, the thirteenth-century Persian poet, as well as the surprisingly powerful writings of figures who remain relatively obscure, such as William Law, the eighteenth-century English theologian. In these remarks, I can touch only lightly on the content of the book; but to provide a sense of its method and its flavor, we'll peer into the crucial first chapter, which Huxley titles "That Art Thou." That chapter reveals Huxley's essentially neo-Vedantic outlook, his vision that it resonates with core spiritual traditions throughout the world, and his extraordinary range of reading to support that assertion.

Tat Tvam Asi

The chapter title is a translation of the Sanskrit phrase "Tat Tvam Asi," from the *Chandogya Upanishad*, composed in India at an undetermined time prior to the sixth century BCE. That document relates the story of the young scholar Svetaketu, fresh from his studies and full of learning and self-importance, confronting his father, Uddalaka, who tells him that he still has no awareness of what is most important. Svetaketu still does not comprehend what Uddalaka calls "that knowledge by which we hear the unhearable, ...perceive what cannot be perceived and know what cannot be known." The father instructs Svataketu to bring him the fruit of a large nyagroda tree, to break it open and find the seeds, and then to break open the seeds and see what he finds—which is nothing at all. "My son," says Uddalaka, "that subtle essence which you do not perceive there—in that very essence stands the being of the huge nyagrodha tree.... In that which is the subtle essence, all that exists has its self. That is the True, that is the Self, and thou, Svetaketu, art That" (pp. 3–4).

The divine, in other words, exists, animates and is one with all that is, *and* it is the deepest part of who we are—who each of us is. As Huxley employs the Hindu terminology, "the Atman, the immanent eternal Self in each of us, is one with Brahman, the Absolute Principle of all existence; and the last end of every human being is to discover the fact for himself, to find out Who he really is" (p. 2).

In saying that our innermost nature is essentially divine, Huxley takes a neo-Vedantic stance, but in embracing what he called "the psychology that finds in the soul something similar to" divine Reality as well as "identical with" it, he casts a broad net and can mobilize mystical sensibilities and commentary from many traditions. God, says the Anglican priest William Law, "is present to thee in the deepest and most central part of thy soul" (p. 2). For Huxley, the perennial philosophy teaches that we must "know the spiritual Ground of things not only within the soul, but also outside in the world, and beyond world and soul, in its transcendent otherness" (p. 2). The quest for that direct perception, however, often begins within; in any case, the ultimate realization is of a divine unity in each of us and in all reality, a "oneness that is the ground and principle of all multiplicity" (p. 5).

In the 20 dense pages of that initial chapter, in support of the universality of that direct perception of the divine oneness behind the manifest world—whether they speak of it directly or hover around it—Huxley cites or quotes, besides the *Upanishads*, the Greek or Hellenistic philosophers Plato, Aristotle, and Plotinus; the early Jewish scholars Hillel the Elder and Philo of Alexandria; the Taoist *Book of Chuang Tzu;* the *Lankavatara Sutra,* a foundation of Zen Buddhism; the Chinese Zen Masters Yung-chia Ta-Shih and Sen T'sen; the Indian sage Shankara, who systematized the teachings of the *Upanishads*; the Persian Sufi saint Bayazid of Bistun; Rumi; the Indian poet-saint Kabir; St. Paul; Meister Eckhart; St. Bernard of Clairvaux; St. Catherine of Genoa; the anonymously written fourteenth-century *Theologica Germanica;* the Flemish mystic John of Ruysbroeck; the Anabaptist leader Hans Denck; the Quakers George Fox and William Penn; and the much-cited William Law. He also makes references to beliefs of the Maori of New Zealand and the Oglala Sioux, and to deeply embedded elements in the structure of Indo-European languages.

The Perennial Philosophy takes up not only the essential character of mystical or spiritual experience, and paths to achieve it, but what those who have achieved it have to say about the nature of the divine and its relationship to the worldly and the human, and about our human condition in the world and how we might best negotiate it. It treats, that is, of psychology, metaphysics and ethics. In the process, Huxley confronts enduring dilemmas of spiritual life, such as free will, good and evil, time and eternity, the value of prayer and ritual, the place of suffering, and what is meant by salvation and by immortality. By the end, he has constructed a quite coherent distillation of what could plausibly be the philosophical fruits of a universal spiritual quest. How successfully he has done that has been a point of discussion and contention for nearly seven decades. But to have launched such a conversation is in itself certainly a remarkable achievement.

The spiritual quest did not deter Huxley from his social criticism. In the years after the War, he renewed his critique of industrialized, technological society; and long before it became a popular cause, he took up the case for environmentally sustainable energy, arguing that the natural world must be treated as "a complex and beautifully coordinated living organism" (cited in Sawyer, 2002, p. 134). He worked still more closely with Krishnamurti—together they established a primary school—and he continued to write novels, art criticism, social commentary, history, and screenplays. He also explored the paranormal, occasionally visiting psychics and investigating hypnosis and phenomena such as extra sensory perception and telekinesis. And along with meditation and yoga, he also tried various experiential therapies. According to his friends, this phase of his life seems to have brought Huxley a personal peace: they saw him as exuding a serenity and loving-kindness; his wife Maria said that she found him "transformed, transfigured" (cited in Sawyer, 2002, p. 151).

The Doors of Perception

It was at just this time, the early 1950s, that Huxley's spiritual search turned more experiential, with his discovery of psychedelic drugs. He read of the studies of Humphry Osmond, a British psychologist living in Saskatchewan, who was studying mescaline, which is a synthetic form of the active substance in peyote, the cactus used by indigenous peoples in Mexico. It was Osmond, in fact, who later, in a letter to Huxley, coined the term "psychedelic." The two met in Los Angeles in 1952 and formed a friendship that continued for the rest of Huxley's life. Some months after that meeting, Huxley took mescaline, supplied by Osmond.

The experience prompted Huxley's other main work on mystical experience, a small volume published in 1954 called *The Doors of Perception*. The title is from verses of William Blake: "If the doors of perception were cleansed every thing would appear to man as it is, Infinite." Huxley interpreted his psychedelic journey in the framework of the perennial philosophy. It gave him, he felt, a direct experience of that divine oneness that is the Ground of all that is; it pushed him beyond mere intellectual concepts, to a powerful intuitive awareness of the central perennial insight. "The Beatific Vision, *Sat Chit Ananda*, Being-Awareness-Bliss—for the first time," he said, "I understood, not on the verbal level, not by inchoate hints or at a distance, but precisely and completely what those prodigious syllables referred to" (p. 18).

He knew that the experience was not enlightenment: it was too fleeting and partial, not sufficiently a result of moral transformation. But he thought that it prompted an invaluable spiritual insight, particularly in a moment in which three flowers in a small glass vase glowed with what he called "pure Being" or "the divine source of all existence" (p. 18), and even the furniture "shone with the Inner Light, and was infinite in its significance" (p. 22). For that moment, he believed, the doors of perception were cleansed.

It was in this work that Huxley advanced the theory of the relationship between mind and brain with which he remains identified, a theory that has its forebears in William James, the French philosopher Henri Bergson and others. We refer to it now as the "transmission" or "filter" theory. By its terms, the brain does not produce consciousness, or at least the farther reaches of it. Consciousness pervades the universe; it is all around us. Our individual awareness is part of the whole; potentially, we have access to all awareness. We are, as Huxley puts it, "potentially Mind at Large" (p. 23). The brain and nervous system function to protect us from being overwhelmed by that awareness, to transmit and filter it, and to focus us on the practical necessities of incarnate life. They serve as what he called a "reducing valve" that reinforces the needs of biological survival. We assume that what filters through that valve is the whole of reality, but actually it is only a trickle. Visionary experiences can bypass the filter, whether they occur spontaneously, or as a result of spiritual practice, or by means of hypnosis or certain substances.

All of this pointed to greater possibilities for the human spirit than the reigning social or scientific theories often assumed. Lectures that Huxley gave in 1960, in San Francisco, on what he called "human potentialities" helped to inspire Richard Price and Michael Murphy, creators of the Esalen Institute—and with that, helped spark the human potential movement that flowered in the following decades.

6.1 Aldous Huxley. (Aldous and Laura Huxley papers [Collection 2009], Copy/Item issue/Negative #: YRLSC_2009_00193. UCLA Library Special Collections, Charles E. Young Research Library, UCLA.)

Island

For Huxley, contemplation flows into ethics: spiritual awakening, he argued more frequently, was fundamental to social betterment. His final major testament was the novel *Island*, published in 1962, the year before his death. It was a utopian rebuttal to his own dystopian *Brave New World*, suggesting a possible mystical means to avoid the robotic, authoritarian society that he had depicted 30 year earlier. Society on the fictional island of Pala is a synthesis of East and West, founded by an Indian Buddhist and a Scottish physician.

In Pala's established social world, *tat tvam asi* is the heart of philosophy, science wisely serves ecological needs, and religious dogmas are rejected. Tantric and contemplative practices keep the populace deeply attentive to the present moment, and a sacred mushroom, used sparingly and reverently, helps them stay aware of the divine cosmic order, "the dance of endless becoming and passing away," the "pure Being" of the One beyond the manifestations of the many, the ultimate identity of any mind with "Mind at

119

Large." The islanders achieve harmony with nature and among themselves, as well as personal, spiritual liberation.

Ultimately, their experiment fails, crushed by outside, militarized forces greedy for the island's oil, allied with rebellious religious dogmatists within. But Huxley saw the possibilities that it envisioned as valid and feasible; as Jeffrey Kripal observes, this book was his final legacy, expressing his mature hopes for the good society (2008). In sending a copy to a friend, he wrote this in an accompanying letter: "Essentially this is what must be developed—the art of giving out in love and intelligence what is taken in from vision and the experience of self-transcendence and solidarity with the Universe" (cited in Sawyer, 2002, 182).

In the literary world, the critical reception of *Island* was less than enthusiastic, and as novelist, Huxley continues to be remembered more for the more cynical *Brave New World*, which *Island*, in part, rebuts. In truth, much of the mainstream intellectual world reacted negatively to Huxley's entire mystical turn, seeing him as a once-brilliant novelist "bogged up neck-deep," as one reviewer put it, "in his mystical dreams and fantasies" (cited in Sawyer, 2002, p. 159).

But in other circles, his *Perennial Philosophy* has had a profound impact, launching the new perennialism, which was taken up in studies of religion and mysticism, and embraced by transpersonal psychology and associated cultural movements.

Perennialists after Huxley, and Their Critics

The new perennialism, of course, has also had its critics. Here we can only glance at this often complex discussion and at a few of its prominent participants—but enough, perhaps, to gain a sense of the contours of debate.

At the heart of the new perennialism, to repeat, was the notion of a core mystical experience common across religious traditions. In the early 1960s, the scholar of mysticism W.T. Stace affirmed that core experience, defining it as a sense of the ultimate unity of all existence in a divine presence and delineating what he saw as its essential characteristics. "In this general sense of a unity which the mystic believes to be in some sense ultimate and basic to the world," he wrote, "we have the very inner essence of all mystical experience" (1960, p. 132). In the mid-1970s, the scholar of religion Huston

Smith carried the definition of a common core further, particularly in his book *Forgotten Truth*, which bears the subtitle *The Common Vision of the World's Religions*. That "common vision" was very much like Huxley's definition of perennial philosophy: unlike modern materialism, it held that the visible world is rooted in another ontological dimension of reality, which we refer to as spiritual, and that what we look for in the beyond we also seek in the depths of our souls. The center of the self, writes Smith, "is in some way identical with that of creation at large," with what he calls "Being Unlimited." The highest human attainment—and our deepest, natural longing—is the sense of oneness with the divine, attained through love or through a mystical realization of that underlying unity, of "at-one-ment" (1976/1992, p. 111).

Smith also takes up Huxley's transmission or filter theory of the brain— "the brain," he says, "breathes mind like the lung breathes air" (p. 63)—and argues that science itself now points to the existence of realms beyond our ability to discern through the senses, realms that transcend our normal categories of space and time. Modern science and spirituality, he believes, point in parallel directions.

This orientation has been a major element in transpersonal psychology, especially in its formative years, and also in the broader transpersonal movement that draws from it. Abraham Maslow, whose work was critical in the formation of the field, affirmed the perennialist stance: "[T]o the extent that all mystical or peak-experiences are the same in their essence and have always been the same," he wrote, "all religions are the same in their essence and have always been the same...." Maslow called this "something common" the "core-religious experience." (1964, p. 20). Stanislav Grof maintains that his research shows empirically "that, in its farthest reaches, the psyche of each of us is essentially commensurate with all of existence and ultimately identical with the cosmic creative principle itself"—a conclusion which he finds "in far-reaching agreement with the image of reality found in the great spiritual and mystical traditions of the world, which... Aldous Huxley referred to as the 'perennial philosophy'" (1998, p. 5). And Ken Wilber took up this stance, defining the "perennial philosophy" as this "unity consciousness" and "the doctrines that purport to explain it," and affirming that "[t]here is much evidence that this type of experience or knowledge is central to every major religion—Hinduism, Buddhism, Taoism, Christianity, Islam and Judaism—so that we can justifiably speak of the 'transcendent unity of religions' and the unanimity of primordial truth" (1985, p. 3). More superficial manifestations and interpretations, of course, will vary—Wilber emphasizes that more later on—but the deeper psychological structures and stages of spiritual insight, which he attempts to delineate, he sees as the same across cultures.

However, as we indicated in our discussion of R.M. Bucke, trends in intellectual life in the last three decades—and particularly in the academic world—have not been so friendly to the perennialist stance. What is sometimes referred to as the "post-modern turn" emphasizes the differences among cultures, not the sameness, and is often suspicious of any search for universal truths, seeing it as only the imposition, often oppressive, of one culture's system of values over another's. The related trends of contextualism and constructivism reign supreme in the academic world: they argue that specific cultural, political and linguistic contexts are what determine human experience, that our experience is "constructed" out of those elements, which are local in nature, leaving little space for universal values or understanding. There can thus be no single "unity consciousness" or essential mystical experience, much less a universally shared array of doctrines that explain them; there can be no "transcendent unity of religions."

Some scholars of religion had long been cautious about the perennialist aspiration, feeling that it was prone to erase essential differences, even in mystical experience itself. In the late 1970s, Steven Katz made the constructivist case: "There are NO pure (i.e. unmediated) experiences..." he declared. [T]he experience itself as well as the form in which it is reported is shaped by concepts which the mystic brings to, and which shape, his experience." (Cited in Kelly et al., 2007, p. 511). Even within the transpersonal movement, we find the influence of a constructivist approach; more recently Jorge Ferrer has questioned the viability of perennialism and its "privileging," as he calls it, of a single unitive vision, of a oneness with the divine. Spiritual history, he argues, reveals a variety of metaphysical worlds, and the "claim that mystics of all ages and places converge about metaphysical matters is a dogma that cannot be sustained by the evidence" (2002, pp. 93–94).

Concluding Remarks

How might we negotiate this dispute between perennialists and their critics? Some recent scholars of religion have looked for a middle ground, acknowledging the range of cultural differences, but still conserving some element of sameness (see, for example, Forman, 1990; Kripal, 2016). A clue to a reconciling stance in this debate, I believe, is to be found in Aldous Huxley's own outlook towards his work. In a letter written near the end of his life, he summed up his essential posture, invoking the term invented by his grandfather: "I remain," he said, "an agnostic who aspires to be a Gnostic—but a gnostic only on the mystical level, without symbols, cosmologies or a pantheon" (cited in Sawyer, 2002, p. 188). In his aspiration to be "a Gnostic," Huxley affirms what constructivism often denies, that is, that there is a form of direct experience of spiritual truth, beyond reason and the normal functions of intellect, a form that transcends the symbols created through language and culture.

In its more extreme forms, I would say, constructivism rests on materialistic assumptions about the relationship of mind to brain. It does not allow for the transmission or filter theory; it does not see consciousness as a fundamental principle of the universe, in which our individual consciousness is embedded as part of the whole. But half a century of transpersonal psychology, and a full century of related studies of the paranormal, indicate that filter theory must be taken seriously, and that distinct non-ordinary states of consciousness may reach beyond the cultural forms that constructivism assumes give shape to all we know.

In the light of such investigation, we can view that "mystical level" that Huxley refers to as a distinct state of consciousness, operating by different rules than our normal states of awareness. What that "noetic"—or knowing—mystical level takes in, as William James stated over a century ago, is "ineffable"; it cannot be captured in the words and symbols in which we conceive our experiences, and which, as constructivists correctly point out, are indeed created out of a cultural matrix. Acknowledging the limitations of any such system of words and symbols, Huxley remains "agnostic"— that is, in a state of suspended judgment—with respect to pantheons and cosmologies, to all the religious symbols and language with which we justify our religious rituals and fight our religious battles. "Give us this day our daily Faith," writes the Old Raja in *Island*, the founder of Pala's utopian society, "but deliver us, dear God, from Belief" (p. 65). In this sense, Faith is confidence in our capacity to have that Gnostic, direct experience, and in the presence of that ineffable spiritual reality that it reveals. Belief, on the other hand, says the Raja, "is the systematic taking of unanalyzed words much too seriously."

In truth, the central insight of constructivism—that our perceptions are shaped by our limited selves at least as much as by any external reality—is hardly a radically innovative notion; it a longstanding recognition in intellectual life, certainly shared by creative spirits such as James and Huxley. In a foreword to a book by Krishnamurti, Huxley made the case against taking words too seriously. Words and symbols are necessary for us—necessary to art, science, law, philosophy, and civilization itself—but their value is as tools or instruments, not as rigid beliefs. They are, he said "a provisional convenience." They stand only inadequately for things and events (p. 2); we should never identify "purely verbal constructions with facts" or imagine "that symbols are more real than what they stand for." There is certainly a place for religious symbols and rituals: they can form legitimate paths to the realization of the divine—as long as they are recognized as human constructs, rather than as divinely ordained absolutes. But any philosophical or religious or political system, Huxley thought, should put us on guard: it is "a standing invitation to take symbols too seriously" (Krishnamurti, 1954, pp. 9–11).

The same, of course, would apply to his own ideas, and to his synthesis of the perennial philosophy. Huxley recognized, as fully as anyone, that the system of philosophy he presents us with must be held lightly and tentatively, that it could never be complete or absolutely true. But that by no means negates the value of the endeavor. Even as strong a critic as Jorge Ferrer acknowledges that "the ecumenical search for common ground" is "an important and worthy enterprise" and that some perennialist claims might well be valid (2002, p. 111). Holding its conclusions lightly, recognizing that they will always need revision, the effort to define commonality in human religious experience engages us, I would say, in a process that is vital, indeed essential, for these conflicted times, and also focuses us on central and undeniably perennial questions about the human condition.

No one in our epoch has contributed to that effort more fruitfully than this man, who carried the lineage of both T.H. Huxley and Matthew Arnold, of both scientific progress and the questioning of it; few have asked those sweeping questions with such self-awareness, and surely none with greater erudition, than Aldous Huxley.

PART II

Transpersonal Psychology and Beyond

CHAPTER SEVEN

The Birth of "Transpersonal"

The basic idea of transpersonal psychology may be infinitely profound, but it can be stated simply: Our individual ego, our sense of a personal self, and the psyche that sustains it, is imbedded in an interconnected cosmos; our personal psyche reaches into, and is penetrated by, a collective consciousness, a natural ambience, a spiritual foundation and context. Our individual consciousness stretches, then, beyond the personal; it has dimensions that are *trans*-personal. A fuller understanding of the human psyche must take account of those connections, of the psyche's reach into the wider realms of consciousness, as exemplified in extraordinary human experiences that stretch the bounds of our awareness. We are dealing here, then, with a scientific and empirical study of mind oriented towards spirit—a spiritual psychology. My intention in this chapter is to look at the rise of this field in our contemporary world—under the name of "transpersonal psychology"—examining trends that fed its formation, as well as some of its implications for our broader worldview.

To be sure, an openness to spiritual realms was not the thrust of mainstream psychology in the twentieth century. It certainly was not the focus of the field at midcentury, when a transpersonal orientation began to emerge as a challenge to the dominant schools of behaviorism and Freudian psychoanalysis. Behaviorism ignored consciousness altogether: it attempted to explain human action with reference to laboratory studies of rats and other lower animals, and its assumptions were entirely materialistic, as biologically based as psychology could be. Behaviorists felt that psychology should be a natural science, focused on what could be observed and measured: actions in response to external stimuli. Traditional Freudian psychoanalysis, for all its vital and profound revelations about the unconscious, was nevertheless founded on the study of psychopathology, of illness and malady. Its picture of human nature was rather dark: motivation was driven by the unconscious, seen as a realm of biological instinct, of sexuality, aggression, and repressed trauma. Psychoanalysis aimed, as Freud famously said, to transform "hysteric misery into common unhappiness" (1895, p. 305).

Tony Sutich and his Circle

We take up our story in 1967, in Palo Alto, California, the home of a remarkable man by the name of Anthony Sutich. At age twelve, Tony Sutich was hit by a baseball bat and subsequently developed progressive rheumatoid arthritis. As a result, he spent the last 50 years of his life incapacitated, confined to a gurney, virtually unable to move. After the ninth grade, he was entirely self-educated (Vich, 1976). But Sutich was an avid reader, and an exceptionally sensitive human being. The education that he forged for himself reflected the three trends that, around 1967, I would argue, came together to form contemporary transpersonal psychology, and to challenge the dominance of behaviorism and psychoanalysis. Those trends were humanistic psychology, psychedelic research, and Asian religions.

Tony Sutich also had a natural talent for counseling: it was displayed, in the beginning, with informal counseling of his own nurses. He eventually developed a private practice, cultivating what he described as a "growth-centered" approach to his work. Rather than attempting to alter external behaviors, or cure diagnosed maladies, he saw himself as helping clients find their own way to a more creative and fulfilling life.

That gave him an affinity for the emerging work of Abraham Maslow, the guiding force of what would be called "humanistic psychology." In the1940s Maslow, then on the psychology faculty of Brooklyn College, began investigating what he saw as exceptionally well-adjusted personalities. His contribution, essentially, focused on the opposite end of the scale of human wellbeing from the studies of clinical patients that had dominated depth psychology. By 1943, he had formulated the basics of his theory of human motivation. Central to that theory was his hierarchy of needs and the concept of self-actualization. As more basic needs are satisfied, he argued, people focus on higher needs, more uniquely human, more in the service of society. They move from a focus on basic needs—physiological requirements, safety—to psychological needs of love and esteem. At the top of this hierarchy, at least in its earlier versions, was what Maslow called "self-actualization": becoming actually what we are potentially, realizing our full capacities. "A musician must make music," said Maslow, "an artist must paint, a poet must write, if he is to be ultimately at peace with himself. What a man can be, he must be" (Maslow, 1943).

Maslow and Sutich met in 1949, when Maslow was on a visit to California. It was a case, Sutich later said, of "immediate rapport" (1976b, p. 28), initiating a close professional collaboration and personal friendship that endured for 21 years, until Maslow's death. Over the next decade, the 1950s, Maslow elaborated his theory of motivation and argued that psychology needed to take into account, and recognize as real, the virtues and greater potentialities of human nature, the higher motives of human behavior: compassion, altruism, justice, love. It needed to balance the study of mental illness with the study of mental health, of what it means to live a full and happy life.

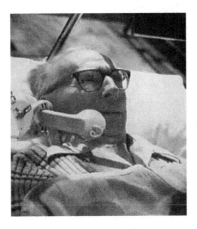

7.1 Anthony Sutich

By the late 1950s, Maslow and allied thinkers, Sutich included, began to form a movement, formally launching the American Association for Humanistic Psychology in 1961. Humanistic psychologists and psychotherapists focused on the notion of personal growth; they referred to their psychology, with its more positive view of human nature and possibility, as the "Third Force in psychology," beyond the two forces of behaviorism and psychoanalysis. Their work spawned a spectrum of new psychotherapies, focused more on the expression of emotions felt in the present than on verbal explorations of the past, and exploring the integration of body and mind. This psychotherapeutic revolution included, for example, Gestalt therapy, bioenergetics, encounter groups, and other approaches; it inspired the human potential movement, with its epicenter at the Esalen Institute, founded in 1962 by Michael Murphy and Richard Price in Big Sur California. By 1967, in collaboration with Maslow, Tony Sutich had helped to spearhead the association and journal that gave professional structure to the field of humanistic psychology.

But also by that time, they had both become somewhat restless with its fundamental tenets. Research and the results of the new therapies, they felt, indicated that the hierarchy of needs did not stop with self-actualization. As Maslow studied people he viewed as self-actualized, he observed that many had had some variety of mystical experience, a rapture accompanied by a sense of awe and meaning. He called these moments "peak experiences," and found that they had transformative long-term effects: they revealed the value of humanity's highest ideals, and stood at the center of authentic religious experience. By this time, the late 1960s, the cultural ambience—certainly the youth culture—had become far more open to spiritual experience, permeated by interest in Asian religions, meditation, aboriginal wisdom, psychedelic revelations, and mystical traditions.

Long before, Tony Sutich's avid literary excursions had taken him into mystical writings from various traditions, especially Asian ones. As early as the 1940s, he was absorbing Advaita Vedantic tracts and Hindu scriptures, as well as readings about Buddhism, Theosophy and Christian Science. At the start of the next decade, his mystical interests were further inspired by the arrival in the San Francisco Bay area of Alan Watts, the British-born interpreter of Asian traditions. As early as 1935 and subsequently, Sutich had had several mystical experiences of his own.

Those readings and experiences contributed to his sense of the limitations of humanistic psychology. By 1966, he wrote, "[m]y longstanding interest in the psychological aspects of mystical experience continued to provoke disturbing questions about basic humanistic theory" (1976b, p. 154). Mystical insight implied that self-actualization was too limited a goal: "It did not adequately accommodate the depths of the cultural turn toward the 'inner-personal' world," he said, "and it gave insufficient attention to the place of man in the universe or cosmos" (1976b, p. 153). Although Maslow saw himself as atheistic, he, too, was convinced of the value of peak and transcendent experiences.

By 1967, Maslow and Sutich were engaged in discussions about the need to incorporate a larger sense of self than the one conceived of in humanistic theory, a self embedded in a larger universe. They thought to call this orientation "transhumanistic," a term they had taken from the evolutionary biologist Julian Huxley. Others joined in these talks, many of which took place in Tony Sutich's living room. They included, prominently, Miles Vich, a strong voice in the humanistic movement. And among the participants was a young psychologist, newly arrived from Czechoslovakia, by the name of Stanislav Grof. It was Grof who suggested the term "transpersonal," which he had used in his own psychological research and included in a lecture given in Berkeley in September of 1967 (Grof, Grob, Bravo, & Walsh, 2008; Sutich, 1976b). Maslow took to the term: "it says," he wrote in a note to Sutich, "what we are all trying to say, that is, beyond the development of the individual person into something which is more inclusive...or which is bigger than he is" (cited in Sutich, 1976a, p. 16). The emerging transpersonal psychology, Maslow insisted, must remain empirical, as a science of mind should (Sutich, 1969a, p. iv); it must be based on concrete research, not merely philosophical speculation. Out of these discussions came the sense that this orientation called for a new journal to explore it. Sutich drafted a statement of purpose and then took on the role of editor. *The Journal of Transpersonal Psychology* was first published in the summer of 1969.

7.2 Abraham Maslow

The featured article in that first issue was Maslow's seminal lecture "The Farther Reaches of Human Nature" (1969a), first given in San Francisco in '67. Sutich called that lecture "the first public presentation of the 'fourth force' in the field of psychology" (Sutich, 1969b, p. 14); it set out the aims of the field. This "fourth force", Maslow asserted, would deal empirically "with transcendent experiences and with transcendent values," values which surpass a limited sense of self (1969a, p. 4). It might examine the highest forms of love and friendship, and other aspects of human potential. With this fourth force would come what he called a "resacralizing" and "respiritualizing" of psychology, an examination not only of peak experiences, but of the experiences, for example, of great mystics, with their "unitive consciousness." "Transcendence," Maslow commented in another piece in that same issue, "refers to the very highest and most inclusive levels of human consciousness...." (1969b, p. 66).

A kindred figure whose related work nourished the field in the first years was the Italian psychologist Roberto Assagioli, developer of what he called "psychosynthesis." Assagioli had come out of the Freudian tradition but later developed a view of the psyche that incorporated collective and spiritual realms. He spoke of four levels of the unconscious, crowned by a "higher unconscious" capable of creative inspiration and transcendent insight. In an article that he contributed to the first issue of the *Journal*, Assagioli embraced the term "transpersonal." That piece was intended, in fact, to parse out just what the word meant (1969); it is an analysis of language and symbols used to signify experiences deemed "supernormal" or transpersonal. In "transpersonal awareness," he wrote, "intuitive awareness comes to replace intellectual, logical and rational consciousness, or better, to integrate and transcend it," leading to "identification with what is seen and contemplated, and to the recognition of the intrinsic unity between object and subject" (1969, p. 39). Ultimately, he indicated, it leads to mystical insight.

Sutich's definition of purpose in the inaugural issue of the journal was a long list of phenomena that might be investigated, but his summation, in the second issue, was that transpersonal psychology would take "an empirical approach" in examining "extraordinary subjective experiences." And one of its "dominant tasks," he noted, would be "some sort of mapping or ordering of states of consciousness transcending the usual states of conscious awareness" (1969c, p. iv).

Stanislav Grof

What such a "mapping" might look like was suggested by work that Stan Grof brought to the mix. He and another participant in those meetings in '67, James Fadiman, represented another trend, apart from humanistic psychology, that influenced this fourth force: research on the effects of psychedelic drugs. That was a field that had captured Tony Sutich's attention as early as the late 1950s. With the onset of the 1960s, psychedelic research had intensified: by 1963, Sutich could write Maslow that "It is going to be hard to talk about 'peak experiences' if one has not gone through the LSD process..." (Sutich, 1976b, p. 122).

Grof's interest in that realm went back to 1956, when he participated in a clinical experiment using lysergic acid diethylamide, or LSD-25. The substance had been sent to his clinic in Prague by Sandoz laboratories, the pharmaceutical company in Basel, Switzerland where it was first synthesized. This particular experiment also utilized strobe lights, which the experimenters illuminated just as the effects of the drug were hitting their peak. At that moment, Grof experienced an "incredible explosion of light," catapulting his consciousness, he later said, "out of my body...." Going into that session, Grof's outlook had been conventionally Freudian; he emerged a mystic. "I had the feeling I had absolutely no boundaries, and I became 'All There Was'..." he reported. "It became absolutely clear to me that what I had been taught at the university—about consciousness being a product of matter, of the neurophysiological processes in the brain—was just not true. Consciousness was something much bigger" (Grof et al., 2008, pp. 157–158).

7.3 Stanislav Grof

Stan Grof had had a classic experience of cosmic consciousness. The episode, he wrote, was a "profound personal transformation and spiritual awakening" (cited in Shroeder, 2014, p. 22), and he resolved to focus his career on such states of consciousness, and related ones, for their healing potential and for what they might tell us about reality itself.

Researchers called these extraordinary experiences "altered" or "non-ordinary states of consciousness." Those years of the late 1960s was the heyday of research on psychedelic drugs: it was not only permitted but funded by governments; there were over 40 research programs throughout Europe and North America (Grof, 1985, p. xv). In 1969, Charles Tart published his pioneering text *Altered States of Consciousness*, which gathered essays that defined general characteristics of these states and explored effects of dreaming, meditation, and hypnosis as well as psychedelic drugs (1969). The book brought some of the basic concepts of transpersonal psychology to a wider public.

None of the psychedelic investigators, however, were as venturous as Grof in attempting to delineate a resulting map of consciousness. By cataloguing experiences from hundreds of journeys, Grof eventually outlined three levels of the unconscious: he called them "biographical," "perinatal," and "transpersonal." The biographical was essentially the Freudian unconscious, the territory of animal instincts, repressed traumas and unconscious perceptions that we accumulate in our lifetimes. Freud had compared the psyche to an iceberg: what was conscious was only the visible surface; the much vaster subconscious was hidden below. But for Grof, the biographical unconscious was analogous to the more accessible surface; below that were two still deeper realms of the unconscious.

In the course of his research with LSD, Grof found repeated instances in which people seemed carried to memories of their own birth, and even to experiences in the womb. The associated consciousness was strong enough, and its effects formative enough, to constitute a fundamental aspect of the psyche, for which Grof coined the term "perinatal," meaning "around birth." We shall explore elements of that realm in the following chapter; for the present, it is sufficient to state simply that Grof saw it as falling into four categories, each tied to stages of the biological birth process. Emotionally charged elements of this perinatal experience, which might be quite different for each of us, could be associated with later characteristics of personality. This perinatal realm of the unconscious was composed not only of our individual birth memories; it readily connected with archetypal experiences and images that might be common to humanity as a whole. As we relive intrauterine oneness with the mother, for example, we might have visions, as well, of cosmic unity; with the titanic struggle through the birth canal, might come a sense of identification with, say, Phoenix rising.

Whether or not they had perinatal experiences, many of Grof's subjects had experiences that seemed to leap beyond what they could know, by ordinary means, in their lifetimes. Grof referred to "experiences involving an expansion or extension of consciousness beyond the usual ego boundaries and beyond the limitations of time and/or space" (Grof, 1975, p. 155).

This was the realm that he called "transpersonal." It might include out-of-body travel, past-life experiences, precognition, clairvoyance, telepathy, identification with the consciousness of animals or plants, encounters with archetypal beings, or full-blown mystical awareness. Grof divided these experiences into categories: some stretched consciousness beyond normal restrictions of time, others beyond normal restrictions of space, and still others seemed beyond assumed objective reality altogether. Examples of those that reached beyond constraints of time included identification with an ancestor, or precognition; those that reached beyond constraints of space included out-of-body experience, and identification with the consciousness of an animal; ones that seemed beyond accepted reality included encounters with spirit guides or archetypal beings from world mythologies, near-death experiences, or a mystical identification with universal mind. Another category was psychoid experiences, which seem to transcend the distinction between mind and matter, or to affect both realms: they would include, for example, synchronicity, supernormal physical feats, poltergeist phenomena, and spontaneous healing.

However we might categorize them, all these experiences indicated that our psyches have access to worlds of consciousness beyond the assumed reach of our body-egos. By this outlook, the iceberg did indeed reach far deeper than Freud had imagined, as it extended into the spiritual dimensions of the psyche.

In 1967, Grof gave lectures in San Francisco and Berkeley that intrigued Sutich. The two of them met at the Esalen Institute, and Sutich was instrumental in bringing Grof into Maslow's orbit. There were only a few copies of Grof's still unpublished manuscript: Sutich either sent one to Maslow (Sutich, 1976b, p. 174) or encouraged Grof to do so. In either case, Maslow was impressed: "I really flipped over it," he wrote to Sutich. "I consider it of the profoundest importance. I called him at once, and he's coming to visit" (Sutich, 1976b, p. 174).

Grof tells a tale of that visit, when it came about. By then, Maslow was living in California. When he arrived at the Maslow home, Grof initially found Maslow's wife Bertha to be rather distant, even cold; as the encounter developed, however, it came out that she was reacting to Maslow's intense excitement over Grof's research. Maslow was recovering from a heart attack, and Bertha feared that his enthusiasm might put his recovery in danger (cited in Page, 2007). In any case, a field was aborning that Maslow would call "a still 'higher' Fourth Psychology, transpersonal, transhuman, centered in the cosmos rather than in human needs and interest..." (1968, pp. iii–iv). It would be a psychology that acknowledged and explored what William James had called "the further limits of our being."

Abraham Maslow died in 1970, just as the field of transpersonal psychology was getting established under that name. As Sutich worked to establish the journal, he also labored to initiate a professional association for the field. By 1972, it had taken form as the Association for Transpersonal Psychology, which continues to this day. Assagioli died two years later, and Sutich two years after that, in 1976. But Grof published *Realms of the Human Unconscious,* which was the first in his prodigious and still continuing output of books, in 1975, and the movement elicited other major new voices.

Asian Influences

One of those new voices was especially influential, and also especially illustrative of the potential uses of that third current, beyond humanistic psychology and psychedelic research, that helped to distinguish the new transpersonal psychology: the influence of Asian religions. Tony Sutich may have come to these interests early, but by the 1960s, as we noted, they had flowered into a broad cultural movement. That decade saw an explosion of interest in Hindu and Buddhist theory and practice, in various forms of yoga, meditation and other practices—and in associated views of the mind. Just as Grof was publishing his first volume, Ken Wilber, then a young man of 26, published his first article in the *Journal,* titled "Psychologia perennis: The Spectrum of Consciousness" (1975). The title is a play on the term *philosophia perennis,* or the perennial philosophy. Aldous Huxley and his Advaita-influenced notion of a perennial philosophy had a major impact on Transpersonal psychology. Maslow cited Huxley as an example of a self-actualized person (1954), and reported that it was Huxley who persuaded him to take up the study of mystical traditions (1968, p. xi). Grof continues to reiterate that the worldview emerging from his observations shows, in his words, "far-reaching parallels" with Huxley's perennial philosophy (see 2000, p. 270, Grof & Grof, 2010, p. 101). As Huxley had attempted to unite Eastern and Western mystical philosophy, Wilber attempted to meld Eastern and Western psychology. His means of doing that was to turn, like Frederic Myers, to an image of the psyche as a spectrum of consciousness.

136

Each band of the spectrum, Wilber argued, represents a different sense of individual identity, stretching from a strong sense of individual, separate ego to identification with universal Mind, or the "ultimate reality of the universe." At each level, there are narrower and broader ways to identify what we define as "self," and what as "other." With this perspective, there is a place for all the competing schools of Western psychology and psychotherapy—psychoanalysis, ego psychology, Jungian analysis, and so forth. They need not be seen as contradictory; rather, each addresses different bands of the spectrum.

Along the way, we encounter what Wilber identified as "Transpersonal bands," in which consciousness stretches beyond the bounds of the individual organism. That is a field of focus in the psychologies of Jung, Maslow, and Assagioli. As we see within our own souls the play of the archetypes in the collective unconscious, we move towards a sense of identity with all of creation. Our identity, says Wilber, "begins to touch that within which is beyond" (1975, p. 121).

7.4 Ken Wilber

But we can go further. Beyond those transpersonal bands is an experience of consciousness itself, of what Huxley would have called "Mind at Large." In this further end of the spectrum, all dualisms, all distinction between self and other, are suspended. And for an understanding of *that*, Wilber turned East, to Hindu notions, with additional references to Zen and Tibetan Buddhism, and Taoism. Ultimately, then, Western and Eastern approaches to the mind, as different as they are, form a "grand complementarity." Growth along the spectrum, as Wilber saw it, is developmental, as it was for Maslow: as we resolve issues on one level, we spontaneously move to another, and to a greater personal fulfillment. For Wilber, a transpersonal psychology is one that accepts the full spectrum, including these higher realms of consciousness.

Wilber elaborated these ideas in a book called *The Spectrum of Consciousness*. He had completed the manuscript in 1973, when he was 23, but it was rejected by some two or three dozen publishers before it finally came out in 1977. Since then, Ken Wilber, who dropped out of graduate school in biochemistry at the University of Nebraska, has become one of the most widely read philosophers of our times, and, it is said, the most widely translated philosophical writer in America, with 25 books translated into some 30 foreign languages.

Some of those writings developed further refinements to the higher realms of consciousness, discerning different levels, drawn from Asian traditions, as one progresses towards pure consciousness. By the time of writing what might be considered his magnum opus, *Sex Ecology, Spirituality: The Spirit of Evolution* (1995), Wilber had identified distinct stages of these higher realms of consciousness, beyond and transcending rationality. The experience of these realms can be cultivated, but it requires an intensive interiority, a deep delving within the self, as in a steady and ongoing practice of meditation. "Progressive internalization," a movement "within and beyond"—that is what draws us of out of narcissism and allows us to transcend the ego (1995, pp. 262, 255). This higher, spiritual unfolding begins with the stage of "vision-logic," a deeper awareness of the processes of rationality, one that reflects on rationality itself, and on the self.

In this analysis of higher realms of consciousness, Wilber builds on a philosophy of structuralism, which distinguishes between surface and deeper structures of thought. Surface structures vary from culture to culture, but deeper structures, such as the ones he outlines here, are universal, cross-cultural, perennial. Instead of depicting a single core mystical experience—as, say, Bucke and Maslow had—Wilber names four general stages of transpersonal development, each representing a distinct type of mysticism: he calls them "psychic," "subtle," "causal," and "non-dual." In *Sex, Ecology, Spirituality*, Wilber illustrates each stage with a particular mystic: respectively, Ralph Waldo Emerson, Teresa of Ávila, Meister Eckhart, and Sri Ramana Maharshi.

At the psychic level, one perceives that the core within each of us is divine—that the self is grounded in God. One comprehends that the individual self is witnessed by something within that is also beyond itself, something eternal that suffuses all being. Emerson calls it the "Over-Soul." Through it, we realize our identity with the whole of creation—that is, with Nature—and with the divine. "The currents of the Universal Being circulate through me;" said Emerson, "I am part or parcel of God."

The subtle level intensifies the sense of union with the divine: Wilber refers to it as "Deity mysticism." It emphasizes less one's identity with the whole of creation, or Nature, more with Spirit beyond Nature. Theresa writes of "seven mansions," or stages of growth. The fifth stage discerns the divine in one's own self, but the sixth dwells with that sense of union, stands in the experience of it, and in the process also experiences raptures and visions. The seventh stage is a "Spiritual Marriage," what Teresa calls a "union of the whole soul with God," entailing a loss of a separate sense of self.

"In the subtle level," says Wilber, "the Soul and God unite; in the causal level, the Soul and God are both transcended in the prior identity of Godhead, or pure formless awareness, pure consciousness as such, the pure Self as pure Spirit" (p. 301). In Meister Eckhart's words, "I find in this breakthrough that God and I are one and the same." "[A]ll images of the soul are taken away," Eckhart continues, "and the soul [is] only the single One, then the pure being of the soul finds resting in itself the pure, formless being of the divine." The self is the Godhead. "[O]ne enters a state of pure empty awareness," explains Wilber, "free of all objects whatsoever" (pp. 307–308).

In the nondual stage, those objects, the entire manifest world, arise again, but are now experienced as perfect expression of Spirit. The formless divine and the world of form are seen to be "not-two," or nondual. As Ramana puts it, "there is nothing that is not the Self. All this world is Brahman." Or Meister Eckhart: "God is all and is one. All things become nothing but God" (p. 309).

With time, and as he responds to criticism, Ken Wilber's ideas grow progressively more complex. In his more recent writings, he speaks less of single, hierarchical stages of conscious development, and more in terms of an array of psychological capacities, each of which might follow its own progressive course of development, at its own rate, more or less independently of others. The single trajectory of a spectrum becomes a far more complex and nuanced "lattice" of developmental lines. Wilber himself speaks of at least four stages of his work. But his perspective, like Bucke's, has remained developmental and evolutionary: individual personal growth is seen within a context of the evolution of human consciousness; personal development reflects evolutionary development. Other writings take his basic insights, and his developmental and evolutionary perspective, into other fields of thought, creating syntheses of tremendous scope, with implications in anthropology, sociology, evolutionary biology, systems theory, even physics, ultimately creating a grand philosophical system.

The Transpersonal Perspective and Cultural Change

Ken Wilber's chasing of the implications of his transpersonal perspective into disciplines beyond psychology, point, finally, to the role of transpersonal psychology in a broader intellectual and cultural shift: the questioning of the materialistic assumptions, and the reinvigoration of a non-doctrinal spiritual perspective, in mainstream intellectual life.

Within the field, there is plenty of variation and fodder for dispute and discussion. Transpersonal psychologists may disagree, for example, on the centrality of the birth experience, or the cross-cultural identity of mystical experience; some object vigorously to the implied hierarchies of Wilber's developmental spectrum, and Wilber himself has dissociated from the term "Transpersonal" in favor of what he prefers to call "Integral" psychology. Jorge Ferrer, with a constructivist-influenced approach that he labels "participatory," offers a broad critique of the field's traditional perennialism and, more generally, its implied assumption of a "pregiven" spiritual reality that is comprehended at various levels of profundity. The alternative, he argues, is to reframe human spirituality as co-creation between multi-faceted human intelligence and "an undetermined mystery or generative power" at the root of life, cosmos and reality. Its measure of value then becomes not the degree of ultimate truth that it encompasses, but the "emancipatory and transformative power" that it creatively "enacts" in the world. (Ferrer, 2017, pp. 9–10).

Discordant though they may sometimes be, the voices of the transpersonal movement converge in a fundamental perspective: that as a full account of reality, the dominant materialist paradigm is limited and ultimately inadequate; and that a more complete account must embrace visions that we customarily call spiritual. Those voices harmonize in the belief that consciousness and intelligence are not simply a product of chemical and physical processes, but rather are fundamental principles that permeate and underlie the physical reality that we know.

With its effort to verify its perspective through empirical procedures, rooted in data and observations, transpersonal psychology challenges mainstream materialism on grounds that materialism must, at least, take stock of; it thus is in a position to spearhead a broader cultural change, a widespread paradigm shift in our view of reality. With its expanded notions of the possibilities and reach—its vastly expanded maps—of human consciousness, transpersonal psychology becomes an epistemology, an empirically based outlook on how we know, for a still unformed but vitally significant paradigm shift in basic assumptions that can deeply reform the whole of our intellectual life. By enhancing our understanding of what James called "the further limits of our being," its "plunge into an altogether other dimension of existence" and its interconnectedness with all of consciousness, transpersonal psychology, if I can borrow words that Abraham Maslow spoke in 1967, might help "resacralize" and "respiritualize" the emerging culture of our times.

CHAPTER EIGHT

Diving Inward:
Holotropic Breathwork and the Bonny Method[1]

Intensified spiritual awareness, as Ken Wilber reminds us, results from internalization, the movement "within and beyond" that draws us beyond the ego. In the world of transpersonal psychology, "internalization" is equivalent to a deeper dive into the subconscious mind, that same element of the psyche that came so forcefully to the attention of psychologists in the 1880s. Depth psychology had established techniques for exploring the subconscious, while the humanistic psychology of Maslow and others, with its attendant psychotherapeutic practices, developed additional approaches, often more focused on present experience and bodily sensations than the psychoanalysis that had preceded it. Transpersonal psychology, by intentionally making use of "altered" or "non-ordinary" states of consciousness, has pushed still further the exploration of psychic depths. The intention of this chapter is to recount the genesis and theoretical foundations of two techniques, especially, that have emerged from transpersonal psychology: the Bonny Method of Guided Imagery and Music (GIM), created by Helen Lindquist Bonny, and Holotropic Breathwork, created by Stanislav and Christina Grof.

These two approaches have a common provenance: both grew out of the experience at the Maryland Psychiatric Research Center (MPRC), where Stan Grof was principal investigator and Bonny was the staff music therapist. The focus of research at the MPRC was the clinical application of psychedelic drugs. In retrospect, of the various psychedelic clinical and research programs then operating throughout Europe and North America, perhaps the most significant was this one in the Baltimore suburb of Cantonsville, the last such program in the United States to close down, as government funding dried up and new prohibitions were imposed in the early 1970s. In addition to its investigation of the physiological effects of the drugs, its therapeutic work with alcoholic and neurotic patients and with others dying of cancer, its studies of the nature of mystical experience, and its revealing efforts to delineate a map of consciousness, the Maryland project gave the initial impetus to these two new psychotherapies that made no use of drugs, and that continue to flourish as transpersonal self-exploration techniques, each with a world-wide following.

In addition to their historical roots, the two techniques bear many similarities, operating with a common, transpersonal philosophical foundation and purview of consciousness, utilizing music as a vehicle for inner exploration, and employing common strategies to initiate, promote, and integrate the client's journey. With its group events open to the public, and buoyed by Stan Grof's international stature as psychologist and thinker, Holotropic Breathwork has cast the broader reach. Both techniques, however, have representatives and trainings in the Americas, Europe, Asia, and Australia; and each has its particular niche, complementary to that of the other: Breathwork is more frequently employed in group workshops, as a tool for occasional self-exploration, while the Bonny Method is more commonly utilized in ongoing individual therapy.

Two Roads to Cantonsville

Helen Bonny and Stanislav Grof were born a decade apart—she in 1921, he in 1931—into radically different worlds. She grew up in Kansas, daughter of a Lutheran minister and a mother who was a pianist and graduate of Oberlin Conservatory of Music, where Helen herself subsequently studied violin. Stan was from Prague, coming of age in an atheistic though non-Communist household; he studied medicine and psychiatry at the venerable Charles University. Among the parallels in their lives, however, is that each was launched on an innovative career by a single epiphany, a transformative mystical experience that demonstrated the reality of higher and non-ordinary states of consciousness.

In Bonny's case, the event was a church retreat in 1948, at which she played the violin—the specific piece was "The Swan" from Saint Saens's "The Carnival of the Animals." Suddenly, she reported, "it was as if the violin was not my own; bow arm and fingers were held in abeyance/obedience to a light and wonderful infusion that created an unbelievable sound I knew I had not ever produced before." The sense of being only a passive instrument for divinely inspired strains continued through her subsequent piece, leaving her with the sense of having experienced a "conversion" in which all sensation took on a new depth, and her inner life, with its beauty and pain, opened wide. The resulting search took her into psychotherapy with hypnosis and humanistic psychology, convincing her of "the power of consciousness exploration" and guiding her towards the study of music therapy (Bonny, 2002, pp. 5–7).

Stan Grof's comparable spiritual opening—his first experience with LSD 25, recounted in the previous chapter—took place eight years later, at the Charles University psychiatric clinic in Prague, shortly after his graduation from medical school. The resulting plunge into his unconscious mind, he later stated, "instantly overshadowed" his Freudian formation, as he was struck by an overwhelming vision of supernatural radiance—something that he now associates with the *Dharmakaya*, or Primary Clear Light, depicted in the *Bardo Thödol*, or *Tibetan Book of the Dead*. His consciousness catapulted into a cosmic drama and identification with the entire universe. From that moment, he left behind the materialistic assumptions of his formal education and determined to dedicate his life to the study of what later was labeled "non-ordinary states of consciousness" (Grof, 2006, pp. xxix–xxxv).

Only after raising a family did Helen Bonny, at the age of 40, undertake studies in music therapy at the University of Kansas, which had established the first graduate program in the field. After completing a master's degree, she served in the offices of the National Association for Music Therapy in Topeka. There she learned of psychedelic research and met Grof and Walter Pahnke, Director of the research program at the MPRC, both of whom had come to town to speak at the Menninger Foundation. In 1969, Helen was invited to join them at the MPRC as music therapist—hired, she later recalled, not only for her knowledge of music therapy, but for her interest in mystical states (2002, pp. 7–8, 46).

After his medical studies, Grof secured a position at the Psychiatric Research Institute in Prague, as principal investigator of a clinical study exploring therapeutic applications of LSD. For ten years he continued his research there, developing his radical map of consciousness that validated transcendent experiences and other unconscious territories often dismissed as psychotic in modern psychology. A two-year fellowship in the United States, beginning in 1967, allowed him time to delineate his findings and brought him to Johns Hopkins University and the Spring Grove Hospital, which spawned the MPRC. When Soviet tanks rolled into Czechoslovakia in August of 1968, crushing the reformist government of the "Prague Spring," Grof defied an order from the authorities to return home and determined to stay in the United States, accepting positions as Assistant Professor at the Henry Phipps Clinic of the Johns Hopkins School of Medicine and as Chief of Psychiatric Research at the Maryland Psychiatric Research Center.

An Expanded Model of Consciousness

It was at the MPRC that Bonny began to learn about the deeper layers of the unconscious mind, as revealed in LSD research. Her arrival was within two years after Grof became involved with the Center. By that time, Grof had fully developed the essential concepts of his map of the psyche, most of which had been charted while he was still in Prague, and he was completing the initial version of the manuscript that eventually became his first book, *Realms of the Human Unconscious* (1975). It is not the role of this chapter to parse out the particular contributions of the various players on the team of the MPRC, but Grof eventually took his place among the leading theorists of non-ordinary states of consciousness and their therapeutic potential. The idea that such states had the potential for psychological healing, indeed, was the centerpiece of the program and lays at the heart, as well, of both Holotropic Breathwork and the Bonny Method.

The purpose of the Maryland program, however, was not only the curing of psychological maladies, but a generic exploration of the human unconscious. As Grof repeatedly stated, the drug had tremendous "heuristic" potential. Under the influence of Walter Pahnke, a minister with a degree from Harvard Divinity School as well as a psychiatrist and physician, the program had a decidedly mystical cast. Pahnke, who directed the program from 1967 until his death in a diving accident in 1971, had gained notoriety for his doctoral experiments at Harvard, under Timothy Leary and Richard Alpert, exploring the effects of psilocybin in stimulating religious experiences.

Grof's work in Maryland reinforced the theoretical foundations that he had laid in Prague and strengthened his sense of LSD's capacity to reveal deep aspects of mind and reality. Early in his research, he had found that responses to the drug varied enormously; LSD did not induce a specific reaction so much as amplify pre-existing elements in the patient's psyche. It was a catalyst that could activate deep, unconscious material—that with the strongest emotional charge—and thus, like dreams, reveal profound elements of the personality (1975, 1980/1994). It also could prompt an "expansion of consciousness," sometimes instigating perceptions and imagery that were "phenomenologically indistinguishable" from profound religious experiences as described in scriptures and mystical texts (1975, pp. 13–14). Tracking the wide range of experiences that emerged in sessions that he had witnessed or investigated, Grof delineated his map of consciousness.

8.1 Helen Bonny and Stanislav Grof, c. 1970

That cartography is now included in the theory and trainings of both the Bonny Method and Holotropic Breathwork: it provides a conceptual orientation towards the totality of experiences that clients of both techniques undergo. We have alluded to it in the previous chapter, but some further account will aid in understanding its therapeutic applications. As initially formulated, it encompasses four levels of LSD experiences and corresponding areas of the unconscious (1975). At the most superficial level, sensations and aesthetic experiences are greatly intensified under LSD, sometimes revealing new dimensions to familiar artistic expression. Psychodynamic life begins to be revealed at the second level, when imagery emerges from the individual unconscious. In LSD sessions, memories and repressed material, from infancy onwards, is not only recalled but vividly relived; symbolic imagery and metaphorical allusions express unresolved inner conflicts. The dynamics at this level are largely compatible with basic concepts of psychoanalysis, though Grof adds a refinement to their interpretation—the concept of COEX, or "systems of condensed experiences," in which similar themes, with a comparable emotional charge, are associated with different periods in the subject's life (and even with other levels of consciousness), structuring his or her perceptions and life experiences.

The radical aspect in Grof's cartography is its positing that the consciousness that is available to each of us extends to memories of birth and even beyond the range of an individual's direct past experience. Its most distinctive element is Grof's analysis of a third, or perinatal, level, associated with biological birth. Together with impressions or actual memories of one's own gestation and birth come perceptions of the proximity of birth and death, and openings to archetypal and transcendent experiences. Such phenomena typically occur in four clusters or matrices, each related to a stage of delivery. The first of these "Basic Perinatal Matrices" (BPMs), corresponding to the period of gestation, before the onset of delivery, typically includes experiences implying a harmony with the enveloping environment, extending to a sense of cosmic unity. The onset of delivery produces the second matrix (BPM II), which is associated with unrelieved pressure, vital threat, and a sense of cosmic engulfment and hopelessness. The following stage, the propulsion through the birth canal (BPM III), corresponds to imagery implying a titanic struggle; and the fourth stage (BPM IV), actual delivery, is associated with ego death, rebirth and renewal. This "universal archetypal sequence," as Grof later referred to it (2000), is at the core of many a spiritual experience and religious myth.

A fourth level of consciousness, the transpersonal, is distinguished by an expansion beyond the usual limits of space and time imposed by the personal ego. The subject might have a sense of experiencing an awareness associated with a time, place, person, being, or category of beings that has not been part of his or her direct experience. Grof originally categorized this wide range of phenomena into two basic categories: those that related to objective reality as we normally understand it, and those that do not. The former might include, for example, clairvoyance, telepathy, out-of-body experiences, or apparent past-life memories, which involve perceptions of the world we acknowledge, albeit by supernormal means. The latter could involve mediumistic encounters with the dead, encounters with archetypal figures, cosmic consciousness, or mystical experiences of the metacosmic Void.

Transpersonal experiences, especially, led to a view of the human psyche, and of human nature, far removed from the Darwinian and Freudian models that dominate in modern thought. Such experiences, as we have noted, implied that consciousness is not simply an epiphenomenon of the individual brain, but a principle pervading all of existence. The attendant view of human nature, as Grof acknowledged in *LSD Psychotherapy*, was closer to a Hindu image than a Freudian one; it portrayed the core of personality not as bestial but divine. Like Abraham Maslow's humanistic psychology, formulated at the same time, psychedelic psychotherapy posited a healthy core in a patient's personality and attempted to access it (1980/1994, pp. 124–125).

In explaining her own conceptions of the psyche, Bonny's early writing alludes not directly to Grof's model, but rather to the four levels of consciousness delineated by Roberto Assagioli. That scheme includes a "lower unconsciousness" composed of physiological and psychosomatic activities, fundamental drives, and pathological compulsions; a more accessible "middle unconsciousness" of impulses, repressed conflicts, and motor reflexes; a restricted level of "ordinary consciousness; and a "higher unconscious" capable of creative inspiration and transpersonal insight (see Bonny & Savary, 1973, pp. 152–157). Later, Bonny began to favor a many-layered "cut log" diagram of mind—one of her own invention—that depicted an ego at the center, expanding outward by means of altered states, through progressively less accessible mental regions, eventually encompassing imagination, creativity, collective unconsciousness, and forms of mystical experience (2002).

In each of these maps of the psyche, higher aspects of mind extend beyond the individual ego into vaster, shared regions, encompassing the Jungian collective unconscious and a realm of "cosmic consciousness" or mystical insight. The common element in them is an expansion beyond the individual unconscious of Freudian theory. For Assagioli, Grof, and Bonny, the psyche is far larger and ultimately more transpersonal than Freud would have allowed. Eventually, both Grof's map and Assagioli's perspective were incorporated into the training for GIM, along with Bonny's "cut log" diagram. Their expanded outlook on the psyche give the Bonny Method and Holotropic Breathwork a shared theoretical, even ontological, framework. Though the two techniques do not depend on that framework for their efficacy, they rest on common philosophical ground.

Non-Ordinary States of Consciousness

LSD provided an entrée into those worlds of consciousness that normally were out of reach of the conscious mind. Since its effects were seen as catalytic, rather than specific to the drug itself, other means, by implication, might have a comparable effect. By the late 1960s, the notion of generic "altered states of consciousness," involving a shift in the pattern of mental functioning, had become a focus of research. Such states were sometimes associated with pathology, but other manifestations of them could involve profound insight. They could be attained through numerous ways apart from the use of substances, including, for example, meditation, hypnosis, and sensory deprivation (see Tart, 1969). In many cultures, unlike in the

modern West, altered states played a major role: they functioned in healing, in the resolution of emotional conflicts, and in creative insight, as well
as in promoting mystical experience (see Tart, 1969, pp. 1–6, 18–21).

Although Grof's early writings focus specifically on LSD and its effects, he
readily recognized that other means could induce similar experiences. His
map of consciousness, he wrote in *Realms of the Human Unconscious*, was
"fully compatible" with other systems, mentioning, in particular, those of
Jung, Assagioli, and Maslow, "as well as mystical schools of various cultures
and ages" (1975, p. 33). Perinatal and transpersonal experiences such as appeared in LSD sessions have been known for centuries, and even millennia;
they have been part of religious visions and are described in scriptures and
other religious documents; they are elements in indigenous rituals, rites of
passage, and healing practices, often prompted by practices such as dancing, fasting, induced pain, and changes in breathing. Within a few years,
Grof was speaking less in terms of LSD experiences and more in terms
of experiences induced in generic "non-ordinary states of consciousness,"
facilitated by a wide variety of means, often without drugs. One of those
means, usually in combination with others, was music, often in the form of
chanting or drumming (1985, 1988).

The Therapeutic Potential of Non-Ordinary States

When LSD was first introduced into clinics, it was not immediately apparent that it offered therapeutic possibilities. Its first suggested use was
for psychiatrists, not for patients: the drug was thought to induce a "model
psychosis," allowing psychiatrists a temporary journey into a schizophren-
ic's inner world, and thus abetting their understanding of their patients'
experience. But that notion soon was discarded, and various papers suggested that LSD could be used as an adjunct to psychotherapy, intensifying
the process (Grof, 1975, pp. 1–2). Before long its use was expanded, as it
sometimes proved effective in reaching patients who were not candidates
for psychoanalysis, and in alleviating the anxieties of dying patients (Grof,
1980/1994, pp. 26–27).

For his part, Grof found that with selected patients who had repeated sessions, a pattern appeared: eventually they would relive traumatic experiences, often regressing to the age at which the experience occurred. The
resulting emotional release and catharsis could free them of previous anxieties and symptoms, apparently resolving deep conflicts. The reliving of

traumatic experience also allowed reevaluation from a more mature perspective, from which the events were no longer overwhelming. In addition, imagery comparable to that in dreams could bring insights into psychodynamic patterns and personal issues. A protocol for serial administration of the drug was developed, initially following psychoanalytic principles. Over time, however, this "psycholytic" therapy, as it was known, strayed away from the psychoanalytic model with different procedures, involving less verbal interaction and including the use of stereophonic music and physical contact (1980/1994, pp. 114, 217).

As the LSD journey entered a perinatal level, patients could experience themselves as dying and being born—a powerfully therapeutic death-rebirth process. They might experience anxiety, fear of death, depression, aggression or other negative emotions, work through them, suffer a kind of ego-death, then experience a sense of emerging—of being reborn—into a more positive, loving, and spiritually enlivened existence. A similar dynamic might take place with transpersonal imagery or perceptions, such as apparent past-life memories or visions of archetypal forces (1980/1994, pp. 285–296).

Among other changes, psycholytic therapy as practiced in Prague began to allow for the therapeutic effect of more mystical experiences. The project that Grof joined in Maryland had taken that element still further, posing the inducing of such peak experiences as a primary therapeutic goal. Utilizing higher doses of the drug, this "psychedelic" therapy regularly involved other elements now incorporated into Holotropic Breathwork and the Bonny Method: the patient's assuming a reclining position, wearing eyeshades, and listening to stereophonic music, and the therapist or sitter's attitude of supporting whatever arises, encouraging completion of the experiential gestalt (1975; 1980/1994).

Music in LSD Psychotherapy

Helen Bonny's task in her new job at the Maryland Psychiatric Research Center was to research and choose music for use in psychedelic sessions. Over time, the team at MPRC had come to see music as an integral part of the "set and setting" required to promote the psychotherapeutic value of the sessions, determining that its use should be continual throughout the session. Bonny and her colleagues tested musical preferences, as well as changes in preferences as a result of listening to music under the influence

151

of the drug. The most effective music for the sessions, by her findings, was Western classical: particularly in the core stages of the session, it could take clients to greater "depths and heights" (Bonny, 1980, 2002).

On the basis of the center's experience in over 600 sessions, Bonny and Walter Pahnke wrote an account of the use of music in psychedelic psychotherapy (1972). Their analysis identified five ways in which music complemented the therapeutic objectives: it intensified the inner exploration, facilitated emotional release, contributed to a peak experience, provided continuity to the session, and directed and structured the journey. Bypassing intellectual resistance and controls, music helped to release and intensify contained and unconscious emotions, ultimately helping the patient achieve the unitive, transcendent experience that was the aim of psychedelic therapy. Although Bonny found classical music particularly effective, the consensus among MPRC's therapists was that the type of music was less significant than musical characteristics such as mood, pitch, dynamics, and structure, and the way those characteristics matched the progressive stages of the session (Bonny, 2002).

Bonny and Pahnke's most important contribution was their analysis of the successive phases of a session, and their matching of musical elements to each phase. Typically, a psychedelic session lasted on the order of 8–10 hours. Music served as its guide, reflecting and reinforcing the session's natural structure through six successive stages. As the session progressed, melodic lines and regular rhythms might give way to more insistent rhythms and dynamic crescendos. The period of the drug's culminating effects would be matched to powerful, exalted musical pieces, followed by quieter, more peaceful strains as the patient savored the experience, and then lighter music to accompany the return to normal consciousness. The resulting contour of musical intensity mirrored the patient's natural response to the drug (Bonny, 1980, 2002).

In this research on the uses of music in psychedelic psychotherapy, principles were established that later were carried over into Guided Imagery and Music and Holotropic Breathwork. The value of music in guiding the session is the most overarching, but the general progression of stages and matching musical characteristics proved applicable in these non-drug therapies as well. Highly discordant music should be avoided at times of peak intensity. Lyrics in the client's native language should also be avoided, since they could be overly directive and could activate the rational mind.

In the same article, Pahnke and Bonny noted that music can be effective in non-drug therapies, pointing, among others, to Leuner's Guided Affective Imagery (Bonny, 2002).

For his part, the use of music in psychedelic psychotherapy had clearly convinced Grof of its effectiveness as a catalyst during sessions. In his first book, he observed that the drug can produce a "hypersensitivity to sounds," allowing subjects to perceive new dimensions in music and triggering powerful emotions (1975, p. 40). Writing a more thorough account of LSD psychotherapy a few years later, he provided a fuller account of music's role, describing it as "an important and integral part" of the process. Referring the reader to Bonny's writings, Grof repeated several of her and Pahnke's observations, including the ways music promotes the therapeutic process and the need to match musical qualities with phases of the journey. He also added observations of his own. "The basic rule," he wrote, "is to respond sensitively to the phase, intensity, and content of the experience, rather than to try to impose a specific pattern on it" (1980/1994, p. 141). While Bonny emphasized the value of classical music, Grof reported, perhaps with some hindsight, that he had grown progressively impressed with the value of ethnic music, particularly elements that, in their native traditions, are associated with the altering of consciousness (1980/1994, p. 143).

Music without Drugs

The music that Bonny programmed for MPRC's psychedelic sessions was classical, both orchestral and choral. Participating in the sessions, she had the idea that the music alone could be used in consciousness-expanding journeys. Later, she recounted the story of first overseeing, serendipitously, a journey without drugs—resulting in her "discovery" of GIM. A visiting therapist who was participating in a psychedelic session came accompanied by his spouse. Bonny suggested that the spouse might gain a feel for the sessions by listening in a relaxed state to some of the music. She asked the visitor to report any images that arose, then proceeded to play the music: to Bonny's surprise, the images kept flowing for three hours (2002, pp. 49–50). Among the visitors to the Center was Hanscarl Leuner, creator of a therapy that he called "Guided Affective Imagery," which utilized prescribed imagistic scenes. Leuner was then exploring the incorporation of music into his approach, and Bonny's experience in volunteering as subject for one of those trial sessions, in 1971, reinforced her sense of the power of music to give rise to both imagery and profound emotions. With his support, she experimented with musical passages intended to evoke Leuner's standard images (2002; Clark, 2002).

By that time, with psychotropic drugs available in the streets and consumed indiscriminately in the emerging youth culture, a backlash against them had taken hold in government circles and in public awareness. With that came objections to their use in psychological research and mental health, and the withdrawal of funding for such efforts. In 1968, the sale of LSD was made a felony offense. In 1970, it was classified as a Schedule 1 drug, officially characterized as habit-forming and without medical value. Many psychedelic research centers had closed down; at the MPRC, a search was underway for non-drug alternatives to psychedelic sessions. In a controlled experiment with alcoholic patients, Bonny prepared a music program of four hours, similar in structure to those used in LSD sessions, but intended for use without the drug. The sessions involved use of headphones and eyeshades, as well as verbal reporting of imagery. Results, at least in some cases, were encouraging, and were found to improve when patients first underwent relaxation exercises, as employed in Leuner's Guided Affective Imagery and other methods. The prior relaxation made emotions more accessible and imagery more vivid. Music alone could induce altered states of consciousness (2002, pp. 10–11, 55–60).

Meanwhile, Bonny had begun using music with people who were not patients, healthy individuals who saw themselves, in Maslow's terms, as on a quest for self-actualization. "My hope," she wrote, "was that many of the actualizing experiences which occurred to people on an expanded drug trip would be possible to them without drugs..." (2002, p. 60). Fortuitously, a snowstorm in 1972, leaving several friends and family trapped in her home, occasioned her first group session, which aimed for a spiritual experience. Further testing with another group, composed of counselors at a drug crisis center, allowed her to experiment with variations in the structure and length of musical programs, and the use or omission of introductory imagery (2002, pp. 61–63).

Soon Bonny was creating various tapes, musical programs with different emotional emphases. In the summer of 1972, she collaborated with Louis Savary, a musician, author, and Jesuit priest, to write *Music and Your Mind*, an account, as they phrased it, of "the use of music in reaching and exploring non-ordinary levels of human consciousness" (Bonny & Savary, 1973, p. 13). Altered states induced only by relaxation and concentration, they argued, allow listeners to hear music with unaccustomed depth, leading them beyond ordinary perception, opening routes to insight, creativity, and transpersonal and spiritual experiences. The book was a practical manual: it provided instructions for induction exercises and for emerging from the experience, offered contextual imagery matched to specific musical selections, and suggested that, whenever conducted in groups, the musical experience be followed by sharing discussions as a means of integration. It recounted, too, many individual journeys: as the music gave rise to imagery, inner conflicts were clarified and resolved, peak and religious experiences attained.

While still working at the MPRC, Bonny entered a Ph.D. program at the Union Graduate School, undertaking as her doctoral project and dissertation the creation of twelve musical programs for self-exploration sessions, and writing about them. In her research, she analyzed mood responses to different musical selections and tested the therapeutic effects of programs. With experimental sessions outside of the MPRC, and helpful input from some colleagues, she refined programs and techniques for her approach, which she christened "Guided Imagery and Music." In 1973, Bonny established the Institute of Consciousness and Music (ICM) to support the practice; by 1975, she was training others in it.

The LSD research program at MPRC was ordered closed in 1971. With the end of that project, both Bonny and Grof began to look beyond Catonsville for their work. As she undertook research for her doctorate and developed GIM, Bonny accepted an offer to establish a music therapy program at Catholic University in Washington, D.C. In 1973, Grof accepted an invitation from Michael Murphy, co-founder of the Esalen Institute, to move to the Esalen campus in Big Sur, California, as resident scholar.

By the time of Bonny's founding of ICM and Grof's move to Esalen, the fundamental philosophy and techniques of both GIM and what later would become Holotropic Breathwork were well established. LSD research had led to a greatly expanded view of the human psyche, and had shown that non-ordinary states of consciousness could lead individual awareness into greater personal depths and transpersonal dimensions, usually expressed in vivid imagery. Such activation of the unconscious had a healing potential, releasing the energy bound in symptoms, whether emotional or psychosomatic. Healing came about through several psychodynamic mechanisms, including abreaction and catharsis, integration of past trauma, experiences of ego death and rebirth, and supportive transpersonal or peak experiences (see Grof, 1988, pp. 219–249). The client's own inner wisdom both located an issue and interpreted the images; the therapist's role was primarily to support and accept the client's process. Though drugs were a primary route to non-ordinary states, such states could be induced by other means as well, particularly music. In such journeys, music could intensify the natural stages of the experience and guide it to completion. Experiment had confirmed the value of techniques such as an induction relaxation exercise, a reclining position, use of eyeshades, occasional physical interventions, and discussion and drawing as means of integrating the experience.

The Development of Holotropic Breathwork

At Esalen, Grof's primary focus was initially on writing; after completing *Realms of the Human Unconscious,* published in 1975, he undertook two follow-up accounts of his LSD research: *The Human Encounter with Death,* written with Joan Halifax, and the compendious *LSD Psychotherapy,* published, respectively, in 1977 and 1980. After that, he produced *Beyond the Brain*, perhaps his magnum opus, which relates the discoveries in non-ordinary states to emerging scientific and philosophical outlooks. At the same time, often in association with his wife Christina, Grof played a major role in organizing and teaching in the educational programs that made Esalen such a vibrant center of alternative thought and culture in the 1970s and '80s.

Originally from Honolulu, Christina Goodale was a 1964 graduate of Sarah Lawrence College, where she had studied with Joseph Campbell. By the time of her first visit to Esalen in 1975, she had been married, borne two children, and was a practitioner of hatha yoga and a follower of Swami Muktananda, a teacher in the Tantric lineage of Kashmir Shaivism. Her own initiation into mystical experience, comparable to those of Bonny and her future husband, came during the birth of her first child, when she experienced an eruption of *kundalini* energy catapulting her into an altered state of consciousness. Comparable visionary experiences followed, including a near-death experience in an automobile accident. Newly divorced, Christina arrived at Esalen, and met Stan Grof, as his marriage to Joan Halifax was at the point of dissolution. His accounts of LSD experiences resonated with her own spontaneous mystical visions. By the end of that year, she and Grof were living together just outside the Esalen campus. Before long, they began their joint work at Esalen, which would include the creation of Holotropic Breathwork. By the end of 1976, the method had attained its mature and lasting form, and was being offered at Esalen in group workshops (Grof & Grof, 2010, p. 177).

Like other components of both Breathwork and GIM, Grof's distinctive use of deep breathing had its origins in the experience with LSD psychotherapy. In the course of psychedelic sessions, Grof had observed, patients would sometimes engage in spontaneous hyperventilation. Deep and rapid breathing was sometimes employed intentionally towards the end of a psychedelic session, when the experience seemed still unresolved—if the client still felt some form of emotional or physical distress. It would again activate the unconscious, resulting in physical as well as emotional responses and symptoms. The therapist's application of physical pressure to the affected area would temporarily exaggerate the symptoms, resulting in further abreaction, emotional release, and a resolution of the psychodynamic gestalt. At Esalen, Grof began using these techniques of hyperventilation and physical intervention independently, without the drug (1980/1994; 1985). In focusing on hyperventilation, Grof was aware of Leonard Orr's incorporation of it into the technique of "rebirthing"; Orr, in turn, had been inspired by Indian *pranayama*, the science of breath. Experimenting with breathing techniques from various spiritual traditions and experiential psychotherapies, the Grofs eventually opted simply for more rapid breathing, which became the key element in Holotropic Breathwork. Hyperventilation itself proved sufficient to relax psychological defenses and release unconscious tensions, drawing out intense emotions and psychosomatic manifestations, allowing their discharge and integration (1988; Grof & Grof, 2010).

Music, Grof found, could deepen the experience and enhance the results. Observing the general principles outlined by Bonny, the Grofs added music to the mix, loosely following the structure that had been developed at the MPRC, timed and modified for use without the drug. With her own strong and wide-ranging musical sensibility, Christina Grof determined the criteria for selection and sequencing of specific pieces. Noting the use of music, drumming and chanting for entering non-ordinary states in many non-Western cultures, the Grofs drew on ethnic and shamanic music, and music from world religious traditions, as well as on Western classical pieces and works of contemporary composers. Unlike Bonny's GIM programs, their selections were seldom tailored to intensify specific emotional reactions, though Grof acknowledged that such specific targeting could be useful if, as in individual therapy, the therapist was aware of a client's immediate emotional concerns and imagistic focus. Initially, the Grofs drew on Christina's collection of music, selecting spontaneously and responding to the group mood in the course of a session. As time went on, responding to the practicalities of group sessions, their colleagues and trainees developed taped programs, following a basic general sequence of mood and intensity.

As in the psychedelic sessions, Grof found that focused bodywork could be especially valuable at the end of session, particularly to bring to the fore and complete unresolved gestalts. Such interventions intensified the breather's physical sensations; the resulting motor and vocal reactions typically promoted discharge of the sensation and release of associated emotions, bringing closure to the session. When a back problem serendipitously limited his own mobility before conducting a large group session at Esalen, Grof turned to the use of dyads: participants would alternately take the role of "breathers" and "sitters." The practice proved successful, providing each breather with a caretaker who remained in ordinary consciousness, attending to the breather's physical needs and sometimes applying bodywork (S. Grof, personal communication, August 9, 2009).

Transpersonal Therapies: The Process of Healing

As their notions of the broader goals of their approaches matured, both Bonny and Grof came to explain them as "holistic," making whole. Healing comes through an integration of divergent aspects of the personality, including ones that extend beyond the ego; it comes through the integration of body, mind, and spirit. Their view of the elements to be integrated included but extended beyond those envisioned in some other approaches that used similar terminology—in Gestalt therapy, for example, which aims to integrate fragmented aspects of the personal ego. Both Bonny and Grof viewed human nature as intrinsically spiritual and saw their therapeutic methods as giving access to transpersonal realms. As Grof explained, "holotropic" therapy—the term, which he coined, means "moving towards wholeness"—entails an expanded sense of human nature, a view that individual consciousness is intimately connected with collective consciousness, and ultimately with awareness of a spiritual context to life. Holotropic therapy, he asserted, eventually becomes a spiritual quest (1985, 1988; Grof & Grof, 2010). Bonny, similarly, described the purpose of GIM as "reintegration, insight, wholeness," and healing as balancing the elements that make up the person, including spiritual ones (2002, pp. 95–96; Abrams, 2002).

And for both Grof and Bonny, the agent of healing was not the therapist but the client, or better said, the client's deepest self. The positive view of human personality—the sense of a healthy core to human nature—that was part of psychedelic psychotherapy and that was central to Maslow's humanistic vision left its imprint on both GIM and Holotropic Breathwork. Both techniques recognize a fundamental tendency towards healing and wholeness in virtually everyone; their goal is to stimulate it through non-ordinary states of consciousness. In his earliest writings, Grof spoke of an "inner radar" activated in such states, a capacity to recognize the issues most ripe for transformative work (1975, p. 216); later, he wrote of an "inner healer," a natural tendency to resolve those issues and seek the wholeness that is the basis of health. Those notions are central in both GIM and Breathwork, vastly diminishing the importance of a therapist's interpretive framework. "All healing," Bonny wrote, "ultimately is self-healing" (2002, p. 273). The effort in both modalities is to accept the imagery and the affect that emerges in non-ordinary states, allowing the dynamic to bring about resolution—to "trust the process" (Bush, 1995, p. 40; Grof, 1988, p. 208). Frequently, the result is a cathartic "death-rebirth" experience, in which an outmoded aspect of the personality is seen to die and a new one to emerge.

Elements of Practice

Despite their shared philosophical ground and their similar structures, GIM and Holotropic Breathwork differ in some fundamentals of their practice, apart from the Breathwork's use of hyperventilation. What follows is a comparison of a few basic elements in the two techniques. Both methods, we should note, have now been available for several decades, and as creative practices, they naturally admit of adaptations and multiple applications (for a sense of the range of adaptations and applications of GIM, see Bruscia & Grocke, 2002). These remarks, then, apply to the more common, classical forms of each approach.

Music

Bonny was a consummate musician; of these two techniques, the Bonny Method gives more primacy to the music, and it generally involves a more precise analysis of musical qualities: the affective impact of pitch, rhythm, tempo, melody, harmony, timbre. Between 1973 and 1989, Bonny created 18 programs, typically of 30–40 minutes duration, each with a specific emotional character or therapeutic intention, all composed entirely of Western classical music (Grocke, 2002). Several of those programs have a canonical status in GIM practice, particularly in its individual form. Some were subsequently modified with Bonny's participation, and her students have created others; but in general, GIM continues to rely on Bonny's own programs, or on meticulous creations in her tradition, utilizing classical pieces.

The structure of programs in the Breathwork, on the other hand, is looser, and employs a wider range of musical traditions, including drumming, world and ethnic music, chants from various spiritual traditions, new age music and film soundtracks, as well as classical pieces. Although Breathwork programs follow a basic general pattern ultimately based on the one that Bonny and Pahnke described in their analysis of LSD sessions, they are devised by many practitioners, all with their varying styles and preferences; each student in the training, in fact, creates one. In comparison to the 40 minutes of music in a typical GIM session, Breathwork programs, in their standard format, normally last for three hours. The vast majority of these programs are intended for group sessions, rather than tailored to the specific needs of clients in individual therapy.

Individual and Group Sessions

Psychedelic psychotherapy was normally practiced in individual sessions, though at times applied in groups. As she developed her drug-free method, Bonny worked with group sessions, but her trainings, from their early stages, emphasized work with individuals. That, she thought, was GIM's "most powerful and effective" application (cited in Clark, 2002, p. 25); group sessions were used largely for introductory presentations. Grof, by contrast, conducted some of his earliest Holotropic Breathwork sessions with individuals (Meadows, 2002), but soon gravitated towards working with groups. Aggregate sessions, he found, created a "strong catalytic energy field" that rendered sessions more effective, as well as making them available to many more participants (1988, p. 199). The Grofs' workshops also benefited from the sometimes catalytic effects of having the combination of a male and a female presence leading the group. Although GIM practitioners have thoughtfully applied and adapted the method for groups and Breathwork practitioners frequently do individual sessions, the

Bonny Method remains primarily a modality for individual therapy and Holotropic Breathwork for group workshops.

Induction

Sessions of the Bonny Method and Holotropic Breathwork follow a similar core structure. The client assumes a reclining position, with eyes closed or vision blocked with eyeshades. The session begins with a relaxation exercise, passes into imagistic "travels" with music, and ends with an integration process. Both modalities frequently use the same or similar introductory relaxation and terminal integration techniques.

Though they may vary within each of two modalities, relaxation techniques normally follow a similar pattern in both. The most common procedures involve a systematic and progressive concentration on different parts of the body. Bonny recommended such a technique in her earliest writing, tracing it to the "progressive relaxation" of Edmund Jacobson and the "autogenic training" of Johannes Schultz, developed in the 1920s and '30s, and subsequently adapted in Leuner's Guided Affective Imagery (Bonny & Savary, 1973, p. 24; Bonny, 1975). Grof endorses a similar procedure, though the specific techniques used in the Breathwork were influenced by Christina Grof's background in Hatha Yoga and in various forms of meditation (1988, p. 205; Grof & Grof, 2010, p. 64).

Dialogue

Although lower-dose psycholytic therapy involved dialogue between subject and therapist, psychedelic sessions usually involved only minimal verbal exchange between subject and therapist during their intense hours. In Grof's estimation, talking during those hours could increase the subject's resistance, interfere with regression, and keep the session more superficial (1980/1994, pp. 105–106, 254).

In the early development of GIM, however, Bonny, collaborating with Daniel Brown, director of a drug rehabilitation center in Massachusetts, found dialogue to be useful in deepening and promoting the experience. Recognizing that talking could be counter-productive, Bonny explored the most effective forms of dialogue, hewing to the principle that as the subject reported imagery, the facilitator should "guide" but not "control" the session. Properly managed with an attitude of "active empathy," dialogue could help concretize the imagery, aid the client in remembering it, and provide material for subsequent reflection (2002, pp. 63–65, 286–292). In Kenneth Bruscia's estimation, dialogue became a "defining feature" of GIM in its individual form (Bruscia, 2002, p. 52). The guide typically takes notes, later shared with the client, on the client's reported imagery and other phenomena evoked in the session.

Perhaps because Breathwork sessions—with their greater length and the intensity added by hyperventilation—more closely approximated work with LSD, Grof continued to discourage verbal exchanges during the sessions, save for communicating immediate needs. On the grounds that "cognition, conceptualization, and verbal exchange seriously interfere with the depth and the flow of the process," discussion in Breathwork is largely confined to preparation and integration, and excluded from the session itself (1988, p. 208).

Integration

In psychedelic sessions, as later in the Breathwork, dialogue became important as the subject was emerging from the experience. If issues were still unresolved—if the subject felt anxiety or physical discomfort—physical interventions, it was found, could facilitate resolution. Focused bodywork, in which the facilitator and client work together to apply pressure on points of physical tension, could bring still latent emotional issues to the surface and complete the psychological gestalt (Grof, 1980/1994, pp. 144–145). At Esalen, Grof began using such bodywork independently of psychedelic sessions, and then incorporated it into Holotropic Breathwork, where it remains a fundamental element of the approach, most frequently applied towards the close of the session. GIM practitioners, too, sometimes make use of bodywork, applying it in the course of sessions to release tensions evoked by the music. The technique, however, remains more central to the Breathwork than to the Bonny Method.

A major element in the integration of psychedelic sessions was artistic expression, in various forms. As the session came to a close, clients would express the experience with drawing, paintings, writing, or some other creative endeavor (Grof, 1980/1994). That principle was incorporated into both GIM and Breathwork. Although clients continue to use other forms of expression, the dominant technique, in both modalities, became mandala drawing, rooted in the work of Joan Kellogg at the Maryland Psychiatric Research Center.

Joan Kellogg came to MPRC as a volunteer in 1971, bringing the technique with her. She encouraged clients to draw in a circle whatever seemed appropriate to them, and she had developed a system for analyzing the results. Helen Bonny recalled being introduced to the mandalas by Grof at a staff meeting (2002, p. 48). Initially, the drawings were used as a means of diagnosing clients, determining their suitability for the therapy. In her very first therapeutic application of music without the drug—the session that she referred to as her "discovery" of GIM—Bonny had her subject draw several mandalas after the session, to represent the experience. In Bonny's own mind, the effect was catalytic, and as she developed her approach, collaborating with Kellogg, she continued to utilize mandala drawing as a fundamental element for integration. In 1977, they jointly presented a case study involving a series of GIM sessions followed by such drawings, demonstrating the mandalas' effectiveness not only in integrating the sessions but also in providing a measure and visual chronicle of therapeutic progress (Bonny, 2002). The same technique proved equally valuable in Holotropic Breathwork, where mandalas had the additional advantage of providing a focus for discussion and interaction in group discussion following the sessions.

Some Concluding Thoughts

With its expansive views of the human psyche's reach and capacities, transpersonal psychology has spawned innovative and effective approaches to self-exploration and psychological healing. Before it was brought to an abrupt halt in the early 1970s, psychedelic psychotherapy had shown measurable success in releasing the effects of trauma and alleviating depression. It proved useful in treating alcoholism and other addictions and helped to resolve psychogenic physical issues. In discharging aggression, it had some success in managing the problems of individuals often considered poor candidates for psychotherapy, such as sociopaths and others displaying various forms of antisocial behavior. At the MPRC and other centers, patients were given over to LSD psychotherapy when other approaches manifestly had failed. Properly administered, the drug had proven especially valuable in alleviating fear of death among terminal patients, relieving the associated depression, withdrawal, tension and sleep disturbances. Artists found that it could greatly intensify aesthetic experience and—as they drew for inspiration on deeper sources in the unconscious—powerfully stimulate creative expression. Many clients found that it could sharply promote religious or mystical experience. Sometimes it resulted in dramatic, highly positive transformations, in emotional liberation and spiritual opening, with long-term positive consequences. Important work had been done in determining pharmacological characteristics and biological effects of the drug, in examining successes and failures, in identifying contraindications and risks, and in refining clinical practices (Grof, 1980/1994; Grof & Halifax, 1977).

It bears mention that, after decades of inactivity, psychedelic psychotherapy is now undergoing a revival. Building on the work done in previous decades, and encouraged by an organization called the Multidisciplinary Association for Psychedelic Research (MAPS), several major universities have undertaken new studies, with more advanced and rigorous investigatory methods. Psilocybin, the active ingredient in psychedelic mushrooms, has been shown to reduce depression and anxiety in patients with life-threatening forms of cancer. Psychedelics are again showing promise in combating addiction, including smoking. Especially robust has been the application of MDMA, a synthetic compound commonly known as "Ecstasy," in the treatment of post-traumatic stress disorder (PTSD), particularly among military veterans (see Grof, 2012; Main, 2016; Schiffman, 2016; Shroder, 2014).

The non-drug techniques derived from psychedelic therapy, such as Holotropic Breathwork and the Bonny Method, may often be less potent than sessions with, say, LSD or psilocybin; but giving access to non-ordinary states, they are powerful tools of psychotherapy and self-exploration. While avoiding the legal and possible psycho-physical complications of drug use, they can lead to many of the same benefits, especially in personal and spiritual growth. Among those who have had ongoing experiences with these states, there is a strong conviction that the benefits are not only to the individual, but to society at large.

The manifold crises of contemporary society, from ever more powerful and plentiful forms of inflicting violence to degradation of the environment, requires—so goes the argument—not only instrumental and political measures, but widespread transformation of the human soul, of habits and attitudes of individuals. By its very nature, holotropic therapy promotes values and a worldview that can reduce conflict and lead to a more harmonious social and political culture. As physical tensions and negative emotions are discharged, aggression and alienation are diminished. There is an increased ability to enjoy life, a greater focus on its simpler pleasures. A more compassionate posture arises, more accepting, even loving, towards others. Competitiveness declines. Cultural differences appear less threatening, more enriching. Egocentric strategies of life, especially those that might harm others, are increasingly seen as superficial and self-destructive. With that change comes a sharper sense of the interdependence of all human life, in its many diverse forms, and of the interdependence of human life with its environmental matrix. There is a stronger sense belonging: of being part of humanity as a whole, part of the miracle of nature. With that comes a corresponding sense of the need for social justice, a greater ecological awareness. Social betterment depends on individual transformation. Holotropic experiences can help to point the way (see Grof, 1980/1994, 2012; Grof & Grof, 2010).

Note

1   An earlier version of this chapter was published as "Holotropic Breathwork and the Bonny Method: The Co-evolution of Two Transpersonal Therapeutic Modalities" in the *Journal of the Association for Music and Imagery (12)*, 2009–2010, 95–117. Copyrighted and reprinted by permission of the Association for Music and Imagery.

CHAPTER NINE

Transpersonal Psychology and the Study of History[1]

One measure of the value of an idea or perspective is its fecundity: how extensively it might be applied not only within but outside of the field of endeavor that gave rise to it. With an initial base in psychology, Ken Wilber soon took his notions of levels or states of consciousness into sociology, theorizing about human cultural development and more particularly, about ways to assess the variety of human religions (1983). Transpersonal thought has had an impact in anthropology, where it brings a more sympathetic, and arguably more psychologically profound, perspective to the examination of indigenous cultures (see, for example, the seminal if controversial work of Harner, esp. 1980). The intention of this current chapter is to suggest uses of transpersonal theory in my own discipline, history.

Especially through the influence of Ken Wilber, transpersonal concepts have been associated with theories of human social development, which implies, of course, human history, or better said, perhaps, *metahistory*—a broad view of historical development. One of Wilber's more elegantly clarifying notions is that of the "four quadrants," which implies that all phenomena can be examined from a perspective that is, on the one hand, either individual or collective, and on the other, either interior or exterior (see, especially, 1995). Put those two sets of alternatives together, and one comes up with four general perspectives. Applying those to human development, Wilber theorizes about different stages in collective evolution, one scale that is "interior" or cultural, another that is "exterior" or socio-political. Cultural development, for example, may pass through different worldviews, from, say, an animistic-magical culture to a scientific-rational one, and then beyond; social systems may evolve from ethnic tribes to feudal empires, agrarian nations, industrial states, and so forth, with various other stages along the way. In a broad sense, then, Wilber is speaking of history.

A more detailed meta-historical perspective, more focused on specific historical episodes, comes from Richard Tarnas, who amply demonstrated his prowess as an intellectual historian with *The Passion of the Western Mind* (1991), a tour through the full unfolding of Western intellectual history, informed throughout by Tarnas's profound grasp of depth psychology. The archetypal perspective that subtly infused that book comes to full flower in *Cosmos and Psyche* (2006), which examines historical events in the light of archetypal astrology. The argument, of course, is highly challenging to the prevailing materialistic worldview, but Tarnas, who is as fully knowledgeable as an astrologer as he is as an historian, makes a forceful case for the correlation of historical events with planetary cycles. From this perspective, epochs of, say, revolution and of conservative reaction, of creative breakthroughs and spiritual awakening, each are reflected in planetary movements. The implication, ultimately, is that forms of transpersonal intelligence, beyond the human, are reflected in human history.

My intention in the remarks that follow is far narrower in scope than the metahistorical speculations of Wilber and Tarnas: it is to demonstrate that specific ideas that have emerged from transpersonal psychology can be useful in the account of equally specific historical events. A case in point is what might be the pivotal speech in American political history, Abraham Lincoln's Gettysburg Address.

The Case of Abraham Lincoln

If ever there were an American president who, by bent and temperament, was in touch with the transpersonal dimension, it is Abraham Lincoln. His famous "melancholy," remarked on by contemporaries and biographers, was seen in his own Romantic era as *liminal*—evidence of contact with the numinous dimensions in his own personality and the cosmos (Wills, 1992). Lincoln was attentive to his own dreams, to the point of sometimes letting them guide his practical actions in family affairs, and his law partner and contemporary biographer described him as alert to portents and omens (Herndon & Weik, 1889). Only two weeks before his own assassination, he had a vivid dream, which he recounted in detail to his assistant Ward Lamon, foreboding the event (Stern, 1940). As the catastrophic Civil War whirled around him, Lincoln, who always remained skeptical of the nostrums of organized religion, nevertheless increasingly saw the War as divinely ordained; while laboring daily to affect its outcome, he mulled continually over its ultimate governance by divine will—a rumination that came to full, public fruition in his Second Inaugural Address.

The War's appalling death toll, and tragedy within his own family, inexorably intensified Lincoln's lifelong preoccupation with death, focusing his mind on its meaning and possible aftermath. Since childhood, his life had been battered by the premature loss of loved ones: His mother died when Lincoln was nine years old; before he reached adulthood, he had lived through the passing of a brother who succumbed in infancy and a sister who died in childbirth. The love of his young manhood, Ann Rutledge, died during their courtship. The second of his four sons, Edward, lived only four years. During the War, in February of 1862, his beloved and favorite son Willie, then 11 years old, died after a feverish illness. As his thoughts on the War matured into the foundation of his immortal funeral oration at Gettysburg, Lincoln remained in deep mourning, twice having his son's body exhumed in order to contemplate the remains (Stern, 1940). In those same months, Mary Todd Lincoln, desperately hoping to contact Willie's spirit, was hosting séances in the White House (Wills, 1992).

9.1 Abraham Lincoln: images of death and rebirth. (Gardner, A., photographer. 1865. Retrieved from the Library of Congress, https://www. loc.gov/item/2007675780/.)

Psychohistory: From Freud to deMause and Grof

Sigmund Freud applied his notions to historical and political figures—most seminally in *Leonardo da Vinci and a Memory of His Childhood*

169

(1910)—and psychoanalysis and its progeny have influenced biography, including political and historical biography, ever since. While loose efforts at explaining historical behavior with psychoanalytic theory have often seemed fatuous, a more disciplined effort to apply concepts derived from modern psychology to the study of history emerged in the later 1950s. In 1957, Harvard historian William Langer gave a landmark address before the American Historical Association, subsequently published in the *American Historical Review*, in which he called for just such an effort, labeling it the "next assignment" (Langer, 1958). The following year saw the publication of Erik Erikson's psychoanalytic account of Martin Luther, which convincingly demonstrated the potential value of the genre and still is regarded as a major classic in the field (1958). Initially, as in those cases, psychohistory focused primarily on the biography of major historical figures—an approach that proved fruitful in accounts of political leaders ranging from Lincoln to Woodrow Wilson, Adolf Hitler, and Malcolm X.[2]

The application of psychological theory to explain collective as opposed to individual behavior might be traced back at least to Freud's own sociological writings, particularly *The Future of an Illusion* (1927) and *Civilization and its Discontents* (1930). With his concepts of archetypes and the collective unconscious, Carl Jung provided notions that begged for historical illustration and for the examination, in light of those notions, of broad social movements. Jung himself took steps in that direction, interpreting major public events of his time, especially the rise of Nazism, in terms of archetypes and their mass appeal.[3]

In the two decades following Langer's address, the use of psychoanalytic ideas to understand the motivation and behavior of historical groups gained momentum. In 1971, Peter Lowenberg published a seminal essay in the *American Historical Review* on Nazi youth, exploring the effects of massive social trauma on later collective behavior. That article established trauma reactions as a central focus of the field. Psychohistory's two principal journals, *Psychohistory Review* and the *Journal of Psychohistory*, both published their first issues in 1973, the latter initially focusing on the history of childhood. Lloyd deMause's studies of the history of childhood, many published in that journal, gave impetus to that field, particularly with an edited volume published in 1974. DeMause's "psychogenic theory of history" posits that childrearing practices generates group fantasies that later are acted out in public life. Some subsequent works apply group process and family systems theory to political and social movements.[4]

Whether focusing on individuals or groups, the field of psychohistory has been decidedly Freudian and psychoanalytic in orientation. Indeed, one of its major practitioners has portrayed it as a "synthesis between the disciplines of history and psychoanalysis" (Lowenberg, 1985, p. 3), a characterization that is descriptively accurate. The field has also been highly controversial, with more enthusiasts in the psychoanalytic community than among mainstream historians. There have been complaints of psychological reductionism, ahistorical analysis, and of too-facile associations between infantile traumas and adult behavior in public life (see, for example, Barzun, 1974; Stannard, 1980). Over time, however, psychohistory has become more established, and its bibliography has grown ample. It also has acquired defenders among highly distinguished historians who are lauded in all quarters of their profession. Preeminent among them, perhaps, is Peter Gay, former Sterling Professor of History at Yale. A cultural and intellectual historian who underwent psychoanalytic training, Gay is the author of *Freud for Historians* (1985), *Freud: A Life for Our Time* (1988), and numerous historical studies, including the multivolume *The Bourgeois Experience: Victoria to Freud*, which is informed with psychoanalytic concepts (1984–1991).

To construct a more transpersonally oriented psychohistory, we might begin with the study of political ideology and rhetoric. As transpersonal psychology plumbs further into the depths of human consciousness, it can clarify motifs that have a strong collective resonance, and that can be mobilized to animate political movements. A case in point is Stanislav Grof's notion of "Basic Perinatal Matrices" (BPMs), with their sequence of associated archetypal imagery leading from death, or near-death, to rebirth. For an illustration of the explanatory power of Grof's concept in the analysis of political rhetoric, we need look no further than to the central oration of American political experience, Lincoln's Gettysburg Address.

Lincoln at Gettysburg

On November 19, 1863, Lincoln took the podium at the site of what remained the Civil War's bloodiest battle, to dedicate a cemetery for the soldiers who had died there four months earlier. There had been some 8,000 deaths on that field in southwestern Pennsylvania, and 50,000 casualties; but the Northern forces had prevailed, bringing new hope to their war effort. As Lincoln rose to speak, Edward Everett, the venerable Harvard classicist and former Secretary of State, had already delivered the occasion's principal declamation, a two-hour performance that well met the audience's high expectations. Lincoln's role was ancillary, to pronounce the formal dedication, and no more. His "Dedicatory Remarks," as they were listed on the formal program, lasted three minutes. They were composed of a mere 272 words, a quarter of the length of the occasion's invocational prayer.

"The power of words," writes historian Garry Wills, "has rarely been given a more compelling demonstration" (1992, p. 25). Lincoln's "remarks" are now viewed as a key document of the American civil religion, second only to the Declaration of Independence in defining the core of a national political consciousness. The Gettysburg Address framed the War as the great test of whether the ideals of liberty and equality, embodied in republican government, could survive anywhere on earth. It spoke of a transcendent purpose behind the great trauma of battle, and of the hope of renewal. The nation, implicitly cleansing itself of the sin of slavery, could not only survive, but rededicate itself to its original ideals and reassert in more pure form its original values. In referring to the Declaration of Independence as the country's founding charter, Lincoln solidified the place of Thomas Jefferson's words as the core statement of national purpose and rededicated American society to the ideals of freedom and equality (see Wills, 1978). To that national Torah he added his own New Testament, introducing the more specifically Christian themes of death, sacrifice and rebirth, and positing a new level of transcendence to national goals (Bellah, 1967). As Robert Lowell pointed out, Lincoln "left Jefferson's ideals of freedom and equality joined to the Christian sacrificial act of death and rebirth" (1964, pp. 88–89). In so doing, he gave expression to the central credo of American civil religion; he articulated a meaning for the American past and a mission for the American future. However well or poorly the country may have lived up to those rhetorical ideals, however the terms might have shifted meanings along their historical way, Lincoln's words remain at the very core of a national political psyche. In times of solemn national ritual and of national crisis, the themes of freedom, natural rights, equality, tolerance, democracy, sacrifice, and divine blessing inexorably re-emerge.

What can explain the power of those 272 words? The persistent myth that Lincoln wrote the address on the back of an envelope attests to a popular sense that the Address was inspired, a result of pure illumination rather than patient craftsmanship. Clearly, the Address carried a message that the society needed to hear. Considered in terms of content alone, it drew meaning from carnage and, with splendid timeliness, isolated thoughts, and sentiments capable of rallying national energies. But content in a speech, of course, is never alone: thoughts and sentiments are always embodied in images, words, and cadences, with connotation and resonance. Unlike, say, the erudite and finely honed but largely forgotten passages of Everett's oration on the same occasion, the Address remains an almost unparalleled fixture of the national canon.

In attempting to probe the secrets of Lincoln's oratorical technique, scholars have advanced numerous explanations, all partially true, many surely playing some role in the speech's effectiveness, but none fully satisfactory. They have pointed to its parallels with classical Greek funeral oratory—the tradition of Pericles's encomium to Athenian democracy—with its praise for the fallen and exhortations for the living. The Greek tradition reveled in antitheses, especially of life and death—the very antitheses that Lincoln invokes so powerfully at Gettysburg (see Cooper, 1932; Hurt, 1980; Smiley, 1917).[5] He set in opposition, as well, word and deed, mortality and immortality. But although he may have identified the deepest polarities of the historical moment, the use of antitheses was by no means uncommon in the political rhetoric of Lincoln's day, and later. Others have argued that in an age of rhetorical efflorescence, Lincoln launched a more spare and muscular form of political speech, without figurative language, shorn of most coupling words (Wills, 1992). Some have noted a high proportion of Anglo-Saxon rather than Latinate terms in the Address (Barton, 1930). But any speech beginning with the phrase "Four score and seven" and ending with a highly complex sentence of 82 words, including four subordinate clauses, is hardly a model of simplicity. (As Strunk and White noted in their classical writer's manual, "The President could have got into his sentence with a plain 'Eighty-seven,' a saving of two words and less of a strain on the listeners' powers of multiplication." [1959, p. 63]). Other critics have pointed to many Latinate terms (see Wills, 1992). Although it is free of formal tropes, the speech displays artful repetitions. Parallel phrases are enunciated in staccato style. Certain words—such as "here," "that," and "dedicate" or "dedicated"—are repeated numerous times, linking successive sentences (Wills, 1992). In general, these repetitions surely have the effect of building the speech's rhetorical power, but rhetoricians have condemned as well as praised some of them (Barton, 1930).

In an age dominated by evangelical Protestantism and in which the King James Bible was the central cultural document, Lincoln's words resonated with scripture. The opening phrase—that complicated rendering of the years since the Declaration of Independence—echoes the familiar Psalm (90:10) allotting "threescore years and ten" to human life, helping to give Lincoln's words a tone of religious dignity (Wills, 1978). The notion of a "new birth" of freedom might have touched his audience's New Testament-inspired sense of the need to be "born again" (John: 3:3). Garry Wills takes the argument of scriptural and religious allusion still further, arguing that Lincoln's use of "our fathers," despite its explicitly political reference, had religious overtones, and comparing the notion of "bringing forth" a new nation to the miraculous conception of Jesus (1978). But the scriptural references, if that they be, are fleeting and rather vague even to be called allusions. They are not explicit, as in many another Lincoln address, such as, for example, his "House Divided" speech of five years earlier. Scholars also point to cultural and intellectual fashions of Lincoln's time as contributing to the Address's resounding reception, such as the mourning conventions of the new rural cemetery movement or Transcendentalism's notion of history as a progressive working out of extramundane ideals (such as equality) (Wills, 1978). Yet the Address remains in the national consciousness, independently of trends in the cultural context of the 1860s.

Surely all of these elements—the conventions of Greek funeral oratory, the use of antitheses, the relatively spare oratorical style, the artful repetitions, the scriptural language, the surrounding cultural and intellectual trends— play some role in contributing to the power of Lincoln's oratory. But a still more profound explanation of the potency of the Address, its lasting hold on national consciousness, may be found on a psychological plane. A clue lies in a factor observed by Robert Lowell in the early 1960s: in a speech to bury the dead, he noted, there is "a curious, insistent use of birth images" (1964, p. 88).

Grof's Basic Perinatal Matrices

For Stanislav Grof, the birth experience is of "paramount significance" in psychic life (1985, p. 197): memories and impressions of it lie deeply buried in both individual and collective unconscious, impelling behavior. In psychedelic therapy and Holotropic Breathwork, as we've noted, clients frequently encounter a "perinatal" realm of the unconscious in which themes of birth and death are not only dominant but intimately intermingled. The entire realm, states Grof, points to "the strong representation of birth and death in our unconscious psyche and the close association between them"

(2000, p. 29); it is, he says, "as if these two aspects of the human experience were somehow one" (1993, p. 28). This mixture of themes of birth and death is a reflection of the actual birth experience, which is, in Grof's view, a life-threatening trauma, the most profound that we endure. As such, it leaves "deep unconscious imprints in the psyche" (2000, pp. 31–32). The perinatal realm, however, cannot be reduced to a reliving of biological birth. Rather, the birth process represents a "core" experience in which its associated archetypal themes can be organized, and which helps to reveal their dynamics (1985, 1988). It provides a conceptual model that allows us to understand deep elements of the individual and collective unconscious. Those elements are naturally organized as a "death–rebirth experience" (1985).

This death–rebirth experience occurs in four "typical thematic clusters" that follow stages of the biological birth process (1985, p. 99). We have alluded before to Grof's Basic Perinatal Matrices, or BPMs, numbered I through IV, but the task at hand now requires us to delve into them more deeply. The first of them, BPM I, corresponds to the fetus's amniotic existence, between conception and the onset of birth contractions (1985, 1988, 1993, 2000). In a healthy generative process, the fetus's interuterine existence is close to ideal, offering full security and protection. The experience is of serenity and tranquility. Those ideal conditions come to an abrupt end with the onset of contractions and BPM II. Suddenly the soon-to-be-born child senses the world closing in: the environment becomes painful and life-threatening. The fetus seems to be caught in an apocalyptic event, raising a sense of overwhelming peril, the specter of death. "It is no wonder," writes Grof, "that death and birth are so closely related in this matrix" (1993, p. 47). BPM III, however, offers an escape, but one requiring intense struggle. The cervix opens, and the fetus begins its passage through the birth canal. Fighting for survival, still experiencing a vital threat, it nevertheless senses purpose, direction, and hope. It must be actively involved in the effort, but an end is in view. The dominant emotional theme has changed from overwhelming peril to titanic struggle. Finally, with BPM IV, actual birth, the fetus becomes the newborn child. He or she has achieved liberation, a new existence, a triumphant redemption that recaptures some elements of BPM I.

In Grof's work with non-ordinary states of consciousness, these perinatal themes are often associated with a wide range of imagery drawn from the subject's biographical experience as well as from mythology, art, religion, politics, and other aspects of collective life. Much of Grof's writing, in fact, involves exploring and classifying this infinitely varied imagery. Birth represents the beginning of individual existence, death its end. In the perinatal realm, they are intertwined. That realm forms a link, an intersection, between the biographical level of the psyche and the transpersonal, the realm beyond our individual existence. In the model provided by the birth experience, the perinatal matrices serve as "organizing principles for material from other levels of the unconscious" (1985, p. 101). They can, Grof reports, "provide us with a doorway to what Jung called the collective unconscious" (1993, p. 29). BPM I might be accompanied, for example, with imagery of nourishing nature, social harmony, or a golden age; BPM II with that of death, the horrors of war, descents into an underworld, and dark nights of the soul; BPM III with epic battles, passionate exertions, and conquest; BPM IV with resolution, rebirth, salvation, and the reclaiming of religious meaning. Especially significant is the pattern of imagery formed by the four matrices, implying a "universal archetypal sequence" deeply rooted in the human psyche (2000, p. 150).

Grof's application of these concepts to the sociopolitical realm and to history is limited, largely focused on asserting the perinatal roots of violence (see 1993 and 2000). The life-and-death struggles of the birth canal, he suggests, "may actually be partially responsible for wars, revolutions, and similar atrocities" (1993, p. 213). In support of that assertion, Grof cites the historical investigations of Lloyd deMause. Grof had been aware of those studies since shortly after the publication of his first book, when deMause contacted him to report the congruity between their independently derived ideas (Grof, 1993, p. 214).

With Freudian premises, deMause had examined the comments of wartime leaders, looking especially for "personal imagery, metaphors, slips, side comments, jokes, scribbles on the edges of documents and so on." Such spontaneous remarks, he said, amounted to "free associations." Eventually deMause found that, with striking frequency, such associations entailed images related to birth. The group fantasies of wartime, he concluded, resurrect feelings of being strangled and trapped in the birth canal, a state that seemingly can be relieved only by violent struggle (deMause, 1982, pp. 91–94). Such fantasies move from a sense of pregnant tension before combat, to explosive relief when battle finally breaks out. DeMause provides numerous instances of birth-related wartime metaphors; examples later cited by Grof include Samuel Adams's speaking during the American

Revolution of "the child of Independence now struggling for birth" and an official message transmitted to Washington announcing the successful detonation of the atom bomb: "The baby was born" (deMause, 1982, p. 97; Grof, 1993, p. 215; 2000, pp. 304–305). DeMause and Grof coincide in this argument: The powerful emotions and energies that are part of our birth experience remain within us, often inadequately integrated. Under certain circumstances, the potentially destructive perinatal energies, particularly those stemming from a sense of overwhelming threat and a need for titanic struggle, can be mustered for individual or collective violence. War can thus be seen, in deMause's words, as "a rebirth fantasy of enormous power" (deMause, 1996). The leader, asserts Grof, is someone who is "under a stronger influence than the perinatal energies than the average person" (2000, p. 308) and who can mobilize them in others.

While DeMause's theoretical framework is Freudian, Grof's analysis of the perinatal matrices, derived from observing thousands of experiences in non-ordinary states of consciousness, is a notion that emerges from transpersonal psychology. That analysis provides a meaningful classification of archetypal imagery in the Jungian collective unconscious—and it admits of a much wider application to the study of history than it has yet been given. From his earliest writings, Grof has noted that the various matrices can be associated with images of sociopolitical conditions and, especially, upheavals (see 1975, pp. 115–149; 2000, pp. 302–303). In his historical overview of Western thought, Richard Tarnas interprets the evolution of epistemology over the last several centuries in terms of Grof's matrices (1991). (The Epilogue to *The Passion of the Western Mind*, then, might be regarded as the outstanding example of transpersonal psychohistory to date.) The archetypal *sequence* of matrices, Tarnas notes, forms a "powerful dialectic" that is often experienced on a collective as well as individual level and can apply to "the evolution of an entire culture" (1991, p. 429).

Potentially, that sequence also has very fruitful applications in the study of political rhetoric. DeMause and Grof have noted isolated phrases pointing to the importance of birth imagery in the comments of political leaders, but an equally significant element in sustained analysis of political rhetoric may lie in the powerful dialectic of transitions from one perinatal stage to another. Since the experience of these matrices is universal and deep within each of us, the associated imagery can be mobilized as a powerful political force, particularly when that imagery indeed reflects the realities of collective life. Some political leaders have instinctively recognized that,

177

and some of the greatest of them have shown an intuitive grasp of elements of that "universal archetypal sequence" which Grof has defined.

Consider, for example, one of the most familiar passages of political rhetoric of the twentieth century, the peroration to Winston Churchill's speech to the House of Commons on June 4, 1940, after the evacuation at Dunkirk (Churchill, 1940). For the British forces, Dunkirk was a narrow escape from the threat of annihilation. Although the worst did not come to pass, thousands of men and essential materiel were lost, and the moment was as dark as any in British history. After reviewing the battle and assessing the subsequent military situation, Churchill raises the specter of a German invasion. In some of his most stirring rhetoric, he then rallies his countrymen to resistance:

> Even though large tracts of Europe and many old and famous States have fallen or may fall into the grip of the Gestapo and all the odious apparatus of Nazi rule, we shall not flag or fail. We shall go on to the end, we shall fight in France, we shall fight on the seas and oceans, we shall fight with growing confidence and growing strength in the air, we shall defend our island, whatever the cost may be, we shall fight on the beaches, we shall fight on the landing grounds, we shall fight in the fields and in the streets, we shall fight in the hills; we shall never surrender, and even if, which I do not for a moment believe, this island or a large part of it were subjugated and starving, then our Empire beyond the seas, armed and guarded by the British Fleet, would carry on the struggle, until in God's good time, the new world, with all its power and might, steps forth to the rescue and the liberation of the old.

With its near strangulation of the British military, Dunkirk represented the classic situation of BPM II—as did the falling of neighboring states, the dire military situation, and the threat of invasion. But in his peroration—with its insistent mustering of the will to struggle, its dogged refusal to surrender, its repeated exhortations to battle however ubiquitous the battlegrounds, and its offering of hope and of growing confidence and strength despite the implacable threat—Churchill's imagery moves forcefully into the elements of BPM III. And with the promised "rescue" in the end by the power and might of the new world, the speech culminates with an image of BPM IV. The eventual result will be not only rescue but "liberation," implying a new life. All will happen "in God's good time," suggesting, however slightly, that both the struggle and the liberation are part of a larger, divinely governed, transcendent order, in which lies the ultimate hope.

Lincoln and the Universal Archetypal Sequence

Much of the power of the Gettysburg Address comes from Lincoln's intuitive mastery of the "universal archetypal sequence," not simply in specific elements and transitions but in its full range. In its brief 272 words, the Address not only immerses us in the entangled themes of birth and death, but leads us, one by one, through all four perinatal matrices, linking them with the national experience and the travail of civil war, using them to forge a sense of national purpose.[6] The opening sentence of the Address, which Lincoln set down as a complete paragraph, corresponds to the first basic perinatal matrix:

> Four score and seven years ago, our fathers brought forth on this continent, a new nation, conceived in Liberty and dedicated to the proposition that all men are created equal.

"Brought forth" is a biblical term, used in the King James version for generation and giving birth. The term's first appearance, for example, is in Genesis, I: 11: "And God said, Let the earth bring forth grass, the herb yielding seed, and the fruit tree yielding fruit after his kind, whose seed is in itself, upon the earth: and it was so." In the Gospel of Luke, I:31, Mary is told that she will "bring forth a son." Lincoln refers to the birth of the nation, but the more subtle emphasis is on conception, as the next phase, "conceived in Liberty," makes explicit. This image of conception at the opening of the Address has been noted before. As Garry Wills observes, "The suggested image is ... of a *hieros gamos*, a marriage of male heaven ('our fathers') and female earth ('this continent'). And it is a miraculous conception..." (1978, p. xv; see also Wills, 1992, pp. 77–79). From the moment of conception brought about by the male fathers and the female continent, the nation is "dedicated to the proposition that all men are created equal." This post-conception phase, Lincoln implies, is undisturbed, even paradisaic—both terms that Grof applies to BPM I. At this point in the Address, Lincoln gives us no hint that the world of liberty and equality is not achieved. At the very least, the nation seemed to itself to be existing in a realm blessed by those virtues. Grof notes that BPM I is linked with images of happy childhood and, socially, a golden age: Lincoln suggests similar associations for the young United States.

The next sentence, however, tells of the sudden onset of pain, threatening the very existence of the nation:

> Now we are engaged in a great civil war, testing whether that nation, or any nation so conceived and so dedicated, can long endure.

Lincoln not only introduces the theme of war, but raises the threat of national death: Can the nation "long endure"? With that sentence, we are brought suddenly into the imagery of the second perinatal matrix, dominated by the theme and threat of death. Lincoln continues with that theme for the next three sentences—which are linked to the previous one as a single paragraph—focusing on the site of the cemetery and the act of burying the dead:

> We are met on a great battle-field of that war. We have come to dedicate a portion of that field, as a final resting place for those who here gave their lives that that nation might live. It is altogether fitting and proper that we should do this.

The image of death, the result of war and the battlefield, is reinforced by the short, staccato sentences, and the repeated references to the site of the cemetery: This is a "final resting place"; men "gave their lives" here; the dedication of the battlefield as a cemetery is "fitting and proper." In this short second paragraph devoted to themes of the second matrix, Lincoln has indelibly linked the theme of death to his earlier theme of birth. Nevertheless, he gives us a hint of hope: the men gave their lives, but the nation still "might live." With that brief suggestion of hope, he marks the transition to the third perinatal matrix.

People in non-ordinary states immersed in the second matrix, Grof remarks, often see "the futility of life without spirituality" (1993, p. 53). Emerging from images of that matrix, Lincoln's rhetoric, in his next sentence, takes a leap into the transpersonal:

> But in a larger sense, we can not dedicate—we can not consecrate—we can not hallow this ground.

Lincoln employs three verbs—"dedicate," "consecrate," and "hallow"—climbing to progressively higher states of numinosity: "consecrate" is a more sacred term than "dedicate," and "hallow," or make holy, the most sacred of the three. The reference serves to put death and our earthly travails into a spiritual context. The principal theme of the third matrix is struggle, struggle towards an emerging goal. With his following two sentences, Lincoln suggests that not only death but the struggle of battle has a larger, transpersonal meaning:

> The brave men, living and dead, who struggled here, have consecrated it, far above our poor power to add or detract. The world will little note nor long remember what we say here, but it can never forget what they did here.

The struggle of the soldiers at Gettysburg, Lincoln then argues, must become the struggle of all, of the living. In urging the active involvement of the living in the struggles of the dead and of the War, Lincoln expresses the core aspect of the third matrix:

> It is for us the living, rather, to be dedicated here to the unfinished work which they who fought here have thus far so nobly advanced.

The repeated use of the word "here," referring to the cemetery—Lincoln uses it six times in the course of the Address—is a recurring reminder that the struggle is one of life and death. But in the first phrases of the final sentence of the address, by far its longest, Lincoln asserts that the great struggle has a greater purpose, though he does not yet define it:

> It is rather for us to be here dedicated to the great task remaining before us—that from these honored dead we take increased devotion to that cause for which they gave the last full measure of devotion—that we here highly resolve that these dead shall not have died in vain—

In these staccato exhortations, Lincoln insistently rephrases the need for struggle, linking it with sense of purpose: We must be "dedicated" to a "great task," take "increased devotion" to "that cause" for which the dead soldiers devotedly gave their lives, and "highly resolve" that they not have died in vain.

181

Finally, in the following phrase, Lincoln moves to the fourth perinatal matrix, announcing that the great, transcendent purpose is rebirth:

> that this nation, under God, shall have a new birth of freedom....

In discussing characteristics of BPM IV, Grof states that it provides "a sense of reclaiming our divine nature and cosmic status" (2000, p. 54). With the simple phrase "under God," which he certainly said at Gettysburg but which may not have been in his first written draft (see Wills, 1993), Lincoln reasserts that the national rebirth is divinely advocated if not ordained. The Gettysburg Address followed the Emancipation Proclamation by some ten months, and the "new birth of freedom" to which he refers is above all the eradication of slavery. With that, the nation is to be born again and indeed reassert its "cosmic status" and national purpose as the protector of not only of the political liberty in which it was conceived, but of the equality to which it was originally dedicated:

> —and that government of the people, by the people, for the people, shall not perish from the earth.

The great purpose of the War, Lincoln asserts, is the preservation of popular, republican government, made possible by a necessary rebirth of its original ideals. In the classic form of the fourth matrix, the rebirth is a redemption that reclaims elements of the first.

"A deep experiential encounter with birth and death," writes Grof,

> is regularly associated with an existential crisis of extraordinary proportions, during which the individual seriously questions the meaning of existence, as well as his or her basic values and life strategies. This crisis can be resolved only by connecting with deep, intrinsic spiritual dimensions of the psyche and elements of the collective unconscious. (1985, p. 100)

For Abraham Lincoln, who bore heavily the burdens of wartime leadership, the Civil War was, personally, just such an existential crisis. It forced him to question the meaning of the nation's existence, its basic values and strategies. The Gettysburg Address represents the distillation of a personal process of both questioning and questing that he underwent during the

War. That process pushed him to connect with spiritual dimensions of his own psyche, and with elements of the collective unconscious. It involved a deep encounter with death, in which he perceived, on some level, the archetypal connection between death and birth, and even the universal archetypal sequence represented by the perinatal matrices.

In articulating the nation's struggle in terms that follow that sequence, Lincoln portrayed the Civil War as a kind of rite of passage. Such rites are almost universal in indigenous cultures, practiced at times of critical change in individual or cultural life. Their "common denominator," writes Grof, "is a profound confrontation with death and subsequent transcendence" (2000, p. 225). They typically attempt to induce a "psychospiritual death and rebirth"—dying to an old role and being reborn into a new one (2000, pp. 9–10). In Christianity, this basic theme of death and rebirth is clearly related to the Resurrection and the Johannine need to be "born again," but it is still more universal, applied in other religious and esoteric systems. And in all of those systems, it is seen as healing and transforming. Through symbolic death and rebirth, the psyche can be liberated from sin or the unbearable tensions of life (Grof, 2000, pp. 52, 109). With that redemption comes forgiveness and compassion.

Carrying this analysis further, we might argue that the luminous sanity of Lincoln's Second Inaugural Address—his other speech that is incontestably part of the national canon—owes something to that process of personal evolution that he himself had undergone, and into which he was attempting to lead the nation. In the Second Inaugural, Lincoln displays some of the principal characteristics of psychological health as described by humanistic and transpersonal psychology. Rather than attributing all evil to the enemy—the common projection of wartime, especially after a war so bloody and bitter as that one—he acknowledges the participation of his own side in the source of the conflict. That source he has now explicitly identified as the sin of slavery. The divine punishment is appropriately meted out to both sides, to the South for holding slaves, to the North, implicitly, for participating in the national and economic system that sustained it. The entire process of sin and justice is placed in a transpersonal context, as a product of the "providence of God"; yet clear human action is called for, and that action must be dominated not by vengeance but compassion: "With malice towards none; with charity for all; with firmness in the right, as God gives us to see the right...." Rather than speaking of the South as other, as still the enemy, Lincoln identifies with the entire nation, exhorting his countrymen "to bind up the nation's wounds; to care for him who shall have borne the battle, and for his widow and his orphan—to do all which may achieve and cherish a just and lasting peace among ourselves, and with all nations."

Conclusion

Lincoln had spoken to an audience at Gettysburg of some 15,000 people (Wills, 1992). In the immediate aftermath, he himself saw the speech as a "failure" and the public as "disappointed"—so he confided to Ward Lamon (cited in Sandburg, 1939, v. II, p. 472). Everett apparently thought otherwise: he wrote a note to Lincoln saying that "I should be glad if I could flatter myself that I came as near to the central idea of the occasion in two hours as you did in two minutes" (cited in Stern, 1940, p. 788). Immediate editorial comments often followed party lines; not a few were hostile or dismissive. But the speech was widely reproduced in print, in rural and small-town weeklies as well as the urban dailies, reaching readers across the country. By the time of the Second Inaugural Address 16 months later, it had begun its march to the core of the national canon. Charles Francis Adams, Jr., a representative of the skeptical New England intellectual elite, recorded, after the latter speech, what was to become the American consensus: "That rail-splitting lawyer is one of the wonders of the day. Once at Gettysburg and now again on a great occasion he has shown a capacity for rising to the demands of the hour which we should not expect from orators or men of the schools" (cited in Edwards & Hankins, 1962, pp. 86–87). By the early twentieth century, a quintessential man of the schools, the Earl Curzon, Chancellor of the University of Oxford, could refer to the Gettysburg Address and the Second Inaugural as two of the three "masterpiece[s] of modern English eloquence" (cited in Barondess, 1954, p. 47). And by the time Carl Sandburg was writing his biography of Lincoln in the 1930s, the Gettysburg Address had become, in Sandburg's words, "The Great American Poem" (cited in Edwards & Hankins, 1962, p. 87).

Why did the Gettysburg Address resonate so powerfully in American consciousness? Because it succinctly articulated a national meaning and artfully expressed a transcendent good that could emerge from the trauma of civil war: the rebirth of freedom and equality. And what was the secret of Lincoln's artful expression? All the factors that historians have identified may well have played a role, but underlying them is a factor revealed by transpersonal psychology, with its enlarged models of the psyche. At a time of extraordinary crisis, Lincoln questioned, for himself, the very meaning of the nation's existence. The relentless encounter with death, on levels both personal and social, pushed him into contact with spiritual elements of the psyche, especially the primordial intermixture of death and birth. Drawing intuitively on the collective unconscious, Lincoln used imagery that tapped into the death-rebirth experience expressed in the spiritual life of many cultures. His intuitive grasp of that experience was so strong that he expressed it, concisely but completely, in terms that follow what Stanslav Grof has identified as a universal archetypal sequence of thematic clusters characteristic of the perinatal realm of the psyche. Lincoln touched in succession on core elements of each of that sequence's four matrices. The extraordinary response to the speech, its persistence over time in the national consciousness, its central place in American civil religion, are evidence, drawn from political history, of the power of those elements in the collective unconscious. They are indicators, as well, of how the study of political rhetoric, and the field of psychohistory itself, might be enriched by incorporating ideas from transpersonal psychology. Ultimately, we might hope, the recognition of such indicators could portend a mutually enriching dialogue between the transpersonal movement and the discipline of history.

Notes

1 An earlier version of this chapter was published as "Transpersonal Psychology and the Study of History: A Reading of the Gettysburg Address" in *The Journal of Transpersonal Psychology*, 36(1), 2004, 1–17.

2 In the year before Langer's address, Alexander and Juliette George had published a psychoanalytic study of Woodrow Wilson (1956). Charles Strozier, founding editor of the *Psychohistory Review*, is the author of *Lincoln's Quest for Union: A Psychological Portrait* (1982). No epoch has garnered more attention from psychohistorians than the Third Reich, and no person more than its leader. See, for example, Rudolph Binion's *Hitler Among the Germans* (1976) and Robert Waite's *The Psychopathic God: Adolf Hitler* (1977). Victor Wolfenstein's *The Victims of Democracy: Malcolm X and the Black Revolution* (1981) is another major work of the genre.

3 See Jung's *Essays on Contemporary Events: The Psychology of Nazism*, published in 1946. Especially notable are the Preface and Epilogue,

and the essays titled "Wotan" (originally published in 1936), "After the Catastrophe" (1945) and "The Fight with the Shadow" (1946). All are included in *Civilization in Transition*, volume 10 of Jung (1964).

4 Some notable studies of historical group processes are Rudolph Binion's examination of German society's response to Hitler (1976), George Kren and Leon Rappoport's work on the Holocaust (1980), Robert Jay Lifton's account of Nazi doctors and their behavior (1986), and Charles Strozier's exploration of the psychology of fundamentalism (1994). David Beisel's study of the origins of World War II makes use of family systems theory (2003).

5 Wills (1992) presents these various analyses of Lincoln's rhetoric, and my brief account of them relies heavily on his study. His analysis of the parallels between Greek funeral orations and Lincoln's Address is in Chapter 1: "Oratory of the Greek Revival," 41–62.

6 There are several extant versions of the Address, with slight variations. Stenographic accounts differ on Lincoln's spoken words. It is not certain that we have his delivery text, the written version that he spoke from; but if we do, he apparently departed from it. Lincoln revised the text after the fact at least four times. The last of these revisions, written in his own hand at the request of historian George Bancroft, was intended to be lithographed for sale at the Baltimore Sanitary Fair of February, 1864. As the final text that Lincoln authorized, it is generally accepted as representing his ultimate preference. It is the version most widely reproduced and the one used in this analysis. (See Wills, 1992, pp. 191–203.)

An Apologia

A different dimension: These chapters have been written out of the premise that "the further limits of our being" do indeed "plunge into an altogether other dimension of existence" from the world of our everyday, sensible awareness. As religious traditions of all descriptions have done for millennia, they assume that a primary purpose of human life is to gain some cognizance of that dimension, and to grow in it, to deepen our awareness of its presence and functions in our lives. No doubt there are personal temperaments that have no need for such a pursuit; but if a "mystical" or "supernatural" or "spiritual" realm is fundamental to reality, and human life is distinguished by its capacity to comprehend, in some measure, its own wider contexts, then the striving to be in harmony with that realm is surely a fundamental element in what it means to be human. Civilizations, in all times and everywhere, have defined themselves by their own particular style of that pursuit—as expressed in the beliefs that give it identity, the literature and/or ritualistic practices that give it meaning, the architectural monuments that embody its aspirations. That alone is testimony to the inescapable nature of this striving, and to its call to us—be it soft or loud, whether in a whisper or a shout—as we each strut and fret our hour on this earthly stage.

In previous epochs, particular social styles of religious belief, and the civilizations of which they are the core, have been free to develop in relative isolation, reinforcing their society's trust in their absolute truth, in their singular superiority as a definition of the real. When the different civilizations met, it often was in violent confrontation—only reinforcing, on each side, the view of its own society as central, as civilization itself at war with barbarism. But we live now in times characterized by the interpenetration of civilizations—the constant exposure, in a globalized world, to beliefs and styles of worship originally rooted in different regions of the planet. However disruptive the process might be to both culture and politics, this constant familiarization, both direct and virtual, has the effect of lending legitimacy to what has been regarded as entirely "other," and to undermine the absolute truth claims of one's own native systems of belief.

With its awareness of world religious and wisdom traditions, the trans-personal perspective has risen in this globalizing environment. It has taken hold in societies that have grown progressively more secular, and thus more independent of their formerly dominant religious orthodoxies. And it may be no accident that this rising vision has been strong in the United States, with its tradition of separation of church and state, and its constitutional mandate to permit a pluralism of religious outlooks, to "make no law respecting an establishment of religion or prohibiting the free exercise thereof." To the degree that it lives up to these ideals, such a society, by implication, lends legitimacy to different spiritual outlooks, and grants to the individual citizen the authority to decide among competing claims of truth. As we have seen throughout these pages, transpersonal thought accepts, in William James's phrase, "the reality of the unseen" (1902/1929): It grants an element of validity, especially a deeper psychological validity, to claims of religious truth; but it also recognizes the severe limitations of those claims, whenever they are tied inextricably to verbal formulations.

The transpersonal perspective has arisen, too, in societies whose more elite intellectual life is dominated by modern science. It incorporates a sharp awareness of the value of scientifically established truth claims; it embraces the procedures and instrumental truth-value of those claims, even as it rejects the strictly materialistic worldview that is sometimes assumed to be allied with them. It looks to science itself, in its more advanced and theoretical expressions, to undermine a scientifically outmoded scientism.

What, then, is the appeal of this perspective, which flouts both religious orthodoxies on the one hand, and the materialistic paradigm on the other? Which embraces the longing for spiritual awareness, but rejects the dogmas and hierarchies of organized religion? Which accepts the premises and respects the procedures of modern science, but sees contemporary science as pointing in a direction that recognizes a non-material foundation to reality? And which sees a resolution to these polarities in the ever-unfolding but never-ending effort to penetrate the mysteries of the human psyche? Why is a growing segment of contemporary Western society inclined look for direct experience of mystical realms, but to seek it apart from traditional religious organizations, or perhaps through several different paths of spiritual practice? What are some of the dynamics behind the fact that so much of the modern Western population, especially its younger members, describe themselves as "spiritual but not religious"?

A Personal Story

The broad, sociological answers to those questions, I am not prepared to address in any comprehensive fashion. Instead, as closure to these ruminations, I offer my own personal story, with its particular limitations, and with whatever ways it might reflect the dynamics, if not the particulars, of the personal stories in the hearts of others. Contemporary scholarship emphasizes the notion that every narrative, every interpretation of truth, is formed by a particular, limited human consciousness; and it looks for authenticity in a writer's explicit awareness of some of the specific cultural influences that have shaped his or her perceptions. Let us hope that the tale that follows is justified on those grounds.

I grew up, I sometimes like to say, in the thirteenth century. The scene was no monastery in medieval Umbria, but a Roman Catholic school in Houston, Texas, in the 1950s. In terms of belief systems, the gap between the two might not have been wide. That Cold War era, before the "opening of windows" represented by the Second Vatican Council, bred an especially dogmatic form of Catholicism—rendered in still more simplified form by the Sisters of Divine Providence, in their formidable black habits with starched white headpieces, to the pliable young minds at St. Anne's School. I vividly recall a depiction on a classroom wall—was it in the fifth grade?—of a polychrome Last Judgment. If I recall correctly, it was mounted on the wall with windows, so that anytime we students glanced out onto the playground, we were reminded of our Final Reward. No doubt there were swaths of blue a the top, with a grey-bearded God the Father benignly welcoming the "good souls"; but what stuck in my mind were those dominant reds and yellows at the bottom, where the "lost souls" suffered the flames of eternal torture—limitless torture, of infinite intensity, forever and ever and ever.

Mind you, I would not say that I gained no benefits from my Catholic early education. The nuns, as I remember them, were certainly good-hearted and well-intentioned, and they were nothing if not dedicated to fulfilling the will of God as they saw it. Instruction was of a decent quality; and out of what they had to offer, I certainly absorbed a sense that there was "something else": a spiritual and moral realm beyond the mundane doings of everyday life, some purpose to living other than the gaining of fame and riches. To this day, I can't escape a certain distant affinity for some of elements of Catholic ritual: few artistic expressions seem more moving to me than, say, the strains of Gregorian plainsong.

No doubt the good sisters told me all that they should have about God's infinite mercy and love; but the dominant sentiment that I absorbed from their teachings was, in short, abject fear. Life was presented as a moral test, to be passed or failed at the moment of death; and those who failed were headed inexorably for eternal damnation. I was close to convinced that my final end was to be among them. Hellfire, in a downright physical form out somewhere in the cosmos, was my ultimate fate.

That, to be sure, is a miserable way to spend one's childhood.

Classmates I certainly had who, pushed through the same educational system, managed to escape such searing scars. By temperament or background, they were not so burdened by the message; they could largely ignore it altogether, or somehow focus on its more hopeful promises of salvation. No doubt I was set up, by an inborn fear-based temperament and by early experience, to absorb the teachings in their most threatening guise.

The fault was not with any failure of familial care. Mine was as loving and attentive a mother as a son could ask for, and her attentions towards me, the youngest sibling, were reinforced by those of my two significantly older sisters. In her Catholicism, my mother was devotional but not rigid. But nearly all lives, it seems, have their primal wounds, and the great one in our family fell suddenly on a morning in late June of 1946. My father, an eminent attorney and prominent civic leader, and as vibrant and warm-hearted a presence as one could imagine, did not wake up. He had died during the night of a massive heart attack, at the age of 40. I had been on the earth, under his loving gaze, for 21 months.

Inexplicably, in my experience, my father had disappeared. At two years old, one's point of reference is only oneself: on some level, I'm sure, I felt that I was responsible for his vanishing. I must have sent him away, by some terrible behavior, though I had no idea what it was. That was my template, and the template with which I entered St. Anne's School.

Somehow, I think, the image of God the Father seeped into the place in my psyche reserved for father, and I lived in fear of sending Him away, and maybe my mother as well, through some other vile if never-understood misdeed. Add to that the threat of hellfire, and the result was a mortal fear of any misdeeds at all. I reacted by striving to be the best and most rule-bound kid that I could possibly be.

But following all the imagined rules in my mind turned out to be a psychologically impossible feat. That was due, in part, to the phrasing of the rules as they came through to me, but it was due mostly to intensely literal way that I received them—compounded, soon enough, by what I now see as a childhood obsessive-compulsive disorder, but what then, in theological parlance, would have been labeled "scrupulosity." Almost any action, in my mind, was in danger of being sinful. As Catholics, for example, we were enjoined from eating meat on Fridays, and directed to attend Mass on Sundays. The doing of one and the not-doing of the other were mortal sins, grounds for eternal damnation. But what if my peanut-butter and jelly sandwich had absorbed molecules of Thursday's chicken from the kitchen counter, or my attention during Mass had wandered away from the priest's words and actions—was I then in full compliance? Or what if, thinking of the new pea-coat that I relished, the thought occurred to me that I should vow to refrain from wearing it; had I just taken such a vow? Was I now required to go without it?

You get the picture. The examples may seem extreme, but the problem was only compounded, in spades, with the onset of puberty. In the popular Catholic theology of that era, sexuality was the projection of all that was uncontrolled and unsubmissive and evil in humanity—all that made it worthy of that red-and-yellow fate depicted on the classroom wall. Anything associated with sexuality, at all, risked mortal sin. The sexual impulse was enmeshed in rules—deadly clear, explicit rules, all expressed as "don't." Dating someone three times in a row, I recall being told, might constitute "going steady," which could be an "occasion of sin." Occasion of sin—that was a crucial concept. It, too, was a sin. It meant willfully putting yourself in any position where you might be "tempted." And the evil deed that might tempt you included what were called "bad thoughts." It wasn't enough not to *do* it—whatever "it" was—it was a sin if you let yourself have a thought about doing it. Even if you didn't think about it, but put yourself in a situation where you *might* think about it, *that* was a sin. Or at least, that's how I took in the teaching. And since an occasion of sin was itself a sin, it stood to reason that an occasion of an occasion of sin was a sin.

One didn't have to go further with this reasoning to realize that the real occasion of sin was life itself. The core message of St. Anne's School—as I, with my temperament and wounds, got it—was something like this: Truth was certain, but revealed to someone else, not me. Outside of that truth was violent suffering for all eternity. The way to enter truth was by accepting authority, totally. Life was a testing ground, loaded with divinely planted obstacles, everywhere. It must be gotten through, above all, without making any wrong moves. The dominant emotion was fear—terror—of the wrong move.

What orientation could be more constraining?

I would like to say that I threw over these imprinted images in a fit of adolescent rebellion, but my flight from them, in truth, was more of a slow drift. Elements of it began back at St. Anne's, but I went from there to a Catholic high school, and then to a Catholic college. The high school, as I recall, did little to help me out of my tangled conundrums; but the ambience at the University of St. Thomas, especially as the liberating effects of Vatican II took hold, was decidedly different. Faculty might disagree with one another, even over theological questions. I majored in English, and the demanding requirements of literary analysis rewarded original ideas. Creative arts, and the study of them, flourished on campus. Students engaged in intense discussions on all sorts of issues, from existentialist philosophy to Great Society politics. My anxiety about not following moral teachings to the letter faded, bit by bit. Gradually, I learned more fully the art of thinking for myself.

Looking back on my slow drift away from Catholic dogma and practice, I'd say now that it was driven by a sense of suffocation. On some deep level, I required the freedom to navigate through the flow of ideas in a way that corresponded to my own proclivities and experience. I needed the liberty to find authority less in external sources, more from within. Once in graduate school, I wrote my doctoral dissertation on the literary and social critic H.L. Mencken, an agnostic (and supremely artful writer) who stated that "the liberation of the human mind has never been furthered" by "pedants and priests." "[I]t has been furthered," he averred, "by gay fellows who heaved dead cats into sanctuaries and then went roistering down the highways of the world, proving to all men that doubt, after all, was safe..." (cited in Boyd, 1925, p. 85).

Mencken's verbal "roistering" was not my style either, but in some fundamental way, I knew that I was a pluralist. Even from early on, I had an inarticulate, gut-level sense that reality stretches far beyond understanding, and that it can be got hold of in many different ways, from many different perspectives. By habit of mind, deep in my core, I sensed a limitation to any mode of expressing truths. I felt suffocated by overconfidence in any single view, and I did not accept that whole categories of people were absolutely wrong. What in the name of God, then, could be more ludicrously implausible than, say, the doctrine of papal infallibility?

Life appeared to me less and less about avoiding wrong moves, and more and more about personal growth, about the progressive enrichment of experience and deepening of capacities. I pursued that growth through varied means, including relationships, reading, travel, the arts, meditation, psychotherapy—and the study of history. History became my profession, or part of it, and I viewed history, in great measure, as a means of personal acquaintance with people whose lives did not cross paths with mine, in all their variability and varied experiences, with all their wide-ranging views of life, linked by themes and emotions that all of us share as human.

Along the way, I certainly encountered my mentors, living and dead. Here I will mention only a couple of them, beginning with William James, whose influence on me is evident throughout these pages. I wrote a master's thesis on James, submitting it back in 1968; different aspects of his work have proven important to me at different stages of my life, before the thesis and ever since. In James's work, more perhaps than in any other written texts, I found a close match to my own instinctive inclinations of temperament and thought. Especially was that true with his defense of pluralism. Consider this passage from *The Varieties of Religious Experience*, which I must have encountered in my first year of graduate school:

> Ought it to be assumed that the lives of all men should show identical religious elements? In other words, is the existence of so many religious types and creeds regrettable?

> To these questions, I answer "No" emphatically. And my reason is that I do not see how it is possible that creatures in such different positions and with such different powers as human individuals are, should have exactly the same functions and the same duties. No two of us have identical difficulties, nor should we be expected to work out identical solutions. Each, from his peculiar angle of observation, takes in a certain sphere of fact and trouble, which each must deal with in a unique manner.... If an Emerson were forced to be a Wesley, or a Moody forced to be a Whitman, the total human consciousness of the divine would suffer.... Each attitude being a syllable in human nature's total message, it takes the whole of us to spell the

meaning out completely.... We must frankly recognize the fact
that we live in partial systems, and that the parts are not inter-
changeable in the spiritual life.... Unquestionably, some men
have the completer experience and the higher vocation, here
just as in the social world; but for each man to stay in his own
experience, whate're it be, and for others to tolerate him there,
is surely best. (1920/1929, pp. 476–478)

Could there be a more articulate refutation to dogmatism, in any form,
than that?

Beginning in those college years, I drifted away from organized religion.
My quest for personal growth might be viewed in terms of Maslow's
ideal of self-actualization: it was about a personally fulfilling life, about
realizing my personal capacities, whatever they may be. A secular stance,
even a materialistic one, was a comfort to me: its denial of an afterlife
implied a far better fate than eternal torture. I felt no investment in
persisting in personal form after my time on this earth: far better not
to be, than to risk misery without end. Towards the spiritual nostrums
of my more New Age-oriented friends I felt a decided resistance: they
seemed intellectually ungrounded, and further, talk of literal spiritual
worlds or beings in any form was too suggestive, for my comfort, of my
early indoctrination.

Despite taking refuge in secularism, however, I never quite lost that primal
sense that there was "something else" beyond the everyday realm presented to our senses. And as Maslow and Sutich discovered for themselves, I
found that my quest for personal growth led on to a spiritual search, of
some kind. Still in graduate school, I took up a practice of meditation—in
the first instance, Hindu-derived Transcendental Meditation. Over subsequent years, I engaged, too, in therapies such as bioenergetics and the
Bonny Method, and in yoga practices. The people I was most drawn to, I
could not help but notice, had a strongly spiritual side; a couple of my clos-
est friends, in fact, threw themselves wholeheartedly into renegade branches of Asian religion and flew off for a time to live in India. My first wife,
Sandy—we were married early in my graduate school years and amicably
divorced nine years later—delved into Jungian psychology. My current
wife, Ginger, is a spiritual seeker of the first order, and eventually urged me
towards a practice of Buddhist-derived Vipassana (Insight) meditation,
which she practices devotedly and now teaches.

During our long courtship, Ginger and I, mostly at her urging, began to look for some spiritually oriented community; we soon affiliated with a Unitarian church, where I eventually took an active role. Although it has its assumptions, Unitarianism seemed as free of dogma as any entity calling itself a church could be; it explored respectfully the world's spiritual traditions; and it imposed no mandates on its participants. It was as close as one could be to "spiritual but not religious" and still have some institutional continuity, with a community that met on a reliable schedule. Where it seemed weak, to both Ginger and me, was in its lack of means to promote some direct spiritual experience.

Even while withdrawing from the forms of institutional religion that I had known in my earlier years, I retained a respect for "religious experience," as James spoke of it—some manner of reaching beyond intellect to recognize a deeper and wider context of our lives. And I had had enough contact with a few exceptional adepts to feel the effects that a deep immersion in such experience could have on an individual human temperament.

Chief among those adepts has been the Fourteenth Dalai Lama. I have had contact with His Holiness on several occasions; on each of them, I could not help but be mightily impressed by the effect that his mere presence has on the people around him, even those with no background in his tradition. In his proximity, burdens lift and spirits soar. My opportunity to witness that most closely was when I had the good fortune to play host to the Dalai Lama on his visit to Yale University in the fall of 1991 (Figure E.1).

By then I was well into my career as a university teacher and dean of students. In my role as Dean of Jonathan Edwards College at Yale, I had invited His Holiness to visit the University. That invitation followed my trip to his home base of Dharamsala, India, on a journey organized by the Institute of Noetic Sciences, where our relatively small group had an audience with His Holiness at his monastery. My intention with the invitation was to demonstrate to Yale students, in their intellect-dominated and intensely busy world, the power of presence that a truly advanced spiritual adept might exude—and thus, by extension, to give them some perspective on their own busy pursuits, some hint that those intellectual and careerist preoccupations, for all their value, might not be fundamental. I was by no means disappointed. There is a great deal to say about that visit, but in this context I'll report on only two incidents, illustrating His Holiness's effect on the students, and on me personally.

195

E.1 The author with His Holiness the Dalai Lama, Yale University, 1991. (Katherine Lantuch.)

The Dalai Lama engaged in a full day of activities during that visit, in several different forums, one of which was a meeting with some forty or so students of the residential college in the living room of the College Master. By and large, the students there had limited knowledge of the Dalai Lama and his history; as they gathered to meet him, there was understandably a great deal of tension in the room, nervousness about how to act before such an alien dignitary in monastic robes, what kinds of questions to ask in what was billed as a dialogue with students. When His Holiness entered the room, he immediately detected the tension—and he simply laughed. He must, he said, appear very different, but if they and he could simply have a discussion "as one human being to another," he was sure that they would have a very good time. In an instant, the tension in that room blew out of the room's French doors like a wind. Within moments, the students were laughing in His Holiness's mental embrace, speaking to him seriously, playfully, authentically, as he recounted stories of his own youth and his experiences as a leader of his people when he was just their age. His presence did its magic, and as the students, after an unforgettably engaging hour, ebulliently filed out, I was in tears.

A few hours later, the Dalai Lama gave an address before a large gathering at the University's major chapel. As he acknowledged the audience's applause after the talk, his gaze fell in my direction, and I felt—very physically—an instant of stillness, as if time had stopped, and what seemed a mild electric jolt. Later, as I recounted that experience to a friend more knowledgeable in the ways of Asian religions, he called it a "shaktipat," a direct transfusion of energy from a guru, a phenomenon well known in Indian traditions.

The point of this tale about the leader of Tibetan Buddhism is that I carried with me, and had reinforced with time, a sense of the value, the personally transformative effects, of direct spiritual experience. But clearly, despite taking up related meditation practices, I was no Tibetan Buddhist, and would not be. True, I might learn much from Buddhist perspectives on the ways of the mind. But I was both too strongly centered in Western culture, and too rational in my approach to life, to jump wholeheartedly into an Asian religious tradition, with its own component of what I saw as quite alien myths and rituals.

In a sense, then, I was caught between two basic stances: an immersion in Western intellectual life, as lived out at an elite university, and an openness to non-rational spiritual experience, as pursued, largely, outside of the academic world. A major factor that helped to bring those two stances together was my discovery of the work of Stanislav Grof.

My first experience of Holotropic Breathwork was in 1988, with one of Stan and Christina Grof's early trainees; some three years later, I attended my first workshop with the Grofs themselves. From the beginning, my experiences in the Breathwork tended towards the numinous, involving a sense of oneness with the cosmos. My attendance at workshops, however, was only occasional, and I recall a marked resistance towards some of the notions bandied about in the Breathwork community, particularly around past-life experiences and reincarnation. Nevertheless, as I began to search more diligently for ways to reconcile my rational and spiritual leanings, it occurred to me that I might look more closely at Stan Grof's writings.

I was in Mexico at the time, on sabbatical from Yale, teaching for a semester at the Universidad de las Américas, Puebla (UDLAP). Having found that the University library had some of Stan's books, I went rummaging around the relevant shelves—when, literally, a book fell off the shelf at my feet. It was Grof's *Beyond the Brain*. I took it up and then made my way through it, perinatal matrices and all. Not all of Stan's ideas, by any means, made full sense to me at the time; but I was impressed by his general philosophical rationale, his highly sophisticated effort to integrate the spiritual experiences he had encountered in psychological explorations with the scientific grounds of Western thought, and to cast it all into a cohesive worldview. I eventually read further in his writings, and attended more of his workshops, primarily with an eye towards understanding more fully Grof's philosophical ideas and their integration with experiences, personal and transcendent, that he attributed to deeper levels of the psyche. With time, I continued to attend workshops and eventually completed the training as a practitioner of Holotropic Breathwork. Stan Grof had become a mentor and philosophical guide.

Holotropic Breathwork, as we've seen, often involves a "death-rebirth experience." In non-ordinary—what Stan prefers to call "holotropic"—states of consciousness, a participant encounters specific pains and difficulties of her life; brings them into a sharper state of awareness; experiences and expresses, without restraint, the associated emotions; and then comes to a new level of acceptance and resolution of the issue. The central insight of the practice is that, in these more profound states of consciousness, this is a natural dynamic, governed by what Stan has called the "inner healer." Our demons are constantly at play in our subconscious; by bringing them into focus in this way, we exorcise them and move towards a deeper level of awareness, of wholeness, more fully integrated, more able to face with equanimity the past and present storms of our lives. The mantra of the Breathwork is to "trust the process." My own experience with the work, both as "breather" or participant and, even more, as a workshop leader, has solidly confirmed the validity of that approach. Buried within our subconscious is an intelligence that dynamically aims for our own health and wholeness, for a progressively more expansive awareness of our deepest human needs and, further, of our interconnectedness with the fabric of reality, with nature and, ultimately, spirit. Is that not experiential evidence that the "further limits of our being plunge ... into an altogether other dimension of existence from the 'sensible' and merely understandable world"?

My academic field is American intellectual history, in which figures such as the American Transcendentalists and William James loom large, and I began to discern and examine ways in which they were precursors to much of the transpersonal perspective expressed in Stan's and related writings. After moving to Mexico—I transferred from Yale to the UDLAP in January of 1997—I put together courses that traced that history, even incorporating Breathwork and meditation into the curriculum. Those explorations, and that synthesis, eventually became the seeds of this book.

Three Treasures of Spiritual But Not Religious

Such, then, is my own intellectual and spiritual odyssey, as I view it, at least at this time. (In writing this account, I am conscious of imposing a neater order on the past than likely existed as it unfolded in real time; but so goes, inevitably, the writing of history.) Perhaps it explains my own draw towards transpersonal ideas and the posture of "spiritual but not religious." But how viable might these trends prove for others? Are they likely to be perpetuated, over time, in society at large? Can a religious orientation be sustained, in a cohesive, self-conscious way, without grounding in an organized church or institution?

Certainly there are reasons to believe not, and to think of "spiritual but not religious" as a rather shallow and even narcissistic stance. The world's great religious traditions, after all, have matured through eons of accumulated experience, and in the best instances, of refinement in teachings and practice. Religious institutions carry that accumulated knowledge forward, passing it on to subsequent generations. Standing apart from such development, cut off from the ripening of such collective teachings over time, is not an individual at the mercy of momentary whims in his own very restricted culture? Is she not blinded by her own ephemeral purview?

These are weighty questions, inviting the mustering of scholarship and lengthy responses. My intention here is simply to close this narrative with a few thoughts about why the transpersonal perspective, and its allied view of religion, might stand the test of time, continuing to attract a growing number of sincere and serious seekers.

A basic posture of Buddhism offers a suggestion of why that may be so. At the core of Buddhism—so goes the teaching—are the "Three Treasures" of the Buddha, the Dharma, and the Sangha. All are essential for the flourishing of the tradition. The *Buddha,* in this context, refers not only to the historical Buddha, Siddhartha Gautama. More fundamentally, it refers to the Buddha Nature in all of us: that element of divinity, purity and innocence that is in each and every person. The *Dharma* denotes Buddhist scriptures and teachings; but more basically, it refers to any teachings that allow us to recognize that Buddha Nature, and to manifest it in our lives. The *Sangha* is the community that perpetuates and reinforces those teachings, that encourages each of its members to realize their best selves. Without any one of the Three Treasures, a tradition is unlikely to be sustained. As in so many instances of Buddhist psychology, there is a luminous truth to this insight:

the Three Treasures, or something approximating them, are core elements in spiritual growth.

Transpersonal thought represents the *psychologizing* of religion, the sympathetic examination of religious life in terms not of theological doctrine or institutional props, but rather as patterns of personal experience. That lens on religion began in the epoch of R. M. Bucke and William James; it has gained depth and empirical validation in contemporary transpersonal psychology. And it supports, or at least is loosely allied with, a social movement that, despite calling itself "not religious," does exhibit its own versions of the Buddha, the Dharma, and the Sangha.

The Buddha of transpersonal thought is exactly what James pointed to at the turn of the twentieth century: the "further limits" of our own being, which "plunge into an altogether other dimension of existence" from the familiar material world. It is the element of our own psyche that touches the spiritual realm, that senses the presence of the numinous, that is in harmony with the moral order and the wider context of life. The recognition, however vague, of those further limits prompts the "not religious" to call themselves, nevertheless, "spiritual."

In support of that sensibility, there is, indeed, a Dharma. A basic purpose of this book has been to demonstrate that this sensibility can draw on a very rich tradition of thought. That tradition may stretch back through all history; but it has been articulated in our modern culture quite self-consciously since the days of Walt Whitman. It has spawned a sophisticated literature, rooted in depth psychology, that stands in opposition to modern materialism, that validates an openness to realms, in psychology and ontology, that we call spiritual. By focusing, perhaps arbitrarily, on a few key figures in the world of transpersonal psychology, I have restricted my own demarcation of that literature; but as a glance at any current book review would indicate, it reaches far wider than might be suggested by my limited bibliographical references.

Finally, I would say, there is no escape from Sangha. The spiritual but not religious may have an aversion to institutional hierarchies, but they cannot refrain, in their own way, from clustering in communities. Such communities—be they study groups, book clubs, web sites, blogs, nonprofit and informal organizations, or alternative schools—promote a robust exploration of the kinds of ideas discussed in this volume; they bring people together in the mutual reinforcement of their private pursuits of personal growth and spiritual development, along lines compatible with the insights of transpersonal thought. A few examples from my own professional life score the point: Several of the chapters of this book were written initially as lectures for the C.G. Jung Educational Center of Houston; with appropriate modifications, they have been delivered to the Houston Community Group of the Institute of Noetic Sciences, to a Jung study group in The Woodlands, Texas, and at the Hines Center for Spirituality and Prayer, an arm of Houston's Episcopal Cathedral explicitly intended to reach out to the city's population that identifies as spiritual but not religious. I have given related classes at the Naropa Institute of Boulder Colorado, and over the Internet at the Wisdom School of Graduate Studies of Ubiquity University. Organizations such as these, proliferating throughout the country and the world, indeed play the role of sanghas.

One focus of discussion in those sanghas is the more psychological interpretation of spiritual art, mythologies and literature from throughout the world. Examining the experiential patterning suggested by that expression, rather than explicit creeds, reveals a psychological validity to the full gamut of wisdom literature and sacred texts. It throws a light into the workings of our subconscious minds. And it infinitely broadens the dharma, making texts and teachings accessible and relevant to people who stand outside of the traditions from which those expressions rose. In the manner of R. M. Bucke, but perhaps with increasing subtlety, that examination reveals deeper levels of experiential truth behind what are often read as doctrinal pronouncements, or seen as mythical illustrations.

Stripped of explicit doctrinal content, those pronouncements and illustrations remain windows, perhaps still clearer windows, to the transcendent. As examples, allow me to return to some teachings, expressions and images from my Catholic heritage, as I can look upon them now, with more love of life than fear of it.

In the dogma of my youth, salvation was determined entirely by the state of one's soul at the moment of death. The truth in that teaching, I would say now, is that a spiritual quest requires growth; if we engage in it well, we progressively advance, albeit with twists and turns, and finish up wiser in it than we were at the start. Beyond the clouds and the brimstone, Heaven was defined as a state of communion with the Divine, and Hell as separated from it. And so, I'd say now, they are—though I think of them as states of our inner life, and of that divine power as, in part, an aspect of myself.

Of all art forms, music is most removed from rational content and in that sense, speaks most directly to the subconscious mind. Perhaps for that reason, religious music can have more sway over me than other forms of religious expression. I am, for instance, an ardent fan of African-American spirituals. But turning back to that Catholic heritage, I think of the time, years ago, that Ginger and I wandered into a fifteenth-century cloister in Salamanca, Spain. The weathered capitals of its pillars were a tangle of demons and gargoyles; but above, against the pure blue summer sky, we could see white storks atop the spires of the nearby cathedral. As the sun went down, the cloistered Dominican nuns broke into an ethereal Gregorian chant. It was one of the stronger numinous moments that I recall, matched, a few years later, by a similar experience at the monastery at Leyre, in the Spanish province of Navarre, as we heard the evening chants of Benedictine monks reverberate through their church, the rough twelfth-century stone walls artfully, if dimly, lit from below.

E.2 El Greco, *The Savior,* El Greco Museum, Toledo, Spain. (Photo Credit: Scala / Art Resource, NY.)

Another powerful image that comes to mind is a painting by El Greco that we came upon, during another Spanish odyssey, in Toledo. It was a torso of Christ, in portrait style, gazing directly at the viewer, embodying, uncannily, an inexpressible understanding of the human tragi-comedy that it gazed on with acceptance and compassion and love (Figure E.2). Today I might say that the religious enterprise, in great measure, is an unshackling of the constraints and fears that prevent us from feeling ourselves those emotions vividly captured in El Greco's canvas.

The message of that painting is concretized in the image of Christ, but universal beyond Christianity. Its source, as I view it, was the divine—call it the deeper transpersonal—element in El Greco himself, in us all. That message is, as Walt Whitman would have it,

> ....that the spirit of God is the eldest brother of my own,
>
> And that all the men ever born are also my brothers
>
> ....and the women my sisters and lovers,
>
> And that a kelson of the creation is love....

References

Abrams, B. (2002). Transpersonal dimensions of the Bonny Method. In K. Bruscia & D. Grocke (Eds.), *Guided imagery and music: The Bonny method and beyond* (pp. 339–358). Gilsum, NH: Barcelona.

Adams, H. (1918). *The education of Henry Adams.* Boston: Massachusetts Historical Society.

Allen, G. W. (1967). *William James: A biography.* New York, NY: The Viking Press, Inc.

Alvarado, C. S. (2004). On the centenary of Frederic W. H. Myers's *Human personality and its survival of bodily death. Journal of Parapsychology, 68*(1), 3–43.

Anonymous. (2013). *The age of cosmic consciousness.* Clearwater, FL: Transform Publishing LLC.

Assagioli, R. (1969). Symbols of transpersonal experiences. *Journal of Transpersonal Psychology, 1*(1), 33–45.

Bair, D. (2003). *Jung: A biography.* Boston, MA: Little, Brown and Company.

Barondess, B. (1954). *Three Lincoln masterpieces: Cooper Institute speech, Gettysburg address, Second inaugural.* Charleston: Education Foundation of West Virginia, Inc.

Barton, W. (1930). *Lincoln at Gettysburg.* New York, NY: Bobbs-Merrill.

Barzun, J. (1974). *Clio and the doctors: Psycho-history, quanto-history, and history.* Chicago, IL: University of Chicago Press.

Beisel, D. (2003). *The suicidal embrace: Hitler, the allies, and the origins of the Second World War.* Nyack, NY: Circumstantial Productions.

Bellah, R. (1967). Civil Religion in America. *Daedelus, Journal of the American Academy of Arts and Sciences, 96*(1), 1–21.

Binion, R. (1976). *Hitler among the Germans.* New York, NY: Elsevier.

Blood, B. P. (1874). *The anesthetic revelation and the gist of philosophy*. Amsterdam, NY. (No publisher).

Bonny, H. L. (1975). Music and consciousness. *Journal of Music Therapy*, *12*(3), 121–135. Reprinted in Bonny, 2002, 77–92.

Bonny, H. L. (1980). *GIM therapy: Past, present and future implications* (GIM Monograph #3). Salina, KS: The Bonny Foundation.

Bonny, H. L. (2002). *Music and consciousness: The evolution of Guided Imagery and Music*, L. Summer (Ed). Gilsum, NH: Barcelona Publishers.

Bonny, H. L., & Pahnke, W. (1972). The use of music in psychedelic (LSD) psycotherapy. *Journal of Music Therapy*, *9*(2), 64–87. Included in Bonny, 2002, 19–41.

Bonny, H. L., & Savary, L. M. (1973). *Music and your mind: Listening with a new consciousness*. New York, NY: Harper & Row, Publishers.

Boyd, E. (1925). *H. L. Mencken*. New York, NY: Robert M. McBride & Co.

Breuer, J., & Freud, S. (1895/2004). *Studies in hysteria*. London: Penguin Books.

Bruscia, K. E. (2002). The boundaries of Guided Imagery and Music (GIM) and the Bonny Method. In K. Bruscia & D. Grocke (Eds.), *Guided imagery and music: The Bonny method and beyond* (pp. 37–61). Gilsum, NH: Barcelona Publishers.

Bruscia, K. E., & Grocke, D. E. (Eds.). (2002). *Guided imagery and music: The Bonny method and beyond*. Gilsum, NH: Barcelona Publishers.

Bucke, R. M. (1879). *Man's moral nature: An essay*. New York, NY: G. P. Putnam's Sons.

Bucke, R. M. (1883). *Walt Whitman*. Philadelphia, PA: David McKay.

Bucke, R. M. (1991). *Cosmic consciousness*. New York, NY: Penguin Books.

Bush, C. A. (1995). *Healing imagery and music: Pathways to the inner self*. Portland, OR: Rudra Press.

Campbell, J. (1949). *The hero with a thousand faces*. Princeton, NJ: Princeton University Press.

Carpenter, E. (1904). *From Adam's Peak to Elephanta*. New York, NY: E. P. Dutton & Co.

Churchill, W. (1940). Wars are not won by evacuations. In D. Cannadine (Ed.), (1989). *Blood, toil, tears and sweat: The speeches of Winston Churchill*. Boston, MA: Houghton Mifflin.

Clark, M. F. (2002). The evolution of the Bonny Method of Guided Imagery and Music (BMGIM). In E. Bruscia & D. Grocke (Eds.), *Guided imagery and music: The Bonny method and beyond* (pp. 5–27). Gilsum, NH: Barcelona.

Coleman, W. (2006). The self. In R. Papadopoulous (Ed.), *The handbook of Jungian psychology: Theory, practice and applications* (pp. 153–174). London: Routledge.

Cook, E. W. (1992). *Frederic W. H. Myers: Parapsychology and its potential contribution to psychology* (Ph.D. dissertation). University of Edinburgh. (Ms. Cook subsequently adopted the married surname Kelly.)

Cook, E. W. (1994). The Subliminal Consciousness: F. W. H. Myers's approach to the problem of survival. *Journal of Parapsychology, 58*, 39–58.

Cooper, L. (1932). *The rhetoric of Aristotle*. New York, NY: D. Appleton-Century.

Cowley, M. (Ed.). (1959). *Walt Whitman's Leaves of Grass: The first (1855) edition*. New York, NY: The Viking Press.

Crabtree, A. (1993). *From Mesmer to Freud: Magnetic sleep and the roots of psychological healing*. New Haven, CT: Yale University Press.

Daniels, M. (2005). *Shadow, self, spirit: Essays in transpersonal psychology*. Charlottesville, VA: Imprint Academic.

deMause, L. (1974). *History of childhood*. New York, NY: Psychohistory Press.

deMause, L. (1982). *Foundations of psychohistory*. New York, NY: Creative Roots, Inc.

deMause, L. (1996). Restaging fetal traumas in war and social violence. *The International Journal of Prenatal and Perinatal Psychology and Medicine, 10*(4), 229–260.

Draper, J. (1875). *History of the conflict between religion and science.* New York, NY: D. Appleton and company.

Edwards, H., & Hankins, J. (1962). *Lincoln the writer: The development of his literary style.* Orono: University of Maine Press.

Ellenberger, H. F. (1970). *The discovery of the unconscious: The history and evolution of dynamic psychology.* New York, NY: Basic Books.

Emerson, R. W. (1957). *Selections from Ralph Waldo Emerson: An organic anthology* (S. Whicher, Ed.). Boston, MA: Houghton Mifflin Company.

Erikson, E. (1958). *Young man Luther: A study in psychoanalysis and history.* London: Faber and Faber.

Fechner, G. T. (1904). *The little book of life after death* (M. C. Wadsworth, Trans.). Boston, MA: Little, Brown and Company.

Ferrer, J. (2002). *Revisioning transpersonal theory: A participatory vision of human spirituality.* Albany: State University of New York Press.

Ferrer, J. (2017). *Participation and the mystery: Transpersonal essays in psychology, education, and religion.* Albany: State University of New York Press.

Fields, R. (1981). *How the swans came to the lake.* Boulder, CO: Shambala.

Flournoy, T. (1900). *From India to the planet Mars.* New York, NY: Harper & Brothers Publishers.

Fontana, D. (2005). *Is there an afterlife? A comprehensive review of the evidence.* Ropley: O Books.

Forman, R. K. C. (1990). *The problem of pure consciousness: Mysticism and philosophy.* New York, NY: Oxford University Press.

Freud, S. (1910). *Leonardo da Vinci and a memory of his childhood.* In J. Strachey (Ed.), *The standard edition of the complete works of Sigmund*

Freud (Vol. 11, pp. 63–136). London: The Hogarth Press.

Freud, S. (1927). The future of an illusion. In J. Strachey (Ed.), *The standard edition of the complete works of Sigmund Freud* (Vol. 21). London: The Hogarth Press.

Freud, S. (1930). *Civilization and its discontents*

Gallup, G. (2003). *American's spiritual searches turn inward*. Princeton, NJ: George H. Gallup International Institute. Retrieved from http://www.gallup.com/poll/7759/americans-spiritual-searches-turn-inward.aspx

Gauld, A. (1968). *The founders of psychical research*. New York, NY: Schocken Books.

Gay, P. (1985). *Freud for historians*. New York, NY: Oxford University Press.

Gay, P. (1988). *Freud: A life for our time*. New York, NY: W.W. Norton.

Gay, P. (1984–1991). *The bourgeois experience: Victoria to Freud*. New York, NY: Oxford University Press.

George, A., & George, J. (1956). *Woodrow Wilson and Colonel House: A personality study*. New York, NY: John Day Company.

Grocke, D. E. (2002). The evolution of Bonny's Music Programs. In K. Bruscia & D.

Grocke (Eds.), Guided imagery and music: The Bonny method and beyond (pp. 85–98). Gilsum, NH: Barcelona.

Grof, S. (1975). *Realms of the human unconscious*. New York, NY. The Viking Press.

Grof, S. (1980/1994). *LSD psychotherapy*. Pomona, CA: Hunter House.

Grof, S. (1985). *Beyond the brain: Birth, death and transcendence in psychotherapy*. Albany: State University of New York Press.

Grof, S. (1988). *The adventure of self-discovery*. Albany: State University of New York Press.

Grof, S. (1998). *The cosmic game: Explorations of the frontiers of human consciousness*. Albany: State University of New York Press.

Grof, S. (2000) *Psychology of the future: Lessons from modern consciousness research*. Albany: State University of New York Press.

Grof, S. (2006). *When the impossible happens*. Boulder, CO: Sounds True, Inc.

Grof, S. (2012). *Healing our deepest wounds: The holotropic paradigm shift*. Newcastle, WA: Stream of Experience Productions.

Grof, S., with Bennett, H. (1993). *The holotropic mind: The three levels of human consciousness and how they shape our lives*. New York, NY: HarperCollins Publishers.

Grof, S., Grob, C., Bravo, G., & Walsh, R. (2008). Birthing the transpersonal. *Journal of Transpersonal Psychology, 40*(2), 155–177.

Grof, S., & Grof, C. (2010). *Holotropic breathwork: A new approach to self-exploration and therapy*. Albany: State University of New York Press.

Grof, S., & Halifax, J. (1977). *The human encounter with death*. New York, NY: E.P. Dutton.

Gurney, E., Myers, F., & Podmore, F. (1886). *Phantasms of the living* (2 vols). London: Trübner and Co.

Hamilton, T. (2009). *Immortal longings: FWH Myers and the Victorian search for life after death*. Exeter: Imprint Academic.

Harman, W. (1969). The new Copernican revolution. *The Journal of Transpersonal Psychology, 1*(1), 21–29.

Harner, M. (1980). *The Way of the shaman: A guide to power and healing*. New York, NY: Harper & Row, Publishers Inc.

Herndon, W., & Weik, J. (1889), ed. Angle, P. (1942), *Herndon's Lincoln: The true story of a great life*. New York, NY: Da Capo.

Holden, J., Greyson, B., & James, D. (Eds.). (2009). *The handbook of near-death experiences: Thirty years of investigation*. Santa Barbara, CA: Praeger Publishers.

Hubbard, B. M. (1998). *Conscious evolution: Awakening the power of our social potential.* Novato, CA: New World Library.

Hubbard, B. M. (2006). The unfolding story of my discovery of conscious evolution and evolutionary spirituality. Retrieved from http://www.co-intelligence.org/newsletter/BarbMarxHubbardStory.html

Hurt, J. (1980). All the living and the dead: Lincoln's imagery. *American Literature, 52*(3), 351–380.

Huxley, A. (1932). *Brave new world.* London: Chatto & Windus.

Huxley, A. (1944). *The perennial philosophy.* New York, NY: Harper & Row, Publishers, Inc.

Huxley, A. (1954). *The doors of perception.* New York, NY: Harper & Row, Publishers, Inc.

Huxley, A. (1962). *Island.* London: Chatto & Windus.

James, H. (Ed.) (1920). *The letters of William James* (2 vols). Boston, MA: Atlantic Monthly Press.

James, W. (1869, March 10). Planchette. [Unsigned review of E. Sargent, *Planchette: or the despair of science*]. *Boston Daily Advertiser.* included in James (1986), 1–4.

James, W. (1874, November). Review of "The anaesthetic revelation and the gist of philosophy." *Atlantic Monthly, 33*(205), 627–628.

James, W. (1882). On some Hegelisms. *Mind, 7,* 186–208. The essay was later included as a chapter in James (1897), 263–298.

James, W. (1886). Report of the committee on mediumistic phenomena. In James, W. (1986), 14–18.

James, W. (1890a). The hidden self. *Scribner's Magazine, 7*(3), 361–373.

James, W. (1890b/1952). *The principles of psychology.* Chicago, IL: Encyclopedia Britannica, Inc. Original edition, 1890, New York, NY: Henry Holt and Company.

James, W. (1892). What psychical research has accomplished. *Forum, 13,* 727–742. Included in James (1986), 89–106.

James, W. (1894). Letter to the Boston *Evening Transcript*, March 24. Quoted in Allen, 1967, 371–372.

James, W. (1896). Address by the president. *Proceedings of the Society for Psychical Research, 12,* 2–10. Included in James (1986), 127–137.

James, W. (1897). *The will to believe and other essays in popular philosophy.* London: Longmans, Green & Co., Inc.

James, W. (1898). *Human immortality: Two supposed objections to the doctrine.* New York, NY: Houghton Mifflin & Co.

James, W. (1901). Frederic Myers's service to psychology. *Proceedings of the Society for Psychical Research, 17,* 13–23. Included in James (1986), 192–202.

James, W. (1902/1929). *The varieties of religious experience.* New York, NY: The Modern Library.

James, W. (1903). Review of *human personality and its survival of bodily death,* by Frederic W. H. Myers. *Proceedings of the Society for Psychical Research, 18,* 22–33. Included in James (1986), 203–215.

James, W. (1907a). *Pragmatism: A new name for some old ways of thinking.* London: Longmans, Green & Co., Inc.

James, W. (1907b). The energies of men. *Science, 25*(635), 321–332.

James, W. (1909a, October). The confidences of a "psychical researcher". *American Magazine, 68,* 580–589. Included in James (1986), 361–375.

James, W. (1909b). *A pluralistic universe: Hibbert lectures at Manchester College on the present situation in philosophy.* New York, NY: Longmans Green and Company.

James, W., (1909c). Report on Mrs. Piper's Hodgson-control. *Proceedings of the Society for Psychical Research, 23,* 2–121. Included in James (1986), 253–360.

James, W. (1910). A pluralistic mystic. *Hibbert Journal, 8,* 739–759.

James, W. (1962). *Talks to teachers on psychology and to students on some of life's ideals*. Mineola: Dover Publications, Inc. Original edition, 1899, New York: Henry Holt and Company.

James, W. (1986). *Essays in psychical research* (F. H. Burkhardt, F. Bowers, & I. K. Skrupskelis, Eds.) Cambridge, MA: Harvard University Press.

Janet, P. (1903). *L'Automatisme psicologique: Essai de psycologie expérimentale sur les formes inferieurs de l'activité humaine* (4th ed.). Paris: Ancienne Librairie Germer Bailliere et Cie. Retrieved from https://books. google.com/books?id=0usaAQAAMAAJ&printsec=frontcover &dq=pierre+janet+l'automatisme+psycologique&hl=en&sa=X& ved=0CB8Q6AEwAGoVChMI9KOE7pxyAIVlyiICh2FkA PK#v=onepage&q=pierre%20janet%20l'automatisme%20 psycologique&f=false

Jeans, J. (1930/1937). *The mysterious universe*. Cambridge, UK: Cambridge University Press.

Jung, C. G. (1902/1970). *On the psychology and pathology of so-called occult phenomena. The collected works of C.G. Jung: Volume1: Psychiatric studies* (2nd ed., pp. 1–88) (R. F. C. Hull, Trans.). Princeton, NJ: Princeton University Press.

Jung, C. G. (1945/1970). The soul and death. In (E. H. Henley & R. F. C. Hull, Trans.). *The structure and dynamics of the psyche* (2nd ed., pp. 404–415). Princeton, NJ: Princeton University Press.

Jung, C. G. (1949). Letter to Virginia Payne, July 23. Retrieved from http://www.uky.edu/~eushe2/Pajares/jamesjung.html

Jung, C. G. (1961). *Memories, dreams, reflections* (R. Winston & C. Winston, Trans.). New York, NY: Vintage Books.

Jung, C. G. (1964) *The collected works of Carl Jung* (R. F. C. Hull, Trans.). Princeton, NJ: Princeton University Press.

Jung, C. G. (1973). *C. G. Jung letters, v. 1: 1906–1950* (ed. G. Adler, A. Jaffe, trans. by R. Hull). Princeton, NJ: Princeton University Press.

Jung, C. G. (1988). *Erinnerungen, Traume, Gedanken von C. G. Jung*, Aufgezeichnicht und herausgegeben von Aniela Jaffé (Trans. Sonu Shamdasani). Olten: Walter-Verlag. Retrieved from http://www. survivalafterdeath.info/articles/jung/flournoy.htm

Kelly, E. (2001). The contributions of F. W. H. Myers to psychology. *Journal of the Society for Psychical Research, 65.2* (863), 65–90.

Kelly, E. F., Crabtree, A., & Marshall, P. (Eds.). (2015). *Beyond physicalism: Toward reconciliation of science and spirituality.* Lanham, MD: Rowman & Littlefield Publishers, Inc.

Kelly, E. F., Kelly, E. W., Crabtree, A., Gauld, A., Grosso A., & Greyson, B. (2007). *Irreducible mind: Toward a psychology for the 21ˢᵗ century.* Lanham, MD: Rowman & Littlefield Publishers, Inc.

Knapp, K. D. (2017). *William James: Psychical research and the challenge of modernity.* Chapel Hill: University of North Carolina Press.

Kren, G., & Rappoport, L. (1980). *Holocaust and the crisis of human behavior.* New York, NY: Holmes and Meier.

Kripal, J. J. (2007). *Esalen: America and the religion of no religion.* Chicago, IL: University of Chicago Press.

Kripal, J. J. (2008, December). Brave new worldview: The return of Aldous Huxley. *The Chronicle Review,* pp. B7–B9.

Kripal, J. J. (2010). *Authors of the impossible: The paranormal and the sacred.* Chicago, IL: University of Chicago Press.

Kripal, J. J. (2016). Mysticism disputed: Major debates in the field. In A. D. DeConick (Ed.), *Religion: Secret religion* (pp. 295–314). New York, NY: Macmillan.

Krishnamurti, J. (1954). *The first and last freedom.* New York, NY: HarperCollins Publishers.

Kuhn, T. (1962). *The structure of scientific revolutions.* Chicago, IL: University of Chicago Press.

Lajoie, D.H., & Schapiro, S. I. (1992). Definitions of transpersonal psychology: The first twenty-three years. *Journal of Transpersonal Psychology, 24*(1), 79–98.

Langer, W. (1958). The next assignment. *American Historical Review, 63*(2), 283–304.

Lattin, D. (2009). *Distilled spirits: Getting high, then sober, with a famous writer, a forgotten philosopher, and a hopeless drunk.* Berkeley: University of California Press.

Liester, M. B. (2013). Near-death experiences and ayahuasca-induced experiences: Two unique pathways to a phenomenologically similar state of consciousness. *Journal of Transpersonal Psychology, 45*(1), 24–48.

Lifton, R. (1986). *The Nazi doctors: Medical killing and the psychology of genocide.* New York, NY: Basic Books.

Lowell, R. (1964). On the Gettysburg address. In A. Nevins (Ed.), *Lincoln and the Gettysburg address* (pp. 88–92). Urbana: University of Illinois Press.

Lowenberg, P. (1971) The psychohistorical origins of the Nazi youth cohort. *American Historical Review, 76*(5), 1457–1502.

Lowenberg, P. (1985). *Decoding the past: The psychohistorical approach.* Berkeley: University of California Press.

Main, D. (2016). Psilocybin, from magic mushrooms, eases anxiety and depression in cancer patients. *Newsweek*, December 1, 2016. Retrieved from http://www.newsweek.com/psilocybin-hallucinogenic-mushrooms-eases-anxiety-cancer-patients-526952

Main, R. (2006). Religion. In R. Papadopoulous (Ed.), *The handbook of Jungian psychology. Theory practice and applications* (pp. 296–323). London: Routledge.

Martin, S. (2009). *Cosmic conversations: Dialogues on the nature of the universe and the search for reality.* Pompton Plains, NJ: New Page Books

Maslow, A. (1943). A theory of human motivation. *Psychological Review, 50*(4), 370–396.

Maslow, A. (1954). *Motivation and personality.* New York, NY: Harper & Brothers.

Maslow, A. (1964). *Religions, values, and peak experiences.* Indianapolis, IN: Kappa Delta Pi Publications.

Maslow, A. (1968). *Toward a psychology of being* (2nd ed.). New York, NY: D. Van Nostrand Company.

Maslow, A. (1969a). The farther reaches of human nature. *Journal of Transpersonal Psychology, 1*(1), 1–9.

Maslow, A. (1969b). Various meanings of "transcendence". *Journal of Transpersonal Psychology, 1*(1), 56–66.

May, R. M. (1991). *Cosmic consciousness revisited: The modern origins and development of a Western spiritual psychology.* Rockport, MA: Element Inc.

Maynard, S. (2014). *The illumination of Dr. Bucke: A journey beyond the intellect.* Bloomington, IN: AuthorHouse LLC.

McDermott, R. (1993). Transpersonal worldviews: Historical and philosophical reflections. In R. Walsh & F. Vaughan (Eds.), *Paths beyond ego: The transpersonal vision* (pp. 206–212). Los Angeles, LA: Jeremy P. Tarcher/Perigree.

Meadows, A. (2002). Distinctions between the Bonny Method of Guided Imagery and Music (BMGIM) and other imagery techniques. In K. Bruscia & D. Grocke (Eds.), *Guided imagery and music: The Bonny method and beyond* (pp. 63–83). Gilsum, NH: Barcelona.

Miller, D. (2005). Mandala symbolism in psychotherapy: The potential utility of the Lowenfield mosaic technique for enhancing the individuation process. *The Journal of Transpersonal Psychology, 37*(2), 164–177.

Monastersky, R. (2006, May 26). Religion on the brain. *Chronicle of Higher Education,* pp. A15–A19.

Moody, R. A. (1975). *Life after life: The investigation of a phenomenon—survival of bodily death.* Atlanta, GA: Mockingbird Books.

Murphy, G., & Ballou, R. (Eds.). (1960). *William James on psychic research.* New York, NY: Viking Press.

Murphy, M. (1992). *The future of the body: Explorations into the further evolution of human nature.* Los Angeles, CA: Jeremy P. Tarcher, Inc.

Myers, F. W. H. (1880). *Wordsworth*. London: Macmillan.

Myers, F. W. H. (1883). *Essays—modern*. London: Macmillan.

Myers, F. W. H. (1884). On a telepathic explanation of some so-called spiritualistic phenomena. *Proceedings of the Society for Psychical Research*, 2, 217–237.

Myers, F. W. H. (1885). Automatic writing-II. *Proceedings of the Society for Psychical Research*, 3, 1–63.

Myers, F. W. H. (1887). Automatic writing-III. *Proceedings of the Society for Psychical Research*, 4, 209–261.

Myers, F. W. H. (1888). *Essays—classical*. London: Macmillan.

Myers, F. W. H. (1889). Automatic writing-IV—The daemon of socrates. *Proceedings of the Society for Psychical Research*, 5, 522–547.

Myers, F. W. H. (1892a). The subliminal consciousness. Chapter 1: General characteristics and subliminal messages. *Proceedings of the Society for Psychical Research*, 7, 298–327.

Myers, F. W. H. (1892b). The subliminal consciousness. Chapter IV: The mechanism of genius. *Proceedings of the Society for Psychical Research*, 8, 333–361.

Myers, F. W. H. (1892c). The subliminal consciousness. Chapter V: Sensory automatism and induced hallucinations. *Proceedings of the Society for Psychical Research*, 8, 436–535.

Myers, F. W. H. (1893). *Science and a future life: With other essays*. London: Macmillan.

Myers, F. W. H. (1893–4). The subliminal consciousness. Chapter VII: Motor automatism. *Proceedings of the Society for Psychical Research*, 9, 26–128.

Myers, F. W. H. (1895a). The subliminal consciousness. Chapter VIII: The relation of supernormal phenomena to time—retrocognition. *Proceedings of the Society for Psychical Research*, 11, 334–407.

Myers, F. W. H. (1895b). The subliminal consciousness. Chapter VIII: The relation of supernormal phenomena to time—precognition. *Proceedings of the Society for Psychical Research, 11*, 408–593.

Myers, F. W. H. (1900). The function of a society for psychical research: Presidential address to the Society for Psychical Research. Included as Appendix A in Myers (1903/1954), 292–307.

Myers, F. W. H. (1903/1954). *Human personality and its survival of bodily death* (2 vols). London: Longmans, Green and Co.

Nomad, A. (1996). *Cosmic consciousness: The man-god whom we await.* Pomeroy, WA: Health Research Books.

Page, K. (Producer & Director) (2006). *Science of the soul: The story of transpersonal psychology* [Motion picture]. (Available from Transpersonal Media, Dallas Texas).

Perry, R. B. (1935). *The thought and character of William James* (2 vols). Boston, MA: Little, Brown and Company.

Pew Research Center. (2012). Nones on the rise: One-in-five adults have no religious affiliation. Retrieved from http://www.pewforum.org/2012/10/09/nones-on-the-rise/

Prophet, M. L., as recorded by Elizabeth Clare Prophet (1974). *Cosmic consciousness: One man's search for God.* Livingston, MT: Summit University Press.

Rechnitzer, P. A. (1994). *R.M. Bucke: Journey to cosmic consciousness.* Markham: Fitzhenry and Whiteside.

Richardson, R. (2006). *William James: In the maelstrom of American modernism.* New York, NY: Houghton Mifflin Company.

Ring, K. (1980). *Life at death: A scientific investigation of the near-death experience.* New York, NY: Coward, McCann & Geoghegan.

Robinson, D. N. (1981). *An intellectual history of psychology* (revised ed.). New York, NY: Macmillan.

Sandburg, C. (1939) *Abraham Lincoln: The war years.* New York, NY: Harcourt, Brace and Company.

Sawyer, D. (2002). *Aldous Huxley: A biography*. New York, NY: The Crossroad Publishing Company.

Schiffman, R. (2016). Psilocybin: A journey beyond fear of death. *Scientific American*, December 1, 2016.

Schmitt, C. B. (1966). Perrenial [sic] philosophy: From Agostino Steuco to Leibniz. *Journal of the History of Ideas, 27*(4), 505–532.

Scotton, B. (1996). The contribution of C.G. Jung to transpersonal psychiatry. In B. Scotton, A. Chinen, & J. Battista (Eds.), *Textbook of transpersonal psychiatry and psychology* (pp. 39–51). New York, NY: Basic Books.

Scotton, B., Chinen, A., & Battista, J. (Eds.). (1996). *Textbook of transpersonal psychiatry and psychology*. New York, NY: Basic Books.

Shanon, B., Sheldrake, R., McKenna, T., & Ralph Abraham, R. (1992). *Chaos, creativity and cosmic consciousness*. Santa Fe, NM: Bear and Company.

Shroeder, T. (2014). *Acid Test: LSD, ecstacy, and the power to heal*. New York, NY: Blue Rider Press.

Smiley, C. (1917) Lincoln and Gorgias. *Classical Journal, 13*(2), 124–128.

Smith, H. (1976/1992). *Forgotten truth: The common vision of the world's religions*. New York, NY: HarperCollins Publishers.

Stace, W. T. (1960). *Mysticism and philosophy*. London: Macmillan.

Stannard, D. (1980). *Shrinking history: On Freud and the failure of pyschohistory*. New York, NY: Oxford University Press.

Stern, P. (1940). *The life and writings of Abraham Lincoln*. New York, NY: The Modern Library.

Stevenson, I. (1970). *Telepathic impressions: A review and report of thirty-five new cases*. Charlottesville: University Press of Virginia.

Stevenson, I. (1997). *Reincarnation and biology: A contribution to the etiology of birthmarks and birth defects* (2 vols.). New York, NY: Praeger.

Strachey, J. (Ed.). (1955–68). *The standard edition of the complete works of Sigmund Freud*. London: The Hogarth Press.

Strozier, C. (1982). *Lincoln's quest for union: A psychological portrait*. New York, NY: Basic Books.

Strozier, C. (1994). *Apocalypse: On the psychology of fundamentalism in America*. Boston, MA: Beacon Press.

Strunk, W., & White, E. (1959). *Elements of style*. New York, NY: Macmillan.

Sutich, A. (1969a). Editor's note. *Journal of Transpersonal Psychology*, *1*(1), iv.

Sutich, A. (1969b). Some considerations regarding transpersonal psychology. *Journal of Transpersonal Psychology*, *1*(1), 11–20.

Sutich, A. (1969c). Editor's note. *Journal of Transpersonal Psychology*, *1*(2), iv.

Sutich, A. (1976a). The emergence of the transpersonal orientation: A personal account. *Journal of Transpersonal Psychology*, *8*(1), 5–19.

Sutich, A. (1976b). *The founding of humanistic and transpersonal psychology: A personal account* (Unpublished doctoral dissertation). The Humanistic Psychology Institute.

Tarnas, R. (1991). *The passion of the Western mind: Understanding the ideas that have shaped our world view*. New York, NY: Ballantine Books.

Tarnas, R. (2006). *Cosmos and psyche: Intimations of new world view*. New York, NY: Viking.

Tart, C. (Ed.). (1969). *Altered states of consciousness: A book of readings*. New York, NY: Wiley.

Tart, C. T. (Ed.). (1975). *Transpersonal psychologies: Perspectives on the mind from seven great spiritual traditions*. New York, NY: Harper & Row Publishers, Inc.

Taves, A. (2003). Religious experience and the divisible self: William James (and Frederic Myers) as theorist(s) of religion. *Journal of the American Academy of Religion*, *71*(2), 303–326.

Taylor, E. (1982). *William James on exceptional mental states: The 1896 Lowell lectures.* New York, NY: Charles Scribner's Sons.

Taylor, E. (1996a). William James and transpersonal psychiatry. In B. Scotton, A. Chinen, & J. Battista (Eds.), *Textbook of transpersonal psychiatry and psychology* (pp. 21–28). New York, NY: Basic Books.

Taylor, E. (1996b). *William James on consciousness beyond the margin.* Princeton, NJ: Princeton University Press.

Vich, M. (1976). Anthony J. Sutich: An appreciation. *Journal of Transpersonal Psychology, 8*(1), 2–4.

Vich, M. (1998). Some historical sources of the term "transpersonal". *Journal of Transpersonal Psychology, 20*(2), 109.

Waite, R. (1977). *The psychopathic god: Adolf Hitler.* New York, NY: Basic Books.

Walsh, P., & Walsh, S. (2012). *Cosmic consciousness: The personality of God upon creation.* Birmingham, AL: Awakening Books.

Walsh, R., & Vaughan, F. (1993). *Paths beyond ego: The transpersonal vision.* Los Angeles, CA: Jeremy P. Tarcher/Perigee.

White, A. (1876). *The warfare of science with theology in Christendom.* New York, NY: D. Appleton and company.

Wilber, K. (1975). Psychologia perennis: The spectrum of consciousness. *Journal of Transpersonal Psychology, 7*(2), 105–132.

Wilber, K. (1977). *The spectrum of consciousness.* Wheaton, IL: The Theosophical Publishing House.

Wilber, K. (1983). *A sociable god: Toward a new understanding of religion.* New York, NY: New Press.

Wilber, K. (1995). *Sex, ecology, spirituality: The spirit of evolution.* Boston, MA: Shambala Publications, Inc.

Wilber, K. (1999). *One taste: Daily reflections on integral spirituality.* Boston, MA: Shambala Publications, Inc.

Wills, G. (1978). *Inventing America: Jefferson's Declaration of Independence.* New York, NY: Random House.

Wills, G. (1992). *Lincoln at Gettysburg: The words that remade America.* New York, NY: Simon and Schuster.

Wolfenstein, E. (1981). *The victims of democracy: Malcolm X and the black revolution.* Berkeley: University of California Press.

Index

About the Author

A historian of American thought and culture, Mark Ryan was Dean of Jonathan Edwards College and a teacher of American Studies and History at Yale University for more than 20 years. Subsequently, he was Titular IV Professor at the Universidad de las Américas in Puebla, Mexico, where he also served as Dean of the Colleges, *Regente* (Head) of José Gaos College, and Coordinator of the master's degree program in United States Studies. He holds Ph.D. and M. Phil. degrees from Yale, an M.A. from the University of Texas at Austin, and a B.A. from the University of St. Thomas.

Mark's other writings include *A Collegiate Way of Living* (Yale University, 2001), articles in various journals on higher education, and articles in *The Journal of Transpersonal Psychology* and related publications on transpersonal thought. He served for 14 years on the Board of Trustees of Naropa University, and he is the past chair of the Board of Directors of Wisdom University, and the current Chair of the Jonathan Edwards Trust at Yale. Certified by Grof Transpersonal Training as a practitioner of Holotropic Breathwork, he now lives in Houston with his wife Ginger Clarkson, a music therapist and teacher of Vipassana (Insight) meditation. Mark currently teaches and lectures at various venues, especially the C.G. Jung Educational Center of Houston, and online with the Wisdom School of Graduate Studies of Ubiquity University.

Printed in Great Britain
by Amazon

42285140R00145